Philipp Kenel
Social Entrepreneurship in Germany

Political Science | Volume 173

This open access publication was enabled by the support of POLLUX – Informationsdienst Politikwissenschaft

POLLUX Informationsdienst Politikwissenschaft

and a network of academic libraries for the promotion of the open-access-transformation in the Social Sciences and Humanities (transcript Open Library Community Politik 2023).

Vollsponsoren: Technische Universität Braunschweig | Carl von Ossietzky-Universität Oldenburg | Eberhard-Karls Universität Tübingen | Freie Universität Berlin – Universitätsbibliothek | Niedersächsische Staats- und Universitätsbibliothek Göttingen | Goethe-Universität Frankfurt am Main | Gottfried Wilhelm Leibniz Bibliothek – Niedersächsische Landesbibliothek | TIB – Leibniz-Informationszentrum Technik und Naturwissenschaften und Universitätsbibliothek | Humboldt-Universität zu Berlin | Justus-Liebig-Universität Gießen | Universitätsbibliothek Eichstätt-Ingolstadt | Ludwig-Maximilians-Universität München | Max Planck Digital Library (MPDL) | Rheinische Friedrich-Wilhelms-Universität Bonn | Ruhr-Universität Bochum | Staats- und Universitätsbibliothek Carl von Ossietzky, Hamburg | SLUB Dresden | Staatsbibliothek zu Berlin | Bibliothek der Technischen Universität Chemnitz | Universitäts- und Landesbibliothek Darmstadt | Universitätsbibliothek „Georgius Agricola“ der TU Bergakademie Freiberg | Universitätsbibliothek Kiel (CAU) | Universitätsbibliothek Leipzig | Universitäts- und Landesbibliothek Düsseldorf | Universitäts- und Landesbibliothek Münster | Universitäts- und Stadtbibliothek Köln | Universitätsbibliothek Bielefeld | Universitätsbibliothek Erfurt | Universitätsbibliothek der FernUniversität in Hagen | Universitätsbibliothek Kaiserslautern-Landau | Universitätsbibliothek Kassel | Universitätsbibliothek Osnabrück | Universität Potsdam | Universitätsbibliothek St. Gallen | Universitätsbibliothek Vechta | Zentralbibliothek Zürich

Sponsoring Light: Bundesministerium der Verteidigung | Bibliothek der Hochschule für Technik und Wirtschaft Dresden | Bibliothek der Hochschule für Technik, Wirtschaft und Kultur Leipzig | Bibliothek der Westsächsischen Hochschule Zwickau | Bibliothek der Hochschule Zittau/Görlitz, Hochschulbibliothek | Hochschulbibliothek der Hochschule Mittweida | Institut für Auslandsbeziehungen (IfA) | Landesbibliothek Oldenburg | Österreichische Parlamentsbibliothek

Mikrosponsoring: Bibliothek der Berufsakademie Sachsen | Bibliothek der Evangelische Hochschule Dresden | Bibliothek der Hochschule für Musik und Theater „Felix Mendelssohn Bartholdy“ Leipzig | Bibliothek der Hochschule für Bildende Künste Dresden | Bibliothek der Hochschule für Musik „Carl Maria von Weber“ Dresden | Bibliothek der Hochschule für Grafik und Buchkunst Leipzig | Bibliothek der Palucca-Hochschule für Tanz Dresden | Leibniz-Institut für Europäische Geschichte | Stiftung Wissenschaft und Politik (SWP) – Deutsches Institut für Internationale Politik und Sicherheit

Philipp Kenel

Social Entrepreneurship in Germany

An Analysis of the Media Discourse from 1999 to 2021

[transcript]

The research for this book was funded by the Berlin Senate via the Berlin School of Economics and Law.

Bibliographic information published by the Deutsche Nationalbibliothek
The Deutsche Nationalbibliothek lists this publication in the Deutsche Nationalbibliografie; detailed bibliographic data are available in the Internet at https://dnb.dnb.de/

First published in 2024 by transcript Verlag, Bielefeld

Cover layout: Maria Arndt, Bielefeld
Printed by: Elanders Waiblingen GmbH, Waiblingen
https://doi.org/10.14361/9783839473153
Print-ISBN: 978-3-8376-7315-9
PDF-ISBN: 978-3-8394-7315-3
EPUB-ISBN: 978-3-7328-7315-9
ISSN of series: 2702-9050
eISSN of series: 2702-9069

Printed on permanent acid-free text paper.

Contents

List of Tables and Graphs

Acknowledgements

Many people have supported me in the process of my doctoral research and thesis writing, on which this book is based on. In particular, I am grateful to: Claudia Gather, Sigrid Betzelt, Simon Griffiths, Nick Taylor, Angela McRobbie, Simon Teasdale, Will Davies, and privately: to Roland, Anneliese and Samir. Thank you!

Introduction

In the wake of the 2021 election to the *Bundestag* , the *Social Entrepreneurship Netzwerk Deutschland* (*SEND*), Germany's main network and lobby organisation for social entrepreneurs, asked all major parties to respond to some of their claims and to comment on their views and proposals for social entrepreneurship (SE) in Germany.[1] The party representatives responded with video statements, which were published (among other places) on *SEND*'s *Facebook* page between September 21th and 24th. In their statements, all politicians expressed their sympathy for SE, explaining why they consider that SE is important and needed. However, each of them using their own language and linking SE to their specific argumentation and political views.

Armin Laschet of the Christian Democrats (*Christlich Demokratische Union Deutschlands, CDU*) highlights the role of social entrepreneurs as Germany's 'innovators' (SEND 2021a).[2] For him, social entrepreneurs can help to activate society's potential to innovate and to find new solutions for social problems. Olaf Scholz of the Social Democratic Party (*Sozialdemokratische Partei Deutschlands, SPD*) sees SE as an opportunity to foster community ('togetherness'). According to him, social innovation requires the participation of many actors: in social enterprises, the community economy and cooperatives alike. Christian Lindner of the Liberal Party (*Freie Demokratische Partei, FDP*) points out Germany's role as one of the richest countries in the world, but also expresses his fear that economic success alone is not enough and that there is a variety of challenges facing the country. For him, SE has the potential of addressing these challenges – by applying new solutions and entrepreneurial thinking, also in areas that are not strictly linked to the economy. On the other hand, Janine

1 All parties at the time represented in the *Bundestag* were contacted, excluding the far-right party *Alternative für Deutschland* (*AfD*).

2 The video statements were transcribed and translated from German by the author.

Wissler of the Left Party (*Die Linke*) summarises what she understands of SE as: 'common good before profit'. For her, SE can make a contribution to overcome social ills, including poverty, loneliness and ever more precarious jobs. Wissler argues that within the framework of solidarity economies social innovation can play an important role, developing ideas on a small scale that may then serve society as a whole. Finally, Katrin Göring-Eckardt of the Green Party (*Bündnis 90/ Die Grünen, Green Party*) sees social entrepreneurs as agents that are committed to the common good and sustainability, who are building an economy that replaces short-term returns with long-term thinking (SEND 2021a).

Given that this is only a few days before the election and that the campaigners are hoping for votes from the SE community and beyond, it is hardly surprising that all five politicians express their support for SE. But apart from this, the different party representatives clearly demonstrate that they connect certain hopes and political goals with the SE phenomenon or movement. However, what each of the five associates with SE can be quite different from each other – and mirror each party's political goals and broader vision for society. Two rather opposed understandings of and visions for SE that stand out are: Christian Lindner's (*FDP*) claim for entrepreneurial thinking in all areas of society – representing a (neoliberal) glorification of entrepreneurial solutions – in contrast to Janine Wissler's (*Die Linke*) understanding of SE as common good before profits – employing the language of solidarity (of the political left). In short, the support that these different actors express for SE is linked to different political goals and to different underlying understandings of the SE phenomenon and movement.

The much-cited quote by management scholar Dees (2001 [1998]) in one of the first scholarly publications on SE, remains timely: "[t]hough the concept of 'social entrepreneurship' is gaining popularity, it means different things to different people" (Dees 2001 [1998]: 1).[3] While this has mostly been taken as a starting point for discussing definitions of SE and what kind of organisations social enterprises are or should be – which remain to be important aspects – I argue that this matter goes much deeper. Taking a more sociological perspective, it can be noted that the different 'meanings' that are attributed to SE concern not only the underlying understandings of SE but also the broader ideas,

3 Arguably, it was also this article, *The Meaning of 'Social Entrepreneurship'*, which first introduced the SE term and concept to a wider academic community. According to a scientometric analysis by Sassmannshausen & Volkmann (2018), in 2013 this was the most-cited publication on SE.

the political goals and agendas and the visions for society that people connect to SE – as could briefly be illustrated with the statements above. Academic literature, too, offers a variety of such wider interpretations and understandings of SE. To the extent that, sometimes, social entrepreneurship is described as a neoliberal concept, transforming the social and welfare sectors, while at other times, SE is said to represent an alternative to precisely this (neoliberal) capitalist economic model (e.g., Shaw & de Bruin 2013).

The fact that there is such "conceptual confusion", as Teasdale (2012: 99) has framed it, when it comes to the wider political or sociological meaning of SE and the motivation of trying to untangle this for the German context has been the starting point for my research. Being such a fluid and contested concept that might be understood and interpreted in very different ways by different actors, also making it prone to appropriation and even instrumentalisation for various political purposes, I aimed to investigate the idea of SE in Germany *empirically*, in order to contribute to a better sociological understanding and making sense of it – in particular along the following research topics and questions:

- ***Diversity and dominance***: What different understandings of SE can be identified, and what is the dominant representation and perspective of the SE concept in Germany?
- ***Representation and Relevance***: What does a broader audience get to learn about the SE phenomenon? What parts or aspects of SE are given a platform and getting noticed by wider society, i.e., beyond the niche spaces of the SE scene itself?
- ***Development over time***: How has the idea of SE been introduced in Germany in the late 1990s (when the 'social entrepreneurship' term first started to appear), and how has the concept developed over time, until the early 2020s (when interest for SE in the public and in politics has started to increase)?
- ***Notions of 'change' and politics:*** SE seeks to 'change' the *status quo* – but which *status quo* is meant, what shall 'change' and how, and what is the vision for economy and society proposed by SE? What (potential) societal or political role is ascribed to SE, and what is the relationship between SE and the dominant (neoliberal) social and economic model?

Until now, these aspects of SE, i.e., its wider meanings, its normative and political underpinnings, have not been investigated empirically for the German context. Several studies have addressed similar aspects – including those of Parkinson & Howorth (2008), Nicholls (2010), Teasdale (2012), Dey & Teasdale

(2016), or Mason & Moran (2019), among others – but mainly for the United Kingdom (UK). As a result, the findings of these studies can only help to understand SE in Germany to a limited extent, since making sense of SE as a political and sociological phenomenon needs to take into account the political and socio-economic specifics of the respective context.

This is where this book makes an original contribution, explicitly focusing on the concept of SE in Germany, based on empirical research on representations of SE in the media between 1999 and 2021. The study is grounded on the theoretical and methodological framework of 'discourse' and 'discourse analysis'. This approach allows to study the development of ideas and, therefore, proves suitable to investigate the different meanings – in the broadest sense – associated with SE, how these meanings are 'produced' and contested, and how they have developed over time (Fairclough 1992; 2010; Diaz-Bone 2006). The empirical study is an analysis of 349 newspaper articles of general newspapers, published between 1999 (which is when the term 'social entrepreneurship' first appears in the German press) and 2021 (the latest year that my analysis was able to include and which coincides with a growing (political) interest for SE). I argue that newspapers (as part of the mass media) are important arenas for a society, in which 'common' knowledge and meaning(s) are produced.

It must be noted, however, that this choice of data implies that the analysis primarily casts light on certain representations of SE in newspapers. It only grasps some parts and aspects of the SE discourse(s), namely: the part of the SE discourse(s) that is represented in newspaper articles, i.e., the part of SE that journalists and editors find interesting and worth writing about. It is a mediated perspective on SE: SE seen through the eyes of newspapers. Yet, given that this book seeks to portray a certain dominant or 'mainstream' view on SE, and aspects about the SE concept that are getting noticed outside of the niche spaces in which SE, so far, is taking place, this is a valid and suitable choice of data for the research questions outlined above, as I will explain in detail in Chapter 3.

With its distinct approach, this book makes a contribution to SE scholarship mainly in four regards: strengthening sociological research on SE, applying empirical research to better understanding SE in the specific German context, tracing the development of 'common' representations of SE over time and, more generally, contributing to the interdisciplinary study of (socio)economic phenomena.

First, it contributes to sociological perspectives on SE that grasp and study SE as a complex (political) phenomenon, which is 'more' than just a (sub-)

form of entrepreneurship and which has 'wider' meanings and a multifaceted relationship to society. The wider political and socio-economic aspects of SE (not only in Germany) remain understudied, arguably, because most of the literature on SE comes from business administration and management studies (see e.g., Sassmannshausen & Volkmann 2018) – as pointed out by Parkinson & Howorth (2008), Lautermann (2012) or Bruder (2021), among others. Drawing on literature from political economy and sociology and a methodological approach (discourse analysis) at the intersection of sociology and linguistics, this study challenges a take on SE, which reduces SE merely to a variant of entrepreneurship, failing to acknowledge it as a complex social phenomenon and movement. In enquiring the relationship between (representations of) SE and neoliberal capitalism, my study also contributes to connecting SE more strongly to broader discussions in sociology, socio-economics and political economy. The relationship between SE and (neoliberal) capitalism remains ambiguous and an interesting object for study. Hopefully, further sociological work will explore SE's 'political potential' – using Davies's (2014a) terms – and its role in a neoliberal system, which is constantly evolving and is capable to adapt to a changing environment and to absorb its critics, as we know from Boltanski & Chiapello (2007) – but in which others see "cracks and contradictions" (Hall et al. 2015: 20–21), and which yet others already see coming to an end (e.g., Jacques 2016; Stiglitz 2019; Saad-Filho 2020).

Second, this book offers empirical insights for better understanding the SE concept and phenomenon in the specific context of Germany between 1999 and 2021. Especially from a sociological perspective, SE must be understood in interplay with its historical, geographic, political and socio-economic context – as I explain in Chapter 1. Arguably, context-specific aspects still receive too little attention in SE research, as among others, Deforurny & Nyssens (2010) have pointed out from early on (and restated more recently, e.g., in Deforurny et al. 2021). I also want to highlight the explicit empirical perspective offered in this book. So far, the interpretations of SE and its wider political meanings and (potential) role in society for Germany are mainly based on theoretical assumptions, they are most often assumed instead of researched (see, e.g., Ranville & Barros 2021) – or derived from studies from contexts other than Germany (as I will explain in Chapter 2). My study, on the other hand, offers an empirical sociological investigation on how the idea of SE is being constructed in Germany, identifying different understandings as well as the dominant mainstream (media) representations and perspectives of the SE concept.

Third, this book highlights that the idea of SE may change over time and helps to understand the development of the (mainstream view of) SE in Germany in a specific period (between 1999 and 2021). The key contribution of my empirical analysis of representations of SE in newspaper articles lies in the identification of three periods, in which certain perspectives on SE are dominant. From 1999 to 2008, SE is mainly understood as a reform of the welfare infrastructure. Between 2009 and 2014, SE is increasingly conceptualised as part of the economy. From 2015, there are two main currents: one sees SE becoming part of the 'start-up' world and, on the other hand, SE is conceived as a phenomenon that contributes to a social and ecological transformation of the economy. For the German context in particular this periodisation is an important contribution. As I argue in Chapter 2, little has been written about SE as a political phenomenon or movement in Germany – in particular beyond the initial phase of the late 1990s and early 2000s, and about how the idea of SE and what larger parts of society gets to perceive of it has developed over time. Arguably, this also gives political and societal relevance to this book – because even though SE in Germany remains quite marginal and weakly institutionalised interest for SE is starting to grow in the early 2020s.[4]

Fourth, this book is a contribution to (and plea for) the interdisciplinary study of socioeconomic phenomena. Qualitative discourse analysis at the intersection of sociology and linguistics is not the most common methodology to research topics related to business and the economy. Economists and business scholars mainly rely on quantitative approaches. In the past decades, mainstream economics has undergone a severe narrowing in methodological and theoretical perspectives – as pointed out e.g., by Graupe (2013), Ehnts & Zeddies (2016), or van Treeck & Urban (2017). The (over) reliance on neoclassical theory and on mathematical models has been heavily and increasingly criticised in recent years, different movements (led by academics, students and civil society) have emerged, demanding more theoretical and methodological pluralism in the study of the economy (e.g., Aigner et al. 2018). My study's interdisciplinary approach shall help to highlight the potential of discourse (analysis) in order to better understand (socio)economic phenomena and developments – and plea for the case that neighbouring disciplines may help to expand

4 SE has not (yet) attracted significant interest or involvement of policymakers unlike in the UK, for example, where first the *Labour* and then the *Conservative* government have significantly shaped the SE sector. However, as I explain in detail in Chapter 2, interest for SE is growing in different areas of society, especially at the beginning of the 2020s.

the theoretical and methodological repertoire to understand (socio)economic phenomena and developments. On the other hand, my study shall also be an invitation for discourse analysts, who research issues related to the (political) economy, such as SE, less often than other topics (e.g., race or gender relations).

The book is organised as follows. Drawing on academic literature from various disciplines I am going to address the complex 'conceptual confusion' around SE in the first chapter. Even if this is not always explicitly stated (let alone investigated), much of the academic literature on SE offers normative and wider explanations of SE. Some explanations are (seemingly) more definitory, while others more explicitly address the proposed societal or political role of SE. Yet, all explanations of SE carry normative and political meaning (either implicit or explicit), as Section 1.2 will explain, given that the 'social' in SE is value-loaded and linked to a certain understanding of what is 'good' for society. Even though this distinction between a more definitory level and a 'wider' societal-political level is not strictly clear cut, it will serve as a useful framework for organising Chapter 1. Following this logic, Section 1.3 will focus on the more implicit meanings and normative underpinnings in definitions of SE. Next, Section 1.4 will address wider narratives that more explicitly ascribe SE a certain societal function, relating SE to other (established) societal institutions and explaining why SE is necessary. Section 1.5 then addresses literature that links SE to 'bigger', systemic questions – in particular literature that establishes a relationship between SE and neoliberalism. Section 1.6 will emphasise the importance of context (such as historical and political) for understanding SE. In addition, this section highlights the flexibility and malleability of the SE concept and the fact that different actors may link SE to various worldviews and/or political goals. Overall, this first chapter sheds light on the complex and dynamic nature of representations and explanations of SE and highlights the diverse and contested meaning(s) that are attributed to SE and that these might change over time, which is important before coming to the specific case of SE in Germany (see Section 1.7).

Chapter 2 focuses on SE in Germany and addresses particularities of SE in this context. First, Section 2.2 will situate the (untranslated) 'social entrepreneurship' term in this specific setting, explaining that it refers to a distinct movement, which can be (historically) distinguished from other social economy movements. Section 2.3 then addresses this specific SE movement in Germany, offering a brief overview of SE in the media, in academic literature, of the relevant actors in the field as well as of first policy engagements with SE. Section 2.4 focuses on the reception of this specific non-translated (English) term and concept – which was quite sceptical in social science and social economy circles. Arguably, this critique is embedded within a critique of wider political and socio-economic developments, as I will explain in 2.5. In the late 1990s and early 2000s, SE was mainly perceived as part of a neoliberal re-shaping of society – globally and in Germany, which at the time was undergoing substantial social security and labour market reform. Looking forward, however, Section 2.6 argues, that little is known – and little has been written – about SE as a political phenomenon beyond the early 2000s and about the (potential) developments of the SE concept and movement after this initial phase.

In order to study the contested concept of SE in Germany between 1999 and 2021, how the meaning of SE has been constructed and whether it is possible to identify developments in this process, Chapter 3 will introduce the research framework of discourse analysis. Discourse analysis offers a suitable theoretical and methodological perspective to investigate the 'wider' meanings of SE in Germany and their development. Section 3.2 will first introduce the theoretical framework of 'discourse' more generally. Section 3.3 will then explain what it means to *analyse* discourse and focus in particular on *Critical Discourse Analysis* (mainly according to Fairclough 1992; 2010), which, complemented by Diaz-Bone (2006), serves as the principal methodological approach for the empirical study. Section 3.4 will then lay out the concrete operationalization for the empirical research. This includes describing the compiling of the corpus of 349 newspaper articles and the utilised search terms and reflecting on the choice of data (newspaper articles) and what this implies for my research findings as well as explaining the analysis of the data derived from the corpus – and, briefly, addressing ethical considerations and the way that the results will be presented in the following chapters (4–6). During the analysis of the data, three periods in the SE discourse in Germany were identified: the first period from 1999–2008, the second period from 2009–2014 and the third period from 2015–2021. Chapters 4–6 will each be dedicated to one period in chronological order.

Chapter 4 presents the results for the first period, ranging from 1999 (the year in which the first article on SE appears in the German press) until 2008 (when the SE discourse 'shifts' towards the economy, as will be explained in detail in Chapter 5). The first half of the chapter (Sections 4.2-4.4) presents the findings of the analysis mainly in a descriptive way, while the latter half (Sections 4.5-4.7) places the focus on discussing and contextualising the findings, and establishes links to previous academic literature. In the first period (1999–2008), overall, SE in Germany remains quite marginal. A SE field emerges only around 2004, closely connected to the organisation *Ashoka* opening an office in Germany and revolves mainly around a few actors. The dominant version of SE in this early phase – as it is represented in the analysed newspaper articles – is rather person-centred, foregrounding the figure of the social entrepreneur. There are different (to some extent competing) 'wider' narratives about the role of SE in society, what 'change' SE shall bring about and what sort of economy and society SE envisions. Yet, the main perspective is clearly one of SE as a reform of the welfare-producing infrastructure. SE and the concrete social enterprises that are represented in the media largely operate in traditionally 'social' fields or fields of the state (such as education or work integration). Tied to this, social enterprises and entrepreneurs are often compared to – and presented as the more efficient or 'better' solution than – institutions of the state and the non-profit sector, which in turn are often depicted as inefficient or even deficient.

There is a remarkable shift around the years 2008–2009, as Chapter 5 explains, marking the beginning of the second period (2009–2014). According to the media representation, SE is now increasingly understood as belonging to the economy – in contrast to the first period, when SE was mainly seen as part of the welfare-producing 'social' infrastructure (see 5.1 and 5.2) – a development which I will describe as 'sectoral shift'. Related to this sectoral shift, SE is now increasingly linked to debates around business ethics and reform of business education (as Section 5.3 points out). Section 5.4 addresses another main theme in the second period: SE within a discussion around purpose and search for meaning in work, in particular for a 'new' generation of students, for who SE now becomes a career option. Sections 5.5-5.7 present the findings for the second period on definitions and explanations of SE, actors as well as logics and value statements in the analysed articles, at times drawing comparisons to the first period. Finally, Section 5.8 engages in a contextualisation of the findings and discusses, among other aspects, the role of the financial crisis of 2008 for the SE discourse.

Chapter 6 is dedicated to the third period, spanning from 2015 to 2021. From 2015, SE is now often described as a 'trend' among founders and start-ups, appearing next to other forms of entrepreneurship. This might be seen as a continuation or further evolution of the second period, however, SE is now presented not just any part of the economy, but more specifically, as part of the start-up world and as 'founding' (as Sections 6.2 and 6.3 explain). Section

6.4 shows that more actors get involved in the SE discourse, and as more people become familiar with the SE concept certain aspects of SE get institutionalised and normalised. In spite of (new) powerful actors such as *SEND* entering the SE field, this does not seem to settle the contested discussion of what SE is supposed to mean. On the contrary, as interest in SE grows, this rather seems to lead to an expansion of the term (as explained in 6.5). Sections 6.6 and 6.7 focus on politics and policy around SE and around *SEND*. Some of actors and policies see in SE 'more' than a form of entrepreneurship; SE is sometimes portrayed as a movement that propels a transformation of the economy and linked to a specific regional (economic) model. Finally, Section 6.8 engages in a contextualisation of the findings of the third period.

The final chapter summarises and discusses the key insights and findings of both the literature review and of the empirical analysis and shows in which way these make a contribution to previous academic research. Section 7.2 will highlight the central contribution of my study: i.e., having identified three different periods in the newspaper discourse of SE in Germany. Section 7.3 will then discuss that, in spite of having identified periods with a dominant and distinct SE discourse, SE remains sociologically complex and ambiguous. It was found that representations of SE may simultaneously be able to criticise and legitimise the capitalist economic model. Section 7.4 discusses the 'sectoral shift' identified, leading from the first to the second period. I argue that this shift is also a reminder of the diversity of SE, acknowledging that SE takes places in different sectors – and that this is relevant for the sociological understanding of SE. The next section (7.5) will then address interrelations between SE and capitalism and the state. Section 7.6 will address some of the overlaps between SE and other concepts (such as 'sustainability' or 'entrepreneurship') and discuss what these might imply for the future of the SE idea. Section 7.7 will reflect on the data (newspapers) and the methodological approach that served to provide the empirical findings and address their limitations. Finally, Section 7.8 closes with remarks on the political potential of SE.

Chapter 1: The Many Meanings of Social Entrepreneurship

1.1 Introduction: Social Entrepreneurship – Still a 'Messy' Field of Research

This chapter is going to draw on literature on social entrepreneurship (SE) to give an overview of different definitions, explanations, narratives and interpretations of the SE concept. Although it still remains a niche phenomenon, SE has gained popularity around the world in the past two decades. Fuelled by impressive stories of heroic entrepreneurs (labelled as 'changemakers'), and their innovative ventures, such as the *Grameen Bank* founded by Nobel laureate Muhammad Yunus, and promoted by organizations like *Ashoka* and the *Schwab Foundation*, interest in this phenomenon has sparked across different societal spheres, including the media and academia. As a result, there is a growing amount of research on social entrepreneurship in different academic disciplines; Sassmannshausen & Volkmann (2018) even claim that social entrepreneurship is reaching maturity as an academic field itself. Yet, the body of literature on SE appears quite diverse (to put it nicely) – or somewhat 'messy' (to put it less nicely). The literature on SE is spread over various disciplines and makes reference to SE in various geographies, institutional and political contexts. In addition, there is a significant share of 'grey' literature, in particular contributions by support agencies, or foundations, targeted mainly at practitioners and policymakers.

Most SE literature is rooted in business administration, followed by third sector and non-profit studies. Further contributions come from policy studies, economics, geography, politics, sociology, among others (Sassmannshausen & Volkmann 2018; Teasdale et al. 2022). This book mainly approaches the SE phenomenon from a sociological perspective. Yet, the literature that is reviewed in this chapter includes various disciplines, given that authors from different disciplines offer explanations of SE as a social and political phenomenon – even though, this might not always be made explicit, let alone be empirically investigated (e.g., Ranville & Barros 2021).

While most literature is shaped by Anglophone research, it often also transcends geographical boundaries, with SE often being portrayed as a 'global' project or phenomenon (Dacin et al. 2010). Sometimes, a distinction is made between an 'American' and a 'European' school of SE research (Kerlin 2010; 2013; Hulgard 2010; Defourny & Nyssens 2010; 2012). In addition, it needs to be noted that there are overlaps – as well as lack of clarity and delineation – between different terms and concepts, including: social entrepreneurship, social business, social enterprise, social entrepreneur, or social innovation. Therefore, the main focus and object of study in SE literature may vary, with research that either focuses on individuals (entrepreneurs), on organisations (enterprises), or on the process and phenomenon (entrepreneurship) (Danko & Brunner 2010).

Despite the growing body of research and literature thus, there is still much "conceptual confusion" (Teasdale 2012: 99) around SE, in particular when it comes to trying to make sense of SE as a political phenomenon, the 'wider' meanings of SE and what sort of economy and society SE is envisioning. Despite SE being a value-loaded concept (as I will explain in Section 1.2), which advocates for 'change', the political and normative underpinnings of SE are only sometimes overtly and explicitly addressed, remaining understudied. The normativity in SE is rarely researched, with academic literature often reproducing assumptions around SE, instead of questioning and investigating them (Ranville & Barros 2021; Bruder 2021). Overall, the relationship between social entrepreneurship and society remains vague and ambiguous (Lautermann 2012). What is more, the political and normative meanings of SE are in flux and dynamic and can change over time (as Section 1.6 will address in detail). As Teasdale notes:

> The construction of social enterprise is ongoing, and fought by a range of actors promoting different languages and practices tied to different political beliefs. That is, social enterprise is politically contested by different actors around competing discourses (Teasdale 2012: 100).

Sections 1.3, 1.4 and 1.5 shall shed light on these contested meanings around SE; the sections are organised according to what I will call different levels or layers of meaning(s) contained in explanations of SE. Section 1.3 will address definitions of social entrepreneurship, which at first sight appear (or seek) to be merely conceptual or cognitive explanations, but implicitly contain certain theoretical, normative and political underpinnings. Section 1.4 will address descriptions and explanations of SE that are linked to wider narratives and topics, thereby ascribing SE a certain function or role in society and offering a more explicit (sociological) explanation of SE. Section 1.5 will then engage with accounts of SE that outright address the 'bigger' systemic questions around how the phenomenon of SE relates to the (neoliberal) capitalist economic model, explicitly discussing SE in the context of wider political or social developments. It shall be noted that while I use these three conceptual levels or layers to organise the chapter, they shall be regarded as rather loose categories that are not completely clear-cut from each other. Section 1.6 will emphasise and discuss the role of context when it comes to trying to make sense of SE as a sociological phenomenon, and address the fact that different actors may shape SE according to their beliefs. Finally, Section 1.7 will provide a summary of the findings of the chapter and outline this book's empirical analysis of the SE discourse(s) in Germany between 1999 and 2021.

1.2 All Things Social Entrepreneurship Carry Meaning(s) – Always

SE is always tied to certain normative and socio-economic underpinnings and political beliefs – whether or not this is addressed in an explicit way, or merely implicitly. Social entrepreneurs are branded or brand themselves as 'changemakers' (Bandinelli & Arvidsson 2013; Ashoka 2020). However, it remains unclear what kind of 'change' SE actually promotes, and in which way this shapes the economy and society. SE being framed as 'social' is inherently tied to normative and political assumptions – while at the same time, it often remains vague. The 'social' nature of SE and closely related concepts, such as 'social impact' or 'social value' in the context of SE usually means 'for the good of society'. This has already been pointed out, for example, by Cho (2006) and more recently by Ranville & Barros (2021), who also explain that precisely this 'social' nature of SE often remains unclear and ambiguous, and that academic literature also tends to (re)produce this unclarity and ambiguity. Bruder, too, has noted that "[t]he prefix 'social' itself is not a value-free description (2021: 487), instead implying "being beneficial for society and ethically legitimate" (ibid.) and, therefore, is positively connoted.

Assuming that SE contributes to 'the good of society' inevitably raises questions of legitimacy: who gets to define what is to be understood as 'good for society' or 'social', and why? This will, of course, be answered differently by various actors – according to their worldviews and underlying normative and political beliefs. To translate the quote by management scholar Dees (2001 [1998]) into a more sociological perspective: What is considered to be 'social' will be different for different people – and rightfully so: in democratic and pluralistic societies, the 'common good' shall not be determined *a priori* by a certain actor or entity. Instead, different individual and group interests and positions shall be discussed and negotiated in a political process (e.g., Schubert & Klein 2020). A fixed and *a priori* understanding of the common good (set by a specific entity) would, instead, be an indicator for an autocratic system. Therefore, while I agree with Ranville & Barros (2021) who, having analysed SE against contemporary schools of political philosophy, demand SE researchers to be reflexive regarding the normativity in their object of study, I argue that the 'social' being a contested category is a somewhat desirable dilemma for SE that will (need to) persist, even if this might sometimes be unsatisfactory to researchers trying to make sense of SE and to untangle the 'conceptual confusion' that SE presents us with. Overall, such sociological aspects of SE are understudied (Somers 2013). According to Parkinson & Howorth, one reason for this is that "much of the current work has come out of business and management disciplines" (2008: 287), which does not place an emphasis on studying SE "as a complex social movement" (ibid.). Similarly, Lautermann (2012) and Bruder (2021), too, have pointed out the lack of foundation in the relevant social theories and disregard of the normative and political questions about the relationship between SE and society in the study of SE.

At the same time, as indicated in the Introduction, there are many different views on the 'wider' meaning(s) of SE and what sort of 'change' SE promotes or should promote, depending on different understandings of the SE phenomenon and the 'hopes' attributed to it. The following three sections in this chapter highlight the diversity of these understandings as well as their complexity and ambiguity. They show how meanings around SE are being constructed and contested on different levels at the same time, whether it comes to 'simply' defining SE, or explaining the wider political or social role of SE. The next section is going to begin with focussing on the apparently 'simple' level of defining or describing SE, which inevitably (implicitly) linked to certain (world)views and value judgements.

1.3 Describing and Defining Social Entrepreneurship - No Innocent Task

'Social entrepreneurship' is an umbrella term, which is used to refer to a wide array of activities; social enterprises can differ greatly in size, organizational form, or the context they work in. They often operate at the margins and intersections of the state, the market and the third sector, sometimes blurring the boundaries between the three (Ridley-Duff & Bull 2011). SE might stand for a microcredit institution in Bangladesh, a work integration social enterprise in Belgium, a fair-trade chocolate producer in Benin, a kindergarten in Britain, or a tech company in Brazil. SE may also bring different people together – and as its 'practitioners' you may encounter (former) bankers or business consultants as well as activists and social workers, sometimes within the same venture. Considering this heterogeneity of the field and its people, it would be surprising to find that all of them had the same understanding of SE and had the same vision for SE as well as for the economy and society as a whole. The projections onto SE – the hopes that people associate with SE – are many, and often quite different from each other. Definitions are supposed to provide a solution exactly for this problem: establishing a common ground so that everyone can share the same understanding of SE. The task of defining SE plays an important role in literature on SE (Dacin et al. 2010). However, defining SE is never 'neutral' or 'innocent'.[1] Defining SE is inevitably tied to underlying normative assumptions – which also extend to or are linked to wider meanings, as I will explain in the following paragraphs.

Definitions of SE are *per se* normative. They delineate what the 'ideal' or prototypical form of SE is or should be and establish a set of characteristics that determines what is to be considered to be 'social entrepreneurship' and what is not. These characteristics inevitably convey some sort of normative or political meaning(s). As explained in the previous section (1.2), this is linked to the prefix 'social', which always carries both underlying and wider (normative) meanings and political beliefs – even though this might not always be stated, or, perhaps, not even be evident to the authors.

It shall be noted here that this section addresses the issue of defining SE differently than probably most other academic texts. I will have to disappoint the reader that is looking for a specific definition of SE. Selecting a

1 I am borrowing this term from Diaz-Bone et al. (2007: 6) who write: "Discourses, as Said (1978) and Spivak (1987) note, are not innocent explanations of the world".

certain definition as a basis is not my purpose. Quite the contrary, settling on a specific definition would be opposed to my research project, which is analysing how (different) meanings and interpretations are discursively constructed. Put differently, the definitions and explanations of SE that will be discussed in the following have a different function: they are part of the object of study. Nonetheless, as I will explain in Chapter 2, my study strongly relies on Birkhölzer (2015), who defines SE as a distinct (social economy) movement, situating it in a specific time in history (and not necessarily linked to a specific organisational form).

This being said, most academic literature tries to define SE in terms of the 'social entrepreneur' (the person) or the 'social enterprise' (the organisation). There is a vast variety of these definitions; comprehensive overviews are provided, for example, in Dacin et al. (2010: 39–41), listing 37 different definitions, or in Jansen (2013: 39–49), who gives an overview of 29 definitions.[2] Most definitions of SE part from the two constituting words 'social' and 'entrepreneurship', explaining in which way, SE has a 'social' and an 'entrepreneurial' (or 'economic') dimension. This is also somewhat the lowest common denominator of the different definitions. The 'social' character of SE may be described as the pursuit of a 'social mission' or the creation of 'social value'; for example, by Mair & Marti (2006: 37) as "to pursue opportunities to catalyse social change and/or address social needs" by Peredo & McLean (2006: 64) as "creating social value, either exclusively or at least in some prominent way", or by Haugh (2006: 5) as to "trade for a social purpose". However, the 'social' aspect of SE is seldom discussed in detail and can be considered as undertheorized in SE literature. The 'entrepreneurial' dimension of SE associates SE with 'doing business' and 'innovation', among others. For Korosec & Berman (2006: 449) this means to "develop new programs, services, and solutions to specific problems", for Mair & Marti (2006: 37) "involving the innovative use and combination of resources to pursue opportunities", and for Tracey & Jarvis (2007: 671) to "identify and exploit market opportunities, and assemble the necessary resources, in order to develop products and/or services". Due to the combination of 'economic'

2 The overview of 37 definitions presented by Dacin et al. (2010) demonstrates the lack of delineation and the almost interchangeable use of different terms ('social entrepreneurship', 'social enterprise', 'social entrepreneur', 'social business', etc.). Strictly speaking, only 10 of the definitions refer to the term 'social entrepreneurship', while 11 definitions refer to 'social entrepreneur', 4 to 'social enterprise', 2 to 'social business', and 10 definitions even combine the different terms.

and 'social' logics, social enterprises are often described by management scholars and organisational sociologists as 'hybrids' or 'hybrid organizations' (e.g., Hockerts 2006; Heinze et al. 2011; Doherty et al. 2014; Grohs et al. 2016).

Apart from the 'social' and the 'entrepreneurial' (or 'economic') dimension, some definitions of SE include a third domain: one that is often framed as 'governance' and which refers to aspects such as organisational form, control and accountability. In particular, third sector and 'social economy' scholars (most of who are organised in the research networks *EMES* or *CIRIEC*) have advocated for this perspective.[3] The defining characteristics of the 'governance' dimension can, for example, be formulated as "a decision-making process in which voting power is not distributed according to capital shares" (Defourny & Nyssens 2012: 15) or might be inscribed within rules for "the reinvestment of surplus for community benefit" (Haugh 2006: 5). According to Defourny & Nyssens, this "governance [dimension is] specific to the *EMES* ideal-type of social enterprise" (2012: 12), and is sometimes considered to distinguish the 'European' from the 'American' school of thought of SE (as I will further discuss in Section 1.6).

Arguably, prescribing rules for the organisational governance of SE – or *not* – is linked to certain premises and normative underpinnings. More specifically, this is linked to a (normative or political) position on the question of what makes 'good' organisational forms for SE. Whether or not a social aim can be pursued by any organisation – agnostic to its organisational form (including for-profit private enterprises) – or whether this requires a specific organisational setting. 'Governance' aspects, such as participatory governance, democratic decision-making and ownership within organisations and the principle that power should be decentralised – instead of centralised in the hands of a few – comes from a specific historical and political tradition, associated with third sector organisations and cooperatives (e.g., Pearce 2003; Ridley-Duff & Bull 2011). 'Governance' aspects may, therefore, be seen as an expression of a

3 *CIRIEC* stands short for the *The International Centre of Research and Information on the Public, Social and Cooperative Economy*. It is a non-governmental international scientific organization that was founded in 1947 (CIRIEC 2020). *EMES* is an international research network. *EMES* takes its name from the French title of its first research project: *L'EMergence de l'Entreprise Sociale en Europe* (the emergence of social enterprises in Europe), conducted between 1996 and 2000 (Borzaga & Defourny 2001; EMES 2020). Both networks mainly consist of economists, as well as sociologists, political scientists and other scholars, who ascribe to the 'social economy' concept.

certain worldview that positively connotes democratic control and participation of the many, expressing the view that organisations integrating these aspects are better suited in order to ensure the (social) aims of an organization in the long run. On the other hand, not including 'governance' indicates faith in the private enterprise, expressing the view that organisational forms based on capital ownership are suitable for or compatible with the pursuit of social aims.

Furthermore, when comparing different definitions, it quickly stands out that various definitions of SE show very different degrees of detail regarding the 'social' or 'entrepreneurial', or, where applicable, also the 'governance' dimension of SE – and, therefore, place different emphases. The following table illustrates this by comparing four definitions of SE: Dees (2001 [1998]) and Austin et al. (2006), coming from a business administration background, Defourny & Nyssens (2012) representing the 'social economy' approach and *SEND* (2019), the main network and lobbying organisation for SE in Germany. These four definitions were chosen, because they are either highly influential for SE scholarship in general or specifically for the German context. According to Sassmannshausen & Volkmann (2018), Dees' (2001 [1998]) text is the most-cited text on SE overall, while Austin et al. (2006) is the most-cited journal article. Defourny & Nyssens (2012) are main representatives of the *EMES* network, which is highly influential in Europe, both in scholarship as well as in shaping (EU) policy, while *SEND* is currently the leading interest group for social enterprises in Germany.

The table shows which aspects of the three dimensions 'social', 'economic' and 'governance' are included in the definitions of the respective author or organisation:[4]

4 Some texts were reorganised in order to be integrated into the structure of the table. Two things should be noted on *SEND*'s (2019) definition included in the table: First, next to the short definition referenced here, *SEND* has also developed a longer definition, involving different stakeholders, in particular member organisation. Second, before developing this definition, *SEND* (until 2018) relied on a definition by the *European Commission* (of 2014), which in turn has been shaped by the members of the *EMES* network.

Table 1: Three Definitions of SE and Comparing Their Social, Economic and Governance Dimensions

	Dees (2001 [1998]: 4)	**Austin et al.** (2006: 2)	**EMES/Defourny & Nyssens** (2012: 12–15)	***SEND*** (2019)
	Social entrepreneurs play the role of change agents in the social sector, by:	*We define SE as (...)*	*Criteria or indicators for an 'ideal-type' of social enterprises (in Weber's terms) are:*	
Social dimension	*Adopting a mission to create and sustain social value (not just private value),*	*social value creating activity*	*An explicit aim to benefit the community,* *An initiative launched by a group of citizens or civil society organisations,* *A limited profit distribution*	*The primary goal of SE is to find solutions for social challenges*
Economic-entrepreneurial dimension	*Recognizing and relentlessly pursuing new opportunities to serve that mission,* *Engaging in a process of continuous innovation, adaptation, and learning,* *Acting boldly without being limited by resources currently in hand,*	*Innovative*	*A continuous activity producing goods and/or selling services,* *A significant level of economic risk,* *A minimum amount of paid work*	*This is achieved by continuously applying entrepreneurial means, resulting in new and innovative solutions.*
Governance dimension	*Exhibiting heightened accountability to the constituencies served and for the outcomes created*		*A high degree of autonomy,* *A decision-making power not based on capital ownership,* *A participatory nature, which involves various parties affected by the activity*	*Controlling and steering mechanisms ensure that the social mission is pursued internally and externally*

The overview of the four definitions shows different things: first, that, in general, the degree of detail of the defining criteria varies considerably. The definition by Austin et al. (2006) is very short and broad, while e.g., the definition by Defourny & Nyssens (2012) is, in many ways, much more detailed and specific. Furthermore, a definition may offer a detailed understanding of one dimension – but not of all three. For example, Dees' (2001 [1998]) definition provides a quite sophisticated and detailed understanding of the 'entrepreneurial' dimension, with three of the five defining characteristics in his definition referring to this dimension. The 'governance' dimension, on the other hand, remains rather unspecific – in the definition by Defourny & Nyssens (2012), on the other hand, the 'governance' dimension is quite elaborate. It can be argued, therefore, that the degree of detail that different definitions place on different (aspects) of the dimensions of SE is, to some extent, also an expression of emphasis – what is considered to be important. Certain aspects of SE are given (more) importance (over others), which, again, derives from normative underpinnings and political beliefs that are linked to different understandings of SE.

Furthermore, there are many other aspects of definitions that are normatively or politically grounded, as I will briefly illustrate, exemplarily focussing on the definition by management scholar Dees (2001 [1998]). Dees (2001 [1998]) clearly positions SE as a form of entrepreneurship – a perspective that can often be found in SE literature by business studies scholars. Embedding SE within entrepreneurship, however, can be seen as a reduction of the concept – as, to some extent, this perspective fails to acknowledge that SE may have 'wider' political meaning, to which I will come back in Chapters 6 and 7. Dees' (2001 [1998]) definition ascribes certain characteristics to SE that derive from his discussion of entrepreneurship theory, namely that SE implies *pursuing new opportunities* as well as *innovation, adaptation, and learning* and *acting boldly*, i.e., taking risks (see table above). Dees' definition associates SE with newness, innovation, flexibility and risk. Dees' (2001 [1998]) framing of social entrepreneurs as 'change agents' further underlines the notion of SE as something that embraces the new, change and breaking with established habits or practices. What is more, newness, innovation, risk-taking, etc. as defining aspects of SE are also as such presented as positive features. Moreover, Dees' (2001 [1998]) definition in centred around the 'social entrepreneur', the person or agent who engages in social entrepreneurship – in contrast, for example, to 'social enterprise' (as in the definition by Defourny & Nyssens 2012), which implies a stronger focus on the organization, or to 'social entrepreneurship', foregrounding the phenomenon or process. Dees (2001 [1998]), therefore, mainly parts from the individual as the core agent of SE, establishing SE as a process driven by individuals – and not e.g., by collective action. In addition, Dees' (2001 [1998]) definition contrasts 'social value' against 'private value'. While Dees' (2001 [1998]) understanding of 'social value' remains quite vague, the distinction from 'private value' is nonetheless remarkable.[5] Even though the two different types of 'value' are not presented as mutually exclusive – this is indicated by the word 'just' (see Table 1 above), which implies that SE may create both forms of value ('private' as well as 'social') – Dees (2001 [1998]) highlights that 'social value' should be the primary focus. Finally, Dees (2001 [1998]) clearly positions SE as a phenomenon that occurs in the 'social sector'.[6]

This exercise of trying to unpack the sometimes explicit sometimes implicit normative and political meanings within definitions of SE could be continued endlessly. However, the main point has been made: to some extent, all definitions and academic literature on SE carry wider political meaning(s). This has been demonstrated in Section 1.2, discussing the prefix 'social' as well as in Section 1.3, addressing the different dimensions of SE ('social', 'entrepreneurial' and 'governance') and briefly discussing the definition by Dees (2001 [1998]). SE is always a value-loaded concept, even if this may not be explicitly stated by the respective author (appearing implicit and/or opaque) and not be of direct concern to their research. Yet, part of the literature on SE does, in fact, address and overtly discuss explanations and interpretations of the social entrepreneurship phenomenon and its wider meaning(s), or they link SE to certain narratives and political developments (more) explicitly, as I will discuss in the following section.

5 Strictly speaking, Dees' distinction between 'private' and 'social' value also seems hard to reconcile with 'mainstream' neoclassical economic thought (e.g., Friedman 1970). In this perspective, the pursuit of private value (individual and egoistic interest) would, in fact, result in a maximisation of social value anyway, and delineating 'private' from 'social' value should then appear nonsensical to the neoclassical economist.

6 Dees (2001 [1998]) does not further explain the 'social sector' mentioned here. Other terms in social science literature would be 'third sector' or 'non-profit sector' (e.g., Betzelt 2001; Evers & Laville 2004; Defourny & Nyssens 2010).

1.4 Social Entrepreneurship Linked to Wider Narratives

This section is going to focus on academic literature that more explicitly links the SE concept to wider narratives. More specifically, by 'wider narratives', I am referring to SE being explained in a societal context, i.e., when a certain function or role is attributed to SE, and relationships between SE and other (established) societal institutions are addressed. These narratives, explanations or interpretations of SE are, inevitably, connected to specific normative and political views. Again, it shall be noted that these wider narratives of SE are extremely heterogeneous. As already indicated in the Introduction, different actors may link the idea of SE to very different political agendas and broader visions for society. In addition, it must be said that this section will only be able to provide a fraction of all the wider meanings that may be attributed to SE in academic literature and shall by no means be regarded as an extensive or complete account thereof.

A concise overview, which demonstrates the great diversity of these wider explanations of SE in academic literature, is offered by Teasdale et al. (2019: 22–23), who (citing various authors) synthesise that SE has been described as

> a potential solution to area-based deprivation (...); an alternative vehicle for the delivery of publicly funded services (...); a more effective means of international development (...); an additional revenue raising stream for non-profits (...) or a potential alternative to winner-takes-all-capitalism (...); (...) a solution to the failure of markets to distribute goods and services equitably (...); (...) a policy solution to the failure of the state to deliver public services that were responsive to consumers (...); (...) a solution to the failure of the third sector to scale-up (...); (...) a vehicle through which public services can be spun off, allowing greater democratic ownership and control (...) (Teasdale et al. 2019: 22–23).

This overview shows that various authors propose quite different narratives of SE and of the societal and political functions or goals connected to the SE phenomenon. Each narrative or explanation of SE comes with its own system of thought and normative and political underpinnings. Each explanation or narrative comes with its own assessment of a 'problem', a situation which SE is seeking to change or overcome – thereby giving SE a specific role (in relation to other societal institutions). To pick out two of the explanations cited above: introducing SE as an 'alternative to winner-takes-all-capitalism' implies the assumption that capitalism (or a certain form of it) is a problem – one that SE shall help to overcome. Portraying SE as a 'more effective means of international development' implies that current forms of international development are regarded as ineffective – and that the function or *raison d'être* of SE is to offer a 'better' model for development.

Without doubt, these interpretations of SE are embedded in different worldviews, they ascribe SE a certain function or role in a social and economic context and represent very different underlying normative or political stands. Teasdale (2012: 103–106) has identified the following as the main theoretical assumptions behind the different narratives of SE: *state failure* (i.e., the assumption that the state and its institutions are unable to provide adequate welfare for its citizens), *market failure* (i.e., the assumption that the private sector is unable to organise equitable distribution), *earned income approaches* (i.e., the assumption that nonprofits are adopting earned income strategies to compensate for declined funds), *marketization of the nonprofit sector* (i.e., the assumption that nonprofits are becoming more business-like because of a general shift in society towards business ideology) and *voluntary failure* (i.e., the assumption that the third sector is unable to deliver effective welfare services). These theoretical assumptions carved out by Teasdale (2012) show that SE can be connected to very different – even opposed – analyses of contemporary societies and developments. Moreover, different narratives may place SE in completely different sub-systems or sectors of society – for example, 'SE as an alternative to capitalism' places SE in the economic system, giving SE the function to transform the economic model. Whereas 'SE as the delivery of publicly funded services' places SE in the public realm (or at the intersection of the public and the 'traditionally social' or 'third' sector), instead, attributing SE the function of transforming the model of welfare production and distribution.

These sectoral placements also determine the relationships between SE and other actors or institutions – e.g., private businesses, state agencies, nonprofits, etc. – which might be contrasted or linked to SE. When SE is introduced as a 'new' phenomenon in a specific setting, this inevitably comes with a statement about the 'old' (established) actors and institutions in this setting. When SE is explained as an "[approach] to better help individuals and communities beyond those institutionally pervasive and arguably stale welfare state charitable service models" (Dart 2019: 66), this entails a negative image of state institutions. On the other hand, presenting SE as a solution to "the failure of the private sector to allocate resources equitably" (Teasdale 2012: 104) comes with a critical statement about private businesses. The societal functions that SE is given varies in different explanations, narratives and interpretations.

Beckmann (2011: 71–72), for example, offers three different interpretations about SE's functions: First, SE may be considered as a phenomenon that offers a wider perspective on economic activity; SE seeks to (re-)connect private (or economic) value and economic efficiency with social value, which today are often seen as antagonistic. Second, SE may amplify the repertoire of practices and entities that address social challenges by discussing the contribution of private entities (social enterprises) to public benefit. Thus, also questioning the (welfare) state's monopoly on providing social or welfare needs. Third, SE may challenge today's understanding of the areas or issues that traditionally comprise the 'social' or welfare sector, such as health or care. SE also opens up a new spectrum of social challenges and potential solutions (e.g., combating poverty or climate change) (Beckmann 2011: 71–72).

Engaging with these wider narratives around SE also shows that explaining SE in relationship to society and its institutions can never be 'innocent' and that such wider explanations are also tied to questions of legitimacy, i.e., justifying why SE is necessary, or 'good' for society. This is linked to an assessment of the 'problem', for which SE provides a 'solution'. For example, when SE is introduced as an alternative to capitalism, capitalism is automatically described as a problem. The need for an alternative economic model is expressed – this view being based on a specific set of value judgements, normative and political beliefs. Similarly, if welfare state institutions or the way they work are presented as the problem – and SE as a means to change these – the *raison d'être* of SE is legitimised in a quite different way.

However, even if there are very different wider narratives around SE – each coming with different 'problem assessments', sectoral placements and ways of legitimising SE – these different narratives and underlying theories are not necessarily incompatible, as Teasdale (2012: 106) notes. Explanations or narratives of SE might, in fact, combine different theoretical assumptions and ways of legitimising SE. Ranville & Barros (2021) share a similar view when they find many "normative contradictions" (2021: no pagination) in academic literature. This means that wider narratives are not necessarily coherent in the sense of strictly following to the ideal types of theories (e.g., *state failure*) identified by Teasdale (2012: 103–106). This applies to academic literature, but, of course, to other, non-academic discussions about SE as well. To stick with an example of a narrative of SE that has already been introduced: if SE is understood as a form of international development, and legitimised as a necessary form to improve the practices of international development, the underlying theory behind this might be a combination of both *state failure* (assuming that governments in developing countries are failing to provide adequate welfare) and *market failure* (assuming that in the global market economy businesses from the Global South suffer from unequal terms of trade).

Furthermore, it shall be noted that in spite of the diversity of the narratives of and around SE – each with their own theoretical assumptions, functions attributed to, or ways of legitimising SE – there are also similar patterns of argumentation across different narratives. Three shall be pointed out here: SE presented as a 'new' phenomenon, SE as a 'better' way of doing things and SE as 'empowering'. First, SE is mostly introduced as a 'new' way of doing things. The wider narratives of SE also reproduce what I have mentioned previously – the 'new' being somewhat automatically and inherently positive. Related to this is, second, the idea of SE as a 'better' way of doing things. Introducing SE as a 'new' phenomenon in a certain field comes with establishing a relationship to existing ways of doing things, institutions and actors – and since SE (as most often understood) is about bringing positive change, it is presented as the 'better' version compared to the *status quo*. While the problem assessment differs in different narratives (as noted above), the argument is mostly structured in the way that SE provides the way out, being introduced as a response to the identified problem. Third, a common ground across different narratives and theories is often the idea that SE is somewhat (more) empowering. Whether SE is placed in the social/public realm or in the economy, narratives of SE often imply a critique of top-down approaches to the delivery of goods or services and the hierarchies connected to this. SE in different settings is described as an approach to break with hierarchies and dependencies, propagating self-help and capacity building. In this perspective, SE 'empowers' people, making them realize their potential, but also involving them and giving them a voice. Consequently, some authors claim that the empowering aspect of SE also has an impact on higher (democratic) participation of the people engaged in SE. For example, Sievers (2016) stresses the participatory dimension of SE, claiming that 'beneficiaries' or 'service/product users' are more involved in decision-making processes. This may also apply to fostering community spirit and social cohesion, or, as Sievers argues, "collective empowerment" (2016: 79).

This section has addressed wider narratives, which explain SE and attribute certain functions or a *raison d'être* to SE, often in relationship to other (established) institutions or actors. The different explanations or narratives discussed in this section shall by no means be understood as a complete, all-encompassing account of all explanations, narratives or interpretations that may be found in academic literature. Instead, it was the aim to show the diversity and ambiguity of different explanations, narratives and interpretations and their underlying theoretical assumptions – once again, showing that meaning(s) of SE are contested. However, it is also important to note that these different explanations of SE not necessarily propagate a coherent worldview or a specific political agenda, but might in fact be intertwined in a combination of different theoretical assumptions. Moving from Section 1.3 to 1.4, this chapter has tried to demonstrate how the meaning(s) of SE are being contested on different levels – both when it comes to seemingly simple explanations (as, for example, being inherent to definitions) and on a 'wider' scale, within narratives around the functions of SE or explaining why SE is needed. The boundaries between these different levels of meaning, however, are fluid and shall not be overstated. This has become quite evident in this section, as discussing 'wider' narratives quickly reaches into even 'bigger' – systemic – questions. These systemic questions will now be elaborated on in the following section, with a particular focus on how the relationship between SE and neoliberalism has been discussed in academic literature.

1.5 A 'Systemic' Perspective: Social Entrepreneurship in Relationship to Neoliberalism

As explained in the Introduction, the realisation that there are many and quite differing, even opposite, interpretations of the SE concept has been a starting point for this book. Even on a 'systemic' level the interpretations of SE may differ considerably, i.e., when it comes to explaining what sort of economic or social model is envisioned by SE, what sort of social or political developments SE might be part of and what the relationship between SE and neoliberal capitalism is. Academic literature, once again, provides very different answers for this. Shaw and de Bruin (2013), for example, juxtapose two very different systemic interpretations of SE, asking "whether (...) social enterprise is driven by neo-liberal policies or offers an alternative to capitalism" (2013: 738). Without doubt, the relationship between SE and neoliberalism, and whether SE may be considered as part of a 'neoliberal', as part of an 'alternative' or 'social' economic model is a contested debate in scholarly literature (e.g., Hulgard 2010; 2011; Dey & Teasdale 2016; Sievers 2016; Nicholls & Teasdale 2017; Bandinelli 2017) – with many scholars offering a somewhat ambiguous or contradictory explanation of SE as a concept that joins both 'neoliberal' and 'alternative' elements, as will be addressed in this section.

First, it must be noted that 'neoliberalism' is complex and has various understandings to it. Some understand neoliberalism mainly as an ideology, others as a specific (historical) period, as a set of policies, or as a political and economic movement – or as a combination of these (e.g., Rose 1999; Mirowski & Plehwe 2009; Crouch 2011; Davies 2014a; Davies 2014b). Based on different understandings, there are also different views on what represents an 'alternative' to the neoliberal economic and political model. Therefore, different assessments of the relationship between SE and neoliberalism that are mentioned in this section might lack a common underlying understanding or focussing on different aspects of neoliberalism.

A few key features of neoliberalism identified by social science scholars shall be mentioned here. A helpful attempt of summarising the essence of neoliberalism has been made by Crouch (2011), who describes neoliberalism as a specific (historical) period and also as a set of ideas, namely as "the set of economic ideas that have ruled the western world and many other parts of the globe since the late 1970s" (2011: VII). Above all

> that free markets in which individuals maximize their material interests provide the best means for satisfying human aspirations, and that markets in particular to be preferred over states and politics, which are at best inefficient and worst threats to freedom (Crouch 2011: VII).

Davies (2014b) also stresses the political and historical dimensions of neoliberalism and the role of governments in promoting it, explaining neoliberalism as "a form of market fundamentalism, imposed upon developing nations by the United States government and multinational institutions" (2014b: no pagination), which is linked to "the elections of 'new right' political leaders, Margaret Thatcher and Ronald Reagan in particular, in the late 1970s and early '80s" (ibid.). Davies (2017) highlights, however, that this does not mean that under neoliberalism markets (as institutions) were introduced into all areas of society, even though they have expanded into many. Instead, many areas of society and its institutions were transformed and shaped in market-like or business-like ways, which also applies to individuals and organisations. "It is economic calculation that spreads into all walks of life under neoliberalism, and not markets as such", Davies (2017: XIV) recalls – to an extent that economic calculation sometimes replaces politics (as an instrument of governing and making decisions in society). Competition and competitiveness (rather than market fundamentalism) are the defining features of neoliberalism. "[T]he neoliberal state takes the principle of competition and the ethos of competitiveness (which historically have been found in and around markets), and seeks to reorganise society around them" (Davies 2017: XVI). This spread of economic rationality for Davies also marks the crucial difference between neoliberalism and (classical) liberalism. "A defining trait of neoliberalism is that it abandons this liberal conceit of separate economic, social and political spheres, evaluating all three according to a single economic logic", Davies (2014a: 20) explains – a development which can be termed 'economization'. Moreover, areas such as health, welfare, education or security are then increasingly understood in terms of human capital and organised as (private) enterprise (Foucault 2004 [1978/1979]; Rose 1999; Bröckling 2007).

Observers and critics of neoliberalism also point to the important role of the individual and individualism (Foucault 2004 [1978/1979]; Rose 1999; Bröckling 2007). Neoliberalism promotes "responsibilization and entrepreneurialization of the citizen" (Rose, 1999: 139), the individual acts as 'entrepreneur of the self', transferring the rationality of the market economy to the most diverse areas of life, where process optimisation and efficiency become guiding doctrines. The figure of the entrepreneur is a particularly important *motif* for neoliberalism, mainly introduced through the work of Schumpeter (Davies 2014a). Schumpeter presumes "an ideal vision of the heroic, creative entrepreneur" (Davies 2014a: 47) – and this image of the entrepreneur is crucial in applying the ethos of neoliberalism to the individual level, leading, more precisely, "to a psychological emphasis on competitiveness as an essential trait of individuals" (Davies 2014a: 47).

In Schumpeter's understanding, entrepreneurs defy and seek to redefine the set of rules and institutions that organise the economy, what is famously labelled 'creative destruction'. However, this does not mean that entrepreneurs challenge the capitalist model as such – quite the contrary, Schumpeter assumes that entrepreneurs are 'exceptional' and 'uncommon' individuals. Thus, only a small, 'exceptional' minority can be entrepreneurs, which bases the ideal figure of the (Schumpeterian) entrepreneur on the idea of (human) difference and competitiveness – representing the core principle of neoliberalism according to Davies (2014a, citing Schumpeter [1934; 1954; 1976]). In addition, following Schumpeter, the 'creative destruction' caused by entrepreneurs is necessary to allow capitalism to adapt to changing developments and therefore to maintain capitalism itself. Without 'creative destruction', capitalism would succumb to bureaucratic organisation, given that large corporations tend towards this form of organisation, which makes entrepreneurs central agents of neoliberal capitalism (Davies 2014a, citing Schumpeter [1934; 1954; 1976]). More generally, given that the 'creative destruction' in Schumpeter's eyes is a necessary (and therefore legitimate) process, entrepreneurs and entrepreneurial activity justify competitive behaviour (in individuals) as well as profit-making, inequality and the power relations on which the capitalist system relies.

As mentioned above, scholars who have written about SE and neoliberalism not necessarily share the same understanding of neoliberalism that I have outlined here. This being said, several scholars relate SE to (aspects of) neoliberalism (e.g., Cook et al. 2003; Eikenberry & Kluver 2004; Dey 2010; Garrow & Hasenfeld 2014). It should be kept in mind, however, that only a fraction of contributions on SE address such 'systemic' questions concerning the relationship between SE and neoliberalism in the first place, trying to 'make sense' of SE from a social science perspective.

A simple reason for SE often being interpreted as a neoliberal phenomenon may be the fact that the term 'social entrepreneurship' includes 'entrepreneurship', which is so strongly associated with Schumpeterian theory and to a certain ideal image of the 'entrepreneur' – a theoretical background that these scholars are aware of and project onto SE. But there are more reasons for why SE is often interpreted as a neoliberal phenomenon. A main argument for this perspective is that SE is associated with processes of marketization and privatization in the social or public sector (Hulgard 2011), given that SE is mainly driven by 'new', mainly private actors, some of which are market-based. Related to this is a view of SE as the projection or application of principles and logics of the private sector into social or public realms. Dart (2004) sees in SE a vehicle that introduces business thinking and the language of management into nonprofit sectors and organisations. Similarly, according to Dey, SE contributes to "inscribing ideas of efficiency, management savvy and entrepreneurship into the body of the social" (2010: 1). Certainly, there are parallels to the idea of *New Public Management*, as an instrument of introducing and legitimising business methods in the pursuit of social and public objectives (Ridley-Duff & Bull 2011). Furthermore, SE is associated with emphasising the individual and individual responsibility. Through SE, the idea of individual social responsibility may become more important in areas such as welfare, social security, health or education (Hulgard 2011).

As mentioned above, there are perspectives, on the other hand, which interpret social entrepreneurship – or aspects of it – as part of an 'alternative', 'counter movement' or 'counter discourse' to (neoliberal) capitalism (Pearce 2003; Hulgard 2011; Teasdale 2012; Sievers 2016; Longhurst et al. 2016). Pearce (2003) clearly positions social enterprises as part of an alternative economic model. For Pearce, SE contributes to a wider project of creating and establishing a 'social economy' that represents a viable alternative economic system. According to Pearce (2003), this alternative economic system stands against the dominant (neoliberal) capitalist economy and is built on values of the 'third sector', including: co-operation, decentralisation, inclusivity, good work, sustainability and people-centration (2003: 40–44). Hulgard claims that (at least some) forms of social entrepreneurship represent "part of an emerging counter discourse in the sense of a participatory non-capitalist economy" (2011: 202). Sievers (2016), too, highlights aspects of participation and collective action – and that contrary to individualism, SE promotes an idea of 'community' and 'collective empowerment', contributing to community building and fostering community resilience (Sievers 2016). Longhurst et al. describe SE as part of "nascent 'new economic' narratives which represent fundamentally different imaginaries of the urban economy" (2016: 69). According to Longhurst et al. (2016), the dominant neoliberal logic is challenged in four key dimensions: the purpose of economic development, distributive mechanisms, governance and form of economic organisation, with SE "providing a viable alternative to privatization, de-regulation and re-regulation" (Longhurst et al. 2016: 72).

Finally, many authors point out the ambiguities in the relationship between social entrepreneurship and neoliberalism, arguing that SE has both neoliberal and alternative elements, making it an ambiguous concept (Grenier 2009; Beckmann 2011; Hulgard 2011; Teasdale 2012; Sievers 2016; Bandinelli 2017). Bandinelli calls this the "inner ambivalence of social entrepreneurship" (2017: 23). Sievers offers a similar perspective, explaining that different types of logics are contained within the phenomenon of SE. This causes a state of constant ambiguity and contestation: "ambiguities between care and efficiency, between market-oriented activation and just being and between participation and exclusion co-exist and co-develop continually through repeated negotiations" (Sievers 2016: 90). Some authors have argued that SE may also be a combination: that "social enterprise exemplified the 'Third Way' by promising the successful combination of social justice and market dynamism (Nicholls & Teasdale 2017: 332)". Other authors differentiate between different currents of SE – and this is also where actors with different agendas around SE come into play. Teasdale supports this view, describing SE as "a fluid concept which is continually re-negotiated by different actors" (2012: 101). Nicholls (2010) argues that because SE is 'pre-paradigmatic' and that "the field has failed to set any normative boundaries around the term" (2010: 613), this creates a "fluid institutional space for dominant actors to shape and exploit" (2010: 612).

Davies, too, has written about the ambiguities of entrepreneurship (more generally). Theoretically speaking,

> [t]he entrepreneur (...) desires [to re-make] the economic *status quo*(...), including its rules and conditions. For this reason, there is undoubtedly political potential in entrepreneurship to introduce something radically new, and not simply 'more innovation' in the sense favoured by business and neoliberal policy makers. (...). In this respect, entrepreneurship has always posed a tacit threat to neoliberalism, while also being celebrated (Davies 2014a: 197).

Davies (2014a) also explains that when considering actual developments and observations, however, that this 'political potential' or 'threat' posed by entrepreneurship has so far been contained by the capitalist system (i.e., by financially rewarding entrepreneurs) and by business elites, who manage to hold close links to entrepreneurs. With regards to social entrepreneurship, Davies (2014a) indicates that SE might be seen as a minor shift away from the complicit and sustaining role of entrepreneurship for neoliberal capitalism. In this regard, Davies highlights the fact that social enterprises mainly pursue non-monetary goals. However, Davies (2014a) also notes that SE fails to break with the central principle of competitiveness – with SE, too, mostly being centred around a small minority of 'exceptional' individuals.

All in all, the contributions show that SE may, in fact, be an ambiguous phenomenon – and that a single and clear answer to the question "whether (...) social enterprise is driven by neo-liberal policies or offers an alternative to capitalism" (Shaw & de Bruin 2013: 738) seems impossible (and a flawed approach to begin with). Instead, once more there are different (competing) interpretations of SE as a political phenomenon and what it means for society or the economy as a whole. These interpretations may vary according to different actors (and their interests concerning SE) or may vary in different contexts, as will be addressed in the following section.

1.6 The Meanings of Social Entrepreneurship: Context-Specific, Dynamic and Shaped by Different Actors

This book is building, above all, on research contributions that have demonstrated that the meanings of SE are contested in different ways and on different (conceptual) levels and that these may be ambiguous, combining different logics, narratives, or theoretical assumptions; meaning(s) of SE are dynamic and in constant flux. Making sense of SE as a normative and political phenomenon is a complex undertaking – and giving a universal answer to what sort of phenomenon SE is, what sort of 'change' and what economic and social model is envisioned by SE seems impossible or at best flawed. Such a universal answer would ignore the contestations that are taking place on different levels. Instead of trying to find a single answer to what sort of phenomenon SE *is*, whether it is a 'neoliberal' or an 'alternative' movement – which seems impossible, as I have argued – the meaning(s) of SE may be better understood and analysed according to different contexts. This view, stressing the crucial relevance of context for understanding SE – is also sustained by Teasdale et al. (2019), who (citing various authors) explain that "[s]ocial enterprise is a concept that is variably interpreted according to historical, geographical, political, social, cultural and economic factors (...)" (Teasdale et al. 2019: 22).

'Context' is another term that may be understood in different ways and that needs to be briefly addressed. Even though my perspective on SE (research) is one that sees SE as 'more' than a (sub-)form of entrepreneurship – and that entrepreneurship theory is only of limited use for discussing SE – it shall be noted that important contributions have been made on entrepreneurship and context (e.g., by Welter 2011). Welter (2011), for example, has criticised that context is too often disregarded in entrepreneurship research and suggested that researchers pay greater attention to contextual factors. This mainly includes 'where' contexts (i.e., business, social, spatial and institutional factors) and 'when' contexts (i.e., temporal and historical factors) as well as paying attention to the people engaging (or not engaging) in entrepreneurship, e.g., women or entrepreneurs in formerly socialist countries (Welter 2011; Welter & Baker 2021). Based on this critique, in recent years,

> [r]esearchers have embraced the need to measure and model many of the contextual factors that shape whether and how people engage in entrepreneurship and we also seem to have gotten better at describing

> limitations to the generality of our findings that contextualization often implies (Welter & Baker 2021: 1155).

However, many aspects of the interplay of contexts and entrepreneurship still remain understudied. In addition, the main focus of 'context' in entrepreneurship research remains somewhat functional or utilitarian, aimed at understanding how conditions for entrepreneurship may be improved (e.g., in certain regions) or how entrepreneurship can be made more attractive for certain groups (e.g., for women). This strand of research thus, seems somewhat captured within a paradigm of entrepreneurialism, assuming that entrepreneurship is a value as such and politically desirable. Moreover, to some extent, this perspective is also based on the idea of competitiveness, based on the notion that different regions are competing to attract entrepreneurs and/or seeking to 'produce' a high number of or particularly successful entrepreneurs. Naturally, this is a narrower interest in 'context' than in this book. My aim is to making sense of SE as a political phenomenon or movement in relationship to the specific context in Germany. Therefore, the most relevant contextual aspects include the socio-economic, political and policy context in Germany in a specific point in history – namely, when SE was introduced in Germany and during which the SE movement continued to develop (as Chapter 2 will address more in detail).

When it comes to SE in different contexts, I must also mention the work of Kerlin (2010; 2013; 2018) as well as of Defourny & Nyssens (2010; 2012), who have pointed towards differences of SE (and of SE research), mainly between the 'European' and the 'US' context, each having their own history, grown traditions and specific features. The US tradition of SE places a stronger emphasis on the individual (the social entrepreneur), while the European tradition gives more attention to the organisation (the social enterprise). In the US tradition, 'social innovation' and 'earned income' (i.e., revenue generation for social organisations that go beyond donations or state aid) are main themes. Instead, in the European SE tradition, organisational governance (including ideas of democratic organisation of the economy, participation, ownership, decision-making, etc.) is of great importance (Kerlin 2010; 2013; Defourny & Nyssens 2010; 2012), as I have already mentioned in Section 1.3. Related to this distinction is that in Europe, cooperatives were and are considered as part of the SE tradition, which is not always the case in the US – even though this might be changing more recently (Kerlin 2010; 2018). According to Kerlin (2010; 2018), another difference between the two regions is that in many European countries, national governments have been providing strong support for SE, therefore playing a significant and active role in shaping the SE field. By comparison, SE in the US has mainly been driven by private and civil society actors, with foundations rather than national governments shaping the SE field.

This clear division into a 'US' and a 'European' version and school of SE has been criticised and questioned, among others, by Bacq & Janssen (2011). For the research purposes of this book, I also have to make a few critical remarks here. First, it must be noted that the grouping into a single 'European' version of SE certainly comes with a reduction of the national individualities of the different SE scenes and organisations, as Kerlin (2010), Defourny & Nyssens (2010; 2012) and Defourny et al. (2021) have observed, too. For Germany, this seems particularly problematic, since one of the main aspects that supposedly separates 'US' from 'European' SE does not apply, namely that (national) government has supported and shaped the development of a SE field (as noted e.g., by Birkhölzer 2015 or Grohs et al. 2016 and as I will further explain in Chapter 2). Second, the literature that contrasts 'European' and 'US' traditions of SE is primarily focused on organisational models and aimed at explaining the type of organisations (social enterprises) that have emerged and developed in the different regional contexts. My main focus, however, is the relationship between SE and the wider social and political context, and making sense of SE as a political phenomenon (beyond its organisational expressions). Third, given that the main purpose of my empirical analysis is to *understand* SE (conceptually taking a few steps back), I argue that a too fixed notion of SE that already explains what sort of phenomenon SE *is* (as rooted in or belonging to a distinct 'European' tradition) may be harmful for this purpose. Thus, while it is important to highlight the important contributions that were made in this regard, the simple distinction between a 'European' and a 'US' version of SE, seems rather limited for my purpose.

The relevance of context and for understanding SE in Germany, however, is undeniable, and the fact that contextual aspects remain largely understudied presents both a challenge for my research purpose – and a research gap, to which my book makes a contribution to close. The importance of context and the fact that the meanings of SE are dependent on context may also be seen linked to the discussion in Section 1.2. In different societies, understandings of the 'social' and 'the good of society' will differ. What is considered beneficial for a society ('social') must be negotiated by the members of this society and is contingent on the normative, political and also regulatory frameworks of a respective context. Societal values are specific to historical, geographical, political, social, cultural and economic circumstances – and they are also in flux, dynamic and subject to change. For example, in Western Europe, child labour was commonplace during the early industrial era, which saw children aged ten or younger often working about twelve hours a day. Perhaps, a company that would have employed children to work five hours per day would have been considered a 'social' enterprise back then (by exceeding the regulatory and ethical standard of the time, in offering more humane working hours), while today such a company would be frowned upon – and be shut down for illegal activity. SE is described as 'changemaking' (e.g., Ashoka 2020), i.e., bringing about social change. If this is taken seriously, one would also need to answer: '*what* change to *what* society or what system or processes within this society?', as 'social change' is not transferrable from one place or historical context to another. Yet, SE research and interpretations of SE (too) often fail to provide an answer for this. Perhaps, this comes from SE often being presented as a 'global' phenomenon. But for understanding SE as a political phenomenon, this is not very helpful, as 'social change' only makes sense with regards to a specific society, its norms and institutions. Thus, understandings of the 'social' as well as of 'social entrepreneurship' might be different in different places.

Moreover, understandings and meanings associated with SE can also change over time when looking at a single country or society. This is where different actors and interest groups have a crucial role. The SE concept is diverse, fluid and dynamic – and this is a result of different actors shaping it, as different studies, mostly focusing on the UK, have demonstrated (among others, Parkinson & Howorth 2008; Nicholls 2010; Teasdale 2012). In the Introduction, it was also demonstrated that German politicians with different party affiliations may propagate different views on SE. SE may even been appropriated by political actors in different ways, to fit their own ideological views and political goals. As Teasdale (2012) has explained:

> The construction of social enterprise is ongoing, and fought by a range of actors promoting different languages and practices tied to different political beliefs. That is, social enterprise is politically contested by different actors around competing discourses (Teasdale 2012: 100).

For the UK, Nicholls (2010), Teasdale (2012), Kay et al. (2016) and Teasdale et al. (2019) explain how social enterprise policy was promoted by the *New Labour* government in order to contribute to the party's political goals. The *Coalition* government under David Cameron then continued to promote SE, reshaping social enterprise policy in a way to fit its own political purposes. Mason and Moran (2019) go even further, arguing that social enterprise policy was crucial in enacting David Cameron's *Big Society* agenda.[7] Building on Foucault's concept of *governmentality*, Dey & Teasdale (2016) explain that in the UK,

> government used social enterprise to govern the third sector 'at a distance' (...), with power exercised through a network of heterogeneous techniques such as policies, grants, and various forms of intellectual and material support (2016: 488).

Nicholls (2010) also addresses the role of different actors in a specific context and (again, focusing on the UK) addresses four types of resource-rich actors that are interested in and capable of shaping the meaning and development and institutionalisation of SE: government, foundations, fellowship organisations and network organisations. Teasdale, too, has highlighted the fact that different actors shape the 'conceptual confusion' that surrounds SE:

> This conceptual confusion is because social enterprise is a fluid and contested concept constructed by different actors promoting different discourses connected to different organisational forms and drawing on different academic theories (Teasdale 2012: 99).

Both Parkinson & Howorth (2008) and Teasdale (2012) identify competing views and interests surrounding SE between social enterprise practitioners and policymakers. Despite holding differing views than policymakers, practitioners may engage in what Dey & Teasdale (2016) call 'tactical mimicry', i.e., being opportunistic participants in the policymakers' interpretation of SE in order to gain resources and direct them into their social mission. As a result, practitioners may then reinforce and support, but at the same time "challenge and appropriate the normative demands and subject position of social enterprise inscribed in government policies and programs" (Dey & Teasdale 2016: 492). Kay et al. (2016: 221, citing Ridley-Duff & Bull 2011: 103) claim that there are two different 'camps' of SE: a 'radical' and a 'reformist' one. The former with the aim "to subvert the logic of the free market and change relationships between money, land and people" (Kay et al. 2016: 221),

7 Mason and Moran (2019) include a comparative study on developments in the UK and in Australia.

and the latter as one that "accept[s] [market-driven capitalist] globalisation and use it to advance social entrepreneurial enterprises" (ibid.). Furthermore, an emphasis on changing meanings of SE over time is provided by Dart (2019), who writes that:

> As an academic researcher and a consultant, I have observed the drift from social enterprise as 'daring new problem-solving model to improve mission fulfillment' to social enterprise as 'hybrid quasi- commercial structure and operations' (Dart 2019: 67).

What I want to capture in this section thus, is the following: making sense of SE from a sociological perspective needs to be context-specific and to consider the socio-economic and political environment of the respective place(s), in which SE is unfolding. In addition, the meanings of SE are contested, they are dynamic and in constant flux, and because SE is such a malleable concept, different actors are able to promote different aspects of SE. This is the rationale for my empirical research that aims at offering a better sociological understanding of representations of the SE concept in Germany between 1999 and 2021 and to examine different representations, dominant views on SE, how the concept has developed during this time as well as notions of 'change' and the relationship between SE and the current social and economic model of neoliberalism.

1.7 'Conceptual Confusion' as the Starting Point of an Empirical Research Project

This chapter has explained that all definitions, descriptions, narratives and interpretations of SE implicitly contain wider normative underpinnings and political beliefs. Meanings of SE are dynamic and contested – on different levels and simultaneously; SE is inevitably tied to wider narratives, for example, about what should change in a society – even though these aspects are only rarely addressed in academic literature on SE, which, currently, mainly comes from business administration and management scholarship (e.g., Sassmannshausen & Volkmann 2018). There are different views on the relationship between SE and neoliberalism, and what sort of economic and social model SE envisions. Overall, there are different answers to what sort of 'change' SE will or shall bring about. In spite of increasing research on SE, a great deal of 'conceptual confusion' around SE remains. In addition, it was demonstrated that a universal and finite answer to the question of what sort of change SE brings about does not seem to make much sense. The meanings of SE are context-specific, and in each context the contestations of meanings of SE may play out differently. Parts of this process may be opaque and other aspects more explicit; some aspects may be either unintentional or intentional, with certain actors trying to shape and exploit the "fluid institutional space" (Nicholls 2010: 612) in which SE unfolds.

As explained throughout this chapter, this book develops from acknowledging these ambiguities and contestations of SE on multiple layers; the normative and political meanings of SE are not static but flexible and dynamic and dependent upon specific socio-economic contexts as well as positions and interests of different actors. Taking into account these premises, this book explores the contestations of meanings of SE in a specific context: in Germany between 1999 and 2021. Arguably, little is known about SE as a phenomenon or movement in Germany, about its 'wider' meanings – in particular beyond the initial phase of the late 1990s-early 2000s, and about how the idea of SE has developed in Germany over time – and, especially, this is only rarely backed up by empirical research. This is where my book makes a contribution, towards a better sociological understanding of SE in Germany, along four topics:

- ***Diversity and dominance***: What different understandings of SE can be identified, and what is the dominant representation and perspective of the SE concept in Germany?
- ***Representation and Relevance***: What does a broader audience get to learn about the SE phenomenon? What parts or aspects of SE are given a platform and getting noticed by wider society, i.e., beyond the niche spaces of the SE scene itself?
- ***Development over time***: How has the idea of SE been introduced in Germany in the late 1990s (when the 'social entrepreneurship' term first started to appear), and how has the concept developed over time, until the early 2020s (when interest for SE in the public and in politics has started to increase)?
- ***Notions of 'change' and politics:*** SE seeks to 'change' the *status quo* – but which *status quo* is meant, what shall 'change' and how, and what is the vision for economy and society proposed by SE? What (potential) societal or political role is ascribed to SE, and what is the relationship between SE and the dominant (neoliberal) social and economic model?

Understanding these aspects is necessary and helpful to a sociological making sense of SE as a complex social and political phenomenon and movement – and to assess the path that SE might take in this specific context in the future. Next to the academic interest, this endeavour also has practical and political relevance, given that, at the time of writing, SE in Germany is in a particularly interesting position. SE has not (yet) attracted significant interest or involvement of policymakers and remains very weakly institutionalised. Nonetheless, political interest in SE is slowly growing (as I outline in Chapter 2), not least due to increased media interest in the SE phenomenon and lobbying activities by *SEND*. The route that different representations and contestations of the SE concept in Germany might take seems open to various routes, which is why it is relevant and timely to better examine and understand the SE concept in Germany in the recent past and present.

For researching (representations of) the SE concept in Germany (1999–2021) along the above four investigative lines (diversity and dominance, representation and relevance, development over time, notions of 'change' and politics), discourse analysis is a suitable theoretical and methodological approach, as it allows to study the different meanings – in the broadest sense – around SE, how these meanings have been 'produced' and contested, and how they have developed over time (as I will explain in detail in Chapter 3). Discourse analysis will contribute to better understanding the multi-layered and dynamic processes around SE and to identifying potential changes over time. But before diving into the empirical analysis, Chapter 2 will first engage with developments concerning SE in the specific context of Germany.

Chapter 2: Social Entrepreneurship in Germany

2.1 Introduction: 'Social Entrepreneurship' in Germany – Perceived as an 'Imported' Concept and Still Rather Marginal

The social entrepreneurship (SE) movement is, arguably, still at a rather early stage in Germany, and SE has not yet attracted significant attention of resource-rich actors (such as government), as will be explained in this chapter. SE in Germany remains quite marginal and weakly institutionalised; the *Social Entrepreneurship Netzwerk Deutschland* (*SEND*), the main network and lobbying organisation for SE, was only founded in 2017. Until now, there is still few research on SE in Germany from sociology, political economy or socioeconomics. Little is known about SE as a complex social and political phenomenon or movement in Germany (as 'more' than a form of entrepreneurship) – in particular beyond the initial phase of the late 1990s and early 2000s. This is where my study makes an empirical contribution, analysing representations of SE (in the media) and tracing how (representations of) the idea of SE has developed in this specific context. For this purpose, I have conducted an empirical discourse analysis of representations of SE in 349 newspaper articles between 1999 and 2021 (as Chapter 3 will outline). However, before coming to the empirical analysis, the development of SE in the specific context of Germany needs to be addressed, which is the purpose of this chapter. SE in Germany is mainly seen as a somewhat 'imported' concept, which is linked to the English term 'social entrepreneurship' that is mostly used untranslated in the German context. This chapter thus, explores how this 'foreign' term and concept unfolds and interacts with the institutional and ideational setting in Germany.

First, Section 2.2 will situate the 'social entrepreneurship' term in the German context, explaining that it refers to a distinct movement, which can be (historically) distinguished from other social economy movements. Section 2.3

then offers a brief overview of this specific SE movement in Germany, giving a snapshot of SE in the media, academic literature, of its actors and infrastructure as well as of first policy engagements with SE. In 2.4 the reception of this specific non-translated (English) term and concept – which was quite critical in social science and social economy circles – will be discussed. Arguably, this critical reception is due to the wider political and socio-economic context, as I will explain in 2.5. SE was perceived as part of (global) neoliberal developments – and there are overlaps between SE rhetoric (of this initial phase) and reform rhetoric in Germany (revolving around social policy and labour market reform). Looking forward, however, Section 2.6 argues, that little is known about SE beyond the early 2000s.

2.2 How to Make Sense of 'Social Entrepreneurship' in the German Context

In Chapter 1, it was explained in detail that context matters when understanding SE – meanings of SE, and contestations thereof, vary according to geographical, historical, political and socio-economic context. Thus, this section will focus on Germany and explain how to make sense of the English term 'social entrepreneurship' in this specific context. For this, I will mainly rely on Birkhölzer (2015) and Birkhölzer et al. (2015), who by the terms 'social entrepreneurship' and 'social business' – in their non-translated forms – delineate a specific movement that can be distinguished from other social economy movements in Germany.

For Germany, Birkhölzer (2015) proposes a typology of 14 different social enterprise or social economy movements. There is a common core to these social enterprise or social economy movements, which are based on: economic self-help and mutual assistance, charitable help, philanthropy and community initiatives and civic engagement (Birkhölzer 2015; Birkhölzer et al. 2015). However, the different movements can be identified and distinguished according to their specific "identities, shared values and organisational structures" (Birkhölzer 2015: 4) and having developed their own distinct traditions and models.[1] Birkhölzer bases this typology on Weber, integrating a historical

1 This view is also shared by Göler von Ravensburg et al., who explain that different social enterprises in Germany "operate under a wide variety of forms, which emerged in different times and contexts, and against the background of different philosophies or

perspective (2015: 4–24); therefore, all 14 distinct social enterprise or social economy movements in the typology can be situated historically. In addition, Birkhölzer (2015) proposes a loose clustering of these 14 movements into 'older social economy movements' and 'younger social economy movements'. The 'older' social economy movements include traditions that go back to the 19th century, namely:

- The co-operative model (*Das Genossenschaftsmodell*)
- The welfare model (*Das Wohlfahrtsmodell*)
- The model of foundations (*Das Stiftungsmodell*)
- The model of traditional associations (*Das Vereinsmodell*) (Birkhölzer 2015: 4–24).

The 'younger' social economy movements in the typology comprise movements that have been emerging since the 1970s, including:

- The model of integration enterprises (*Integrationsbetriebe*)
- The model of volunteer agencies (*Freiwilligendienste und –agenturen*)
- Models of self-managed enterprises of alternative-, women- and eco-movements (*Selbstverwaltete Alternativ-, Frauen- und Umweltbetriebe*)
- Models of self-help initiatives (*Selbsthilfeunternehmen*)
- The model of socio-cultural centres (*Sozio-kulturelle Zentren*)
- The model of German work integration enterprises (*Beschäftigungs- und Qualifizierungsgesellschaften*)
- The model of local exchange and trading systems (*Tauschsysteme auf Gegenseitigkeit*)
- The model of neighbourhood and community enterprises (*Nachbarschafts- und Gemeinwesenbetriebe*)
- Models of mutual insurance systems (*Versicherungsvereine auf Gegenseitigkeit*)
- **The model of social entrepreneurship (no German translation)** (Birkhölzer 2015: 4–24, emphasis by the author).

---

traditions. They do not act or see themselves as a coherent 'SE sector'; they are organised in separate groups or 'families', with different identities, institutional and legal frameworks, research affiliations, education and training organisations, etc" (2021: 85).

Birkhölzer (2015) and, among others, Hackenberg & Empter (2011) and Birkhölzer et al. (2015) consider the movement referred to as 'social entrepreneurship' as a distinct movement. This also widely matches the self-image or presentation of the actors that constitute the SE field in Germany, who mainly ascribe to the English (non-translated) term 'social entrepreneurship' (e.g., SEND 2019; 2021b). 'Social entrepreneurship' is a commonly-used term among these key actors, e.g., the *Social Entrepreneurship Netzwerk Deutschland*.

While this distinction between different social economy movements may not in all aspects seem completely stringent, it proves helpful. On the one hand, when it comes to assessing the SE field – statistically, for example – some of the defining criteria that are supposed to separate 'social entrepreneurship' organisations from others are hard to uphold (e.g., Christmann et al. 2021). There is, for example, no specific legal form for this social economy movement which would facilitate identifying and delineating specific organisations. However, for my research approach this is unproblematic, since I am investigating precisely the movement and the ideas that gather around the term 'social entrepreneurship' – not statistically, but rather conceptually – for which Birkhölzer's (2015) identification of SE as a distinct social movement proves suitable. The following section shall then give an overview of the distinct SE field that has developed in Germany since the late 1990s until the early 2020s.

2.3 The Development of a Social Entrepreneurship field in Germany

This section will give a short overview of SE in Germany – mainly understood as the movement that is unfolding in Germany under the non-translated term 'social entrepreneurship', as explained in Section 2.2. An overview that comprises two decades can, of course, only be indicative and shall not be read as all-encompassing. In line with the international debate, for Germany, too, it is often assumed that SE is gaining importance. On the one hand, the assumption that SE is a 'growing field' shall be taken with great caution – as Teasdale et al. (2019) have warned about succumbing to the widespread "myth of social enterprise growth" (2019: 35). SE remains weakly institutionalised in Germany. On the other hand, increased attention for SE seems undeniable (see e.g., Halberstadt & Hölzner 2018; Sassmannshausen & Volkmann 2018) – at least in academia and in the media.

Taking newspapers as a proxy, the term 'social entrepreneurship' appears for the first time in the media in 1999.[2] Initially, the interest in SE in the German press is still very marginal: with (on average) only one article per year on SE between 1999 and 2004. Around 2005, the number of articles considerably increases to (on average) seven articles per year. Further surges can be observed in the late 2010s and early 2020s, as the following graph illustrates:

Graph 1: Social Entrepreneurship in German Newspapers – Number of Original Articles per Year in Daily and Weekly Newspapers and News Magazines Containing the Term 'Social Entrepreneurship'

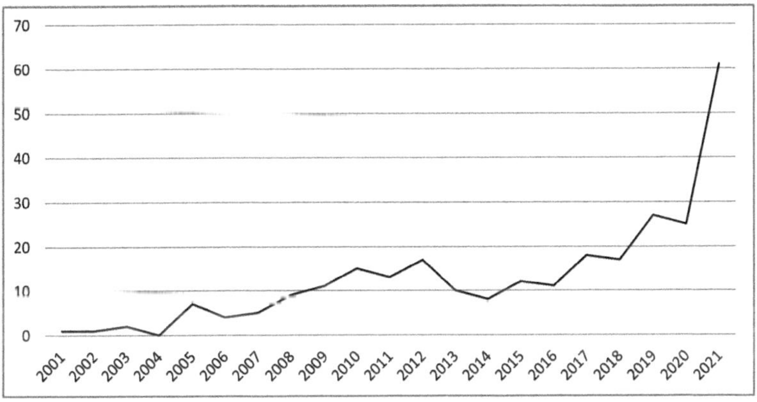

Source: author's representation, based on databases WISO, FAZ archive and SZ archive – selected sources (newspapers available since 2000 or earlier)

Academic literature on SE in Europe dates back approximately to the mid-2000s, with 2006 marking an important year, seeing several important publications (Steyaert & Dey 2019). A few German(-speaking) academics, like Johanna Mair or Kai Hockerts, were involved in the debate from early on (e.g., Mair et al. 2006). First contributions on SE in German or focussing on Germany started to emerge (Achleitner et al. 2007; Faltin 2008) – and a few years later, the first edited volumes with more in-depth conceptual contributions were published, increasingly concerned with discussing the understanding of

2 'Social entrepreneurship' first appears in an article from the 8th of April 1999 in *Die Zeit*, titled: 'KAPITALISTEN DER NÄCHSTENLIEBE'.

the SE phenomenon in the German context (Jähnke et al. 2011; Hackenberg & Empter 2011), as will be further addressed in Section 2.4. Academic publications remained closely linked to the international debate on SE. Mainly taking a European and comparative perspective, the work of the *EMES Network* was and remains significant (e.g., Defourny & Nyssens 2012; Birkhölzer et al. 2015; Göler von Ravensburg et al. 2018; 2021; Karre 2021).

Following suit, empirical studies were trying to assess and measure the SE field and to strengthen the statistical base for SE in Germany. Drawing on large existing studies on civil society, the third sector and commercial entrepreneurship, a meta-study by Scheuerle et al. (2013) tried to better estimate the SE field. Building and expanding on this was a large research project conducted by Jansen et al. (2013). A study by Unterberg et al. (2015) also aimed at better estimating the German SE field – to some extent acknowledging what Teasdale et al. (2019) have described, i.e., that the number of social enterprises is heavily dependent on definition – offering an estimate of between 1,000 and 70,000 social enterprises in Germany (2015: 74), depending on the operationalisation of different criteria such as income sources and 'innovation'. The study by Unterberg et al. (2015) was also intended to make policy recommendations and was funded by the *German Federal Ministry for Economic Affairs and Energy* (*BMWi*) – which can, arguably, be seen as a signal for the growing interest for SE in policy circles, as I will discuss later in the section. The state-owned investment and development bank *Kreditanstalt für Wiederaufbau* (*KfW*), too, has started to derive data on SE from the *KfW-Gründungsmonitor* (Metzger 2019), estimating that 9% of all recent entrepreneurs are now social entrepreneurs. Studies funded by the *European Commission* – closely linked to and/or conducted by members of the *EMES Network* – too, make a contribution to assessing the German SE field (Göler von Ravensburg et al. 2018), and to better understand it from a comparative and in particular European perspective (Borzaga et al. 2020). More recently, additional regional studies were commissioned – for example, Christmann et al. (2021) for Brandenburg.

Nevertheless, mapping the SE field in Germany comes with great uncertainties. As in other contexts (see Teasdale et al. 2019 for the UK), estimates depend on definition, which is – once again – dependent on normative and political assumptions . Among others, the *Social Entrepreneurship Netzwerk Deutschland* e.V. (*SEND*) criticises the fact that unlike most other countries, Germany lacks an official (government) definition of SE, which makes research (among other things, such as targeted funding) difficult.[3] There are no official statistics that record social enterprises and that identify them as such (Maaß & Schneck 2017), which also shows that the institutionalisation of the SE field in Germany is weak. Across different studies, the number of social enterprises may range from a few hundred to more than half a million units (Maaß & Schneck 2017: 10). Drawing on other data (e.g., from the *Global Entrepreneurship Monitor*, as in Bosma et al. 2016) or via conducting original research, the mapping and measuring of the SE field continues (e.g., in projects by the *Euclid Network* or *SEFORIS*, both involving EU funding). These activities are mainly driven by organisations, which sometimes have come up with their own studies (often called 'monitors'). This includes the *Green Startup Monitor* – and, above all, the *Deutscher Social Entrepreneurship Monitor* by *SEND*, which may be considered to combine both research as well as advocacy for SE (Hein 2021). There is occasional overlap or collaboration between the different projects – e.g., since 2020, the *Deutscher Social Entrepreneurship Monitor* by *SEND* is published under the framework of the *Euclid Network* and is in part funded by the *European Commission*.

This brings me to the next aspect of the development of SE in Germany: the most important actors involved in the SE field and the infrastructure they have established for SE in Germany. For the early phase of SE in Germany, two international actors were crucial, especially for allocating resources and creating public awareness for SE: the *Schwab Foundation for Social Entrepreneurship* and, most importantly, *Ashoka* (Rummel 2011; Zimmer & Bräuer 2014). *Ashoka*, the largest and most established fellowship organisation for SE (Nicholls 2010), opened an office in Germany in 2003. However, *Ashoka*'s promotion of SE had reached Germany even before this – as can be observed in the first news article (mentioned above) on SE in Germany (from 1999), reporting, among other things, on *Ashoka*'s international activities (A_1).[4] Also in 2003, a government-funded award for social entrepreneurs (*Startsocial*) was launched. Shortly after, the *Schwab Foundation for Social Entrepreneurship* started activities in Germany, most importantly initiating the award for 'Social Entrepreneur of the Year' from 2005 (*Ashoka* and the *Schwab Foundation* as well as their prominent

3 Hein (2021) has criticised this claim as politically motivated. However, Göler von Ravensburg et al. (2021) seem to agree with *SEND* that there is neither legal definition of SE nor a precise common understanding of the concept in Germany.

4 'A_1' stands for the first article in the corpus, as the chosen way of referencing the news articles that are included in the empirical analysis of this book.

role in the early SE scene will be addressed further in 2.4). The first *Vision Summit* took place in 2007 – these yearly conferences were held until 2016, organised first by the *Genisis Institute* and later by the *Grameen Creative Lab*, and currently, a successor that is also led by Peter Spiegel, the *WeQ Institute*, is planning to re-start the summits (WeQ Institute 2020). Foundations – such as the *Mercator*, the *Vodafone* or the *Bertelsmann* foundation – also became involved in SE from early on. International social investment actors, such as *BonVenture* (since 2003) or *ANANDA impact fund (formerly 'Social Venture Fund'*, in Germany since 2009) also commenced activities in Germany; later, the *Finanzierungsagentur für Social Entrepreneurship* (*FASE*) was established (in which *Ashoka* had a key role).[5] However, the financing infrastructure for SE in Germany remains in its early development stages and programmes of this kind are only available for a small number of SE organisations (Zimmer & Bräuer 2014). *Phineo* – until today the leading social impact measurement consultancy – was established in 2009. Universities started to engage in research and teaching on SE (Leppert 2008; Schwarz 2014). The *Social Entrepreneurship Akademie*, a spin-off that resulted from the cooperation of different higher education institutions in Munich, was established in 2010. *Yooweedoo*, a training programme for students emerged out of the *University of Kiel* (see Wihlenda et al. 2021 for further social entrepreneurship and innovation education programmes at universities in Germany). In later years, student networks also formed around the idea of SE at German universities (including *Infinity Deutschland* and *Enactus*). The organisation *Hilfswerft*, founded in 2014, seeks to promote 'social entrepreneurship education' across universities in Germany.

The early 2010s also saw the founding of new support agencies for social entrepreneurship: *Social Impact* (established under this name in 2011, but with its predecessor, *IQ Consult*, operating since 1994), with several *Social Impact Labs* that provide coworking, coaching, workshops, networking and events, operating regionally (currently in Beelitz, Berlin, Bremen, Frankfurt, Hamburg, Leipzig, Munich, Potsdam and Stuttgart) (Social Impact 2022a). *Yunus Social Business* was founded in Germany in 2011. The global brand *Impact Hub* (providing 'coworking plus', including e.g., networking events and access to a community of other entrepreneurs etc.) also opened local 'hubs' in Germany: the first one in Berlin in 2013; as of June 2022, there are local 'hubs' in Berlin,

5 *FASE* was established as a spin-off by *Ashoka*, with the support of the *Apax Foundation* and the *BMW Stiftung Herbert Quandt* (Ashoka 2013).

Essen, Stuttgart, Munich, Hamburg, Leipzig and Dresden (Impact Hub Germany 2022). Specialised information outlets such as the magazine *enorm* and the website *The Changer* (later *tbd**) were launched.

In 2017, arguably today's leading organisation in the SE field was founded: the *Social Entrepreneurship Netzwerk Deutschland e.V. (SEND)* as a network organisation of and for social enterprises with two main aims: networking for its member organisations (social enterprises) and to lobby for SE in the political realm. It shall be noted that there is considerable overlap between *SEND* and previous SE organisations: *Ashoka, Impact Hub, Social Impact* and *tbd** were heavily invested in founding *SEND*, and *SEND*'s first executive committee mainly consisted of leading personnel of these other organisations. Furthermore, *SEND* emerged out of the *German Startups Association* (*Bundesverband Deutsche Startups e.V.*), the main lobby organisation for commercial start-ups and was initially, in part, funded by the *BMW Foundation* (current funders include: *BMW Foundation, Samsung, KfW Foundation, Bundesverband Deutsche Startups e.V., Schöpflin Foundation*) (SEND 2021b). As said earlier, since its foundation, *SEND* has significantly contributed to the shaping of the SE field, and continues to do so. The yearly *Deutscher Social Entrepreneurship Monitor* (2018; 2019; 2020/21; 2021/22), in the initial years in part funded by *SAP*, makes an important contribution to assessing the field, to knowledge-building on SE, as well as to spreading the knowledge on SE to a wider audience. *SEND* portrays itself as the 'voice of SE' in Germany – *SEND*'s key mission is described on the website as following: *We want to live in a society in which everyone benefits from progress. That's why we connect the social entrepreneurship sector and give it a voice* (SEND 2021b). Furthermore, in 2018 (after a longer planning phase) the *Bundesinitiative Impact Investing* was launched, mainly by actors, who had been involved in the SE field before: *Bertelsmann Stiftung, BMW Foundation Herbert Quandt, Bundesverband Deutscher Stiftungen* and *Phineo* (Bundesinitiative Impact Investing 2020).

Throughout this book, I have argued that in Germany there is still very little government and policy attention or involvement with SE – at least in international comparison and especially compared to the UK. One of *SEND*'s main critiques, precisely, concerns the federal government's lack of a concise strategy for SE (SEND 2021c). Birkhölzer, too, writes that in Germany "[g]enerally speaking, public authorities (...) do not really understand the real needs and problems of social enterprises" (Birkhölzer 2015: 25). A recent comparative report by the *European Commission* supports the view that, unlike in other European countries, there is no specific policy for social enterprises in Germany (Borzaga et al. 2020: 12).[6] More generally, in a comparative perspective, the degree of acceptance of the SE concept in Germany is classified as low. The SE concept is not commonly used, and has only a very limited role next to traditional welfare institutions (Borzaga et al. 2020: 35) – this will further be addressed in Sections 2.4 and 2.5. According to Göler von Ravensburg et al., "[t]here does not appear to be any overt party/political, church or trade-union support (...) except by individuals at a relatively low decision-making level" (2021: 93). As noted in Section 1.6, the fact that in Germany government (so far) has played a minor role in actively addressing the SE field also seems to speak against Germany representing a 'typically European' version or tradition of SE (separating it from the 'US' tradition of SE).

Despite this overall rather low support for SE, there has been some government involvement as well as policies that should be mentioned. First, the European level needs to be taken into account, from which different impulses emerged when it comes to policy directly targeted at SE. In 2011, the EU launched the *Social Business Initiative* (*SBI*) with the aim of improving the environment for social enterprises across Europe. According to Zimmer & Bräuer (2014), however, the *SBI*'s impact in Germany was very limited, partly due to the high administrative demand of the programme and due to little support at the national and *Bundesländer* level – which would have been crucial for the implementation of the *SBI* (Zimmer & Bräuer 2014: 15–16). Judging from the media analysis included in this book (see Chapters 3–7), it can be confirmed that the *SBI* received little public attention/reception in Germany. Currently, the EU is developing a new programme – the *EU Action Plan for Social Economy* (European Commission 2021). Its role and impact for Germany is to be seen in the future.

At federal level, there is still no concise strategy to support SE, however, a few initiatives have been launched aimed at supporting the emerging SE field, which shall briefly be mentioned. In 2011, as part of the *National Engagement Strategy* in order to foster citizen engagement, the *Bundesministerium für Familie, Senioren, Frauen und Jugend* (*BMFSFJ*) initiated a programme to improve financial support for social entrepreneurs in cooperation with the state-owned investment and development bank *Kreditanstalt für Wiederaufbau* (KfW) (BMFSFJ 2011). According to Zimmer & Bräuer (2014) and citing Gebauer & Ziegler (2013), the programme ran until January 2014, with no continuation or

6 Birkhölzer (2015) and Borzaga et al. (2020) argue from a broader understanding of 'social enterprise', however, explicitly including 'social entrepreneurship'.

evaluation known to the authors.[7] Furthermore, the mentioning of SE in the coalition agreements (*Koalitionsvertrag*) between the ruling parties of different federal governments is interpreted as a sign of growing policy support. The coalition agreement between the *CDU*, *CSU* and *SPD* from 2013 declares that social innovations merit support, and that these may also come from social enterprises. The coalition agreement of 2018, also between the *CDU*, *CSU* and *SPD*, takes up the 'social entrepreneurship' term for the first time, and is a little more daring, announcing that the federal government seeks to promote and support social entrepreneurship even more than before (CDU, CSU & SPD 2018). Cagarman et al. (2020), however, note that this general declaration by the government remains abstract (see also: Deutscher Bundestag 2019). This mentioning of 'social entrepreneurship' in the coalition agreement of 2018 was nonetheless seen as a remarkable success for *SEND*'s lobbying work, given that this was only a few months after the organisation had been founded. The coalition agreement for 2021–2025 of the current federal government between *SPD*, *Bündnis 90/Die Grünen* and *FDP* is even more specific than the previous coalition agreement. In the document, the current government promises that it will elaborate a national strategy and improve the legal framework for SE, among other things (Scheper 2021). Yet, at the time of writing, specific steps and measures are still to be seen.[8]

Despite the lack of significant SE-tailored policy at the federal level, however, there are signals indicating that the support for SE is growing in policy circles. For example, the above-mentioned study by Unterberg et al. (2015) was commissioned by the *Federal Ministry for Economic Affairs and Energy* (*BMWi*) with the aim – next to better understanding SE in Germany – of making policy recommendations for better supporting SE. Zimmer & Bräuer (2014) point towards the government funded *Startsocial* award as early as 2003 (which, however is a quite small coaching programme, instead of providing substantial funding). Gebauer & Ziegler (2013) and Zimmer & Bräuer (2014) also raise the question whether the 2000s created the basis for SE in the first place – what is

7 It is also remarkable that several years later, in an official response of the federal government to an enquiry (*Anfrage*) by the *Green Party* in the *Bundestag*, the *BMFSJ* programme is not mentioned (Deutscher Bundestag 2019).

8 When the *Green Party* made an enquiry (*Anfrage*) in the *Bundestag* to the federal government (of CDU/CSU and SPD at the time) in 2019, it responded pointing towards several policies and programmes and explaining that these are relevant for social entrepreneurs (Deutscher Bundestag 2019). However, this does not address the SE sector's demands for programmes tailored specifically to SE.

often associated with cuts in public expenditure (Birkhölzer 2015). This is an interesting perspective, positioning SE as a product of a more general neoliberal era, which will be further explored in Sections 2.4 and 2.5. In terms of specific policy developments, it should also be mentioned that, after a request (*Antrag*) of *Bündnis 90/Die Grünen*, SE was discussed in the *Bundestag* for the first time in 2018. In May 2020, the government's (*CDU*, *CSU* and *SPD*) proposal for better support for SE was approved in the *Bundestag*. During the same government, shortly before the election, nine ministries came together for a joint paper of a social innovation strategy (BMBF 2021). With regards to senior policy staff, two recent developments (after the 2021 elections) should be pointed out: Zarah Bruhn, a social entrepreneur (founder of *Social Bee*, a work integration social enterprise, in particular targeting refugees), well-known and connected in the German SE scene, was appointed Special Envoy for Social Innovation at the *FDP*-led *Federal Ministry of Education and Research* (BMBF 2022). Sven Giegold, a former MEP for *Bündnis 90/Die Grünen* was brought from Brussels into the *Federal Ministry for Economic Affairs and Climate Action* (BMWK 2021). Giegold has expertise in SE and the wider social economy field (e.g., cooperatives).

On the *Bundesländer* level, too, SE has been mentioned in different coalition agreements in different *Bundesländer*. Cagarman et al. (2020) mention, for example, the current coalition agreement in Bavaria (2018–2023) between *CSU* and *Freie Wähler* (CSU & Freie Wähler 2018) – similar to the federal coalition agreement of 2018, with a rather general promise that the government aims to better support SE. More recently, two *Bundesländer* have taken more concrete steps, launching programmes to support SE. The first is '*Sozialinnovator*' in Hesse, in May 2020 (SEND 2021d). The second is 'SocialEconomy Berlin', launched in August 2020 (Social Economy Berlin 2020).[9] *SEND* is an official partner in the development as well as execution of both government-funded programmes – which demonstrates that the organisation has to a great extent successfully assumed the role as the main lobby organisation and contact for policymakers for SE. In Berlin, the state's investment and development bank, *Investitionsbank Berlin* (*IBB*), opened some of its funding programmes to organisations with a non-profit legal form in 2019, in an attempt to include social enterprises. According to *SEND*, five *Bundesländer* are planning new programmes: Bremen, Hamburg, Saxony, Saxony-Anhalt and Schleswig-Holstein (SEND 2022a: 7).

9 Prior to *Social Economy Berlin*, there was also a short pilot programme initiated by the Berlin Senate called *Social Innovation Capital* (SenWEB 2020).

Overall, it can be concluded that, like in other countries, in Germany a SE scene has been developing more or less over the past two decades. While one should be wary of light-hearted assumptions that SE is a growing field – an assumption that is sometimes uncritically (re-)produced by different societal actors, sometimes including academics – interest for SE seems to be increasing in different realms. This certainly includes academic research and – based on my empirical analysis, it can also be confirmed that – attention in the media is increasing (also see Chapters 3–7). Zimmer & Bräuer (2014) see a crucial moment in the Nobel prize win for Muhammad Yunus in 2006, having created awareness for SE globally, including in Germany. Hackenberg & Empter (2011) see great potential for SE in Germany. Beckmann (2011: 71) offers an interesting and more nuanced perspective, arguing that while the development of a statistical or institutional SE field may still be a niche and in its infancy, SE (in Germany) has already gained importance in the public discourse. On the whole, this view is also shared by Grohs et al. (2016) – who remain sceptical, however, claiming that SE's potential to unfold in Germany is limited, given the specific structures of the German welfare state. This brings me to the reception of 'social entrepreneurship' that will be discussed in the next section.

2.4 The (Critical) Reception of the 'Social Entrepreneurship' Movement and Its Actors in Germany

In Sections 2.2 and 2.3, I have explained that under the non-translated term 'social entrepreneurship', a distinct social economy or social enterprise movement can be identified in Germany, starting in the late 1990s-early 2000s. As briefly mentioned in this chapter, many welcomed the idea of SE, including academics involved in the early debate, often from a business studies background (e.g., Achleitner et al. 2007). From this perspective, Germany's long-established social security system was seen in a (overly) statist tradition with highly institutionalized structures, and a patriarchal culture, which did not encourage the responsibility of new approaches and of private actors in the 'social' field (Leppert 2008: 10–12). A supposedly stiff 'German mindset' would, arguably, prescribe that the church and the state are in charge of 'social' issues, making it difficult for new actors entering the stage, such as social entrepreneurs (Achleitner et al. 2007: 12). More traditional public and non-profit organisational forms were often seen as bureaucratic and lacking the ability to innovate (Karre 2021). In this view, SE was seen as a welcome addition to the

German welfare mix, and these publications often advocated for improving the conditions for SE and social entrepreneurs in Germany. The rather optimistic or even euphoric take on SE – assuming that SE is *per se* positive and brings about favourable change (also see Chapter 1) – was often uncritically reproduced and sometimes found its way into academic literature, too (Balgar 2011; Leppert 2011; Heinze et al. 2011). Hackenberg & Empter even pose the question whether SE may be considered a 'royal road' ("*Königsweg*" 2011: 12) for addressing social challenges, allegedly marrying the 'best' features of different worlds: i.e., the (resource) efficiency of the market, the public interest of the state as well as the social ethos of civil society.

Other contributions by academics and societal actors were more critical of SE. This includes most contributions from social science scholars. Here, I will develop these critical or sceptical perspectives on SE in Germany in the initial phase, when the SE term and concept started to appear (i.e., during the late 1990s and early 2000s). Not least due to the 'new' English term 'social entrepreneurship', the concept and movement was (and is) often seen as an 'imported' one, introduced from abroad into the German context with its specific set of institutions and actors. This can be observed, for example, in a reader's letter, which caught my attention during the empirical research process (that will be outlined in Chapter 3). The reader is clearly bothered by the SE term, and – responding to an interview with professor Birger Priddat, in which Priddat uses the term – writes:

> The interview with Birger Priddat in principle is highly informative, but some technical American terms are annoying and hard to understand, even for the educated reader. For example, what is 'social entrepreneurship'? (...) Even more annoying than the professional arrogance of the interviewed professor is the role of the interviewer, who refrains from making the interview understandable for the reader. (A_53_Berliner Zeitung_14.08.2010).[10]

This reader's letter is a good example for how SE was and is often perceived as 'foreign', in particular 'American'. The relationship between SE and 'the US' – or rather of a certain image of the US, the US as a symbol – is an interesting theme in the analysed articles and will be discussed in the empirical chapters (in particular in Chapters 4, 6 and 7).

10 Translated from German by the author.

I argue that in order to understand the reception of SE in Germany – in particular the critical reception – the dominant role of *Ashoka* and its take on SE needs to be highlighted, as well as some features of the early version of SE (discourse) in Germany, as I will explore in the following paragraphs. As previously mentioned, the first generation of funding and support agencies, *Ashoka* in particular, played a vital role in shaping the early SE movement – arguably, introducing the term and concept, publicising it as well as inspiring media stories and academic publications on the topic (Balgar 2011; Hackenberg & Empter 2011; Schwarz 2014). Rummel (2011: 22) goes as far as attesting these funding and support agencies interpretive authority over SE (*'Deutungshoheit'*) at the time. To support this view, Rummel provides an insightful interview sample of Judy Korn of the *Violence Prevention Network*, who explains that she started labelling herself 'social entrepreneur' because of *Ashoka*:

> I got this call by *Ashoka* (...) and after many years of brooding over it, I finally knew what my job was. (...) before I met *Ashoka*, labelling myself as an entrepreneur wouldn't have crossed my mind. But ultimately, that's what it is. And in this way, *Ashoka* has helped me a lot, personally, in defining my job and defining who I am (Rummel 2011: 89).

The excerpt is an example for how the SE term and concept was taken up and internalized by practitioners – demonstrating *Ashoka*'s role in spreading the SE term and idea. This goes beyond engaging in 'tactical mimicry' (Dey & Teasdale 2016, as mentioned in 1.6), in the sense of merely using the SE language for strategic reasons and attracting resources. The interviewee leaves no doubt that *Ashoka* has influenced her identity and (re)presentation as a 'social entrepreneur', suddenly calling 'social entrepreneurship' what she had been doing all along. Rummel goes even further, claiming that – at least for the early phase of SE in Germany – *Ashoka* has constructed and controlled the norms that apply in this (new) field, as well as access to funding, etc. (Rummel 2011: 89).

This version of SE, promoted mainly by support agencies, was taken up and reproduced in the media, and, in part, by academics. Media coverage on SE often revolved around the personal stories of individual entrepreneurs. They would often highlight 'exceptional individuals' and their personal trajectories, sometimes even portraying them as 'heroes' (Rummel 2011; Gebauer & Ziegler 2013). In this way, the early SE discourse in Germany is largely based on a Schumpeterian ideal figure of the entrepreneur, which is an important theme in neoliberalism (as explained in 1.5, see Davies 2014a). In this perspective, only some people can become entrepreneurs, as they are 'exceptional' and 'uncommon' individuals – which establishes difference and competitiveness as essential traits of individuals. Aspects of this individualized and glorifying perspective can also be found in scholarly literature on SE, which often concentrated on individual cases or case studies (Rummel 2011; Schwarz 2014; Birkhölzer 2015). Academic research – case studies in particular – were often focused on the fellows or award winners promoted by *Ashoka* and co. – which often had the role of gatekeepers to provide access to interview partners.

In Chapter 1, it was explained in detail that, at all times, there were and there are different views on SE; it can be various different things to many different people. But for the initial phase of SE in Germany – under this specific English term – there is wide agreement that there was a dominant version of SE – the version promoted mainly by *Ashoka* and a few others such as the *Schwab Foundation* and academics mainly from business schools (Rummel 2011; Gebauer & Ziegler 2013; Schwarz 2014; Zimmer & Bräuer 2014; Birkhölzer 2015; Grohs et al. 2016). The early reception of SE in Germany, therefore, must be understood, above all, as a reception to the specific '*Ashoka*-style' version of SE. This dominant version of SE has been described, among others, with the following features: its focus on the individual entrepreneur, the over-emphasis of SE as new, innovative and changemaking, the focus on scaling and scalability and measuring success quantitatively, as well as a link to elites, etc. (Rummel 2011; Birkhölzer 2015; Voß 2015). The link to (business) elites is, perhaps, the most explicit in the *Schwab Foundation for Social Entrepreneurship*, founded and named after management scholar Klaus Schwab, who is also the initiator of the *World Economic Forum* (formerly *European Management Forum*) that unites high-profile decision makers in Davos, Switzerland every year. The *World Economic Forum* is also seen as a driving force of the idea of competitiveness around the world – and in particular promoting competitiveness between nations, on the basis of their 'productivity' (Davies 2014a).

The strong focus on the individual social entrepreneur as the central agent of SE is a main point of critique (e.g., Rummel 2011; Birkhöler 2015; Grohs et al. 2016). This person-centricity is somewhat inherent to some of the practices of the early support agencies. *Ashoka* and *BonVenture*, for example, fund individuals (and not organisations, projects or enterprises) through personal fellowships. They identify and select their fellows through competitions or awards, which, arguably, contributes to an individualized understanding of SE. In addition, this award culture around SE placed the focus on only a few key figures ('social entrepreneurs') and their ventures – usually those holding awards or fellowships by *Ashoka* and co. Combined with the 'changemaking' narrative around SE, this created a stylised image of a few selected individuals as being 'exceptional' or even as being 'heroes', who have outstanding abilities and personality traits. *Ashoka* and co. actively promoted the narrative of SE as 'new', 'innovative', 'different', or 'changemaking' phenomenon (see also Chapter 1); *Ashoka Germany* brands itself 'home of changemakers' (Ashoka 2020) – with their protégées and allies being these innovative 'changemakers'. While *Ashoka* hardly ever specifies what sort of 'change' they are referring to, it is clear that an inherent assumption is that SE *per se* brings about positive change for society – similar to the assumption that 'social' means 'for the good of society', as was explained in Chapter 1. Birkhölzer (2015: 23), too, criticises the SE scene for overly relying on concepts like 'social mission' or 'social innovation', which are quite vague. As argued in Chapter 1, this is a valid argument, given that 'social' is a normative category and, therefore, very flexible.

The question whether or not SE can or should be seen as a 'new' phenomenon was also contested. Different contributions pointed towards initiatives across history seeking to join a social mission with economic activity, e.g., cooperatives that emerged during the industrial revolution (e.g., Beckmann 2011; Rummel 2011). As I have argued in 2.2, the term 'social entrepreneurship', however, was new at the time and can be situated within a specific time period and be linked to specific actors. Some also pointed towards 'new' aspects or methods, e.g., specific strategies and support structures, language and practices like the focus on scaling/ scalability, or (maximizing) social impact (Rummel 2011).

This aspect of measuring the success (also quantitatively) as well as the focus on 'scale' and 'scalability' has also been described as a feature of SE, and sometimes criticised (Rummel 2011). The promoters of SE in the early years often claimed that the 'change' created by social entrepreneurs is (or should be) not only qualitatively 'innovative', but also quantitatively relevant. In fact, some definitions of SE include 'scalability' or some sort of quantitative 'impact' or 'social impact' as a defining characteristic of SE (see overview in Dacin et al. 2010). SE should provide ideas that can be replicated. This 'social impact' is regarded as something that can be assessed and that, therefore, is quantifiable and scalable. This came, again, with new language, terms and concepts – and also tools, e.g., for impact measurement, such as social accounting or the *Social Return on Investment*.

Another point of critique concerns the network and ties of the support agencies, in particular their links to elites. The *Schwab Foundation* (perhaps, the most explicit case) was already mentioned above, but other SE support agencies, too, seem rather close to the corporate world and to (US) philanthropy and rich donors (Birkhölzer 2018: 37). Voß (2015) highlights the links of SE support agencies like *Ashoka* and others to large corporations or to conservative foundations and consultancies, such as *McKinsey*, *Adenauer Stiftung* or *Bertelsmann Stiftung*, both in Germany and globally. Voß (2015: 69–70) criticises the support and funding of SE by global elites, foundations and multinational companies. The SE actors are often considered to be (too) close to business or to be (too) business-like or profit-driven themselves. According to Karre (2021), this critique often comes from traditional third-sector actors that view the new SE actors as competition and as a way of commercialising social-welfare provision, or even as a means for 'social-washing' business activities. Voß (2015) also draws on criticism against the microcredit movement, which is closely connected to the concept of SE. Feeding into this critique is the fact that different SE actors were not afraid of engaging in partnerships with (big) commercial companies (e.g., the Yunus-Danone-partnership). Arguably, it added to the perception of SE as business-like or being tied to the business world that most of the academics who first engaged with SE in Germany were business scholars, who were also quite optimistic about SE (e.g., Mair et al. 2006 or Achleitner 2007).

Voß (2015) also raises questions of inclusivity here. Based on observations during a prominent SE event, the *Vision Summit* of 2015, Voß remarks that social entrepreneurs often speak of 'we' and 'us' – creating a bond, a feeling of belonging, togetherness, inclusion. Sceptically, though, Voß asks: who is meant by *us*, who is included, and who is not? Who gets to participate in social entrepreneurship? There are a few indications that suggest that the SE movement might be somewhat elitist. The SE scene certainly seems very middle-class, attracting the highly educated with university degrees. English is quite ubiquitous in the scene, often being the main language at meetings, events, summits, etc. – it seems somewhat expected that everybody speaks near-perfect English or is able to nonchalantly switch between German and English . In a (non-representative) study, Jansen (2013), indeed, found that over 80% of social entrepreneurs surveyed were degree-educated and over 11% held a PhD – much higher percentages than the average population (Jansen 2013: 27). Possibly, the critique of the English term 'social entrepreneurship' (as was also addressed above, with the illustrative reader's letter) and of the international orientation of the SE – being strongly associated with internationally operating (US-led) foundations and support agencies as well as with Muhammad Yunus and the microcredit movement – may, arguably, open doors for elements of anti-Americanism,anti-globalism and xenophobia and should be taken with caution. However, legitimate questions about inclusivity and recognition of the specific local context remain unanswered.

Heinze et al. (2013), Birkhölzer (2015) and Grohs et al. (2016) are some of the few that have focused on the relationship between SE and the specifics of the German context. According to Heinze et al. (2013), the relevance of SE in Germany is (and will be) rather limited. They argue that too little attention is given to fact that SE was coined mostly in developing countries (e.g., by Yunus in Bangladesh), in an environment with a different (often weaker) welfare infrastructure. In Germany, with a (comparatively) extensive welfare state and social security provision, therefore, SE remains marginal (also see Grohs et al. 2016). To some extent, Birkhölzer (2015; 2016) offers a similar view, being somewhat sceptical about the importance that SE would have in Germany, relativizing the very euphoric voices of others (see above).

When it comes to the German welfare context, other, more established, actors in the social field need to be mentioned, in particular the large welfare associations (*Wohlfahrtsverbände*), which were rather critical of the emerging SE movement and actors.[11] As Birkhölzer (2015) and Birkhölzer et al. (2015) have explained, there is a long-standing tradition of social enterprise or social economy movements in Germany (see the typology of 13 models introduced above), of which the *Wohlfahrtsverbände* today remain the most important and powerful (Achleitner et al. 2007; Schneiders 2020). To some extent, the *Wohlfahrtsverbände* felt threatened by the emerging SE actors and their narratives, because they were portraying them as the 'dinosaurs' of the social sector, i.e., as being static and lacking innovation. This is understandable, given the rhetoric of the SE actors, presenting SE as a 'new solution' to social challenges, one that is 'better' to the approaches that have been applied so far. This presentation as 'the new and better way of doing things' comes with a certain form of 'othering'

11 There are six large welfare associations in Germany: *Caritas, Diakonie, Paritätischer Wohlfahrtsverband, Rotes Kreuz, Arbeiterwohlfahrt, Zentralwohlfahrtsstelle der Juden in Deutschland*, which also have a shared lobbying organization: the *Bundesarbeitsgemeinschaft der Freien Wohlfahrtspflege* (BAGFW). Some of the welfare associations are, indeed, major corporations, *Caritas*, for example, employs over 600,000 people (Caritas 2020).

(also see Chapter 1), in which existing actors or practices are presented as the 'ineffective other': the 'old way of doing things that did not work'. Naturally, the actors depicted as such would not be very thrilled about this representation. Birkhölzer et al. (2015) explain that the welfare associations (*Wohlfahrtsverbände*) have

> warned against a debate on 'social innovation' and 'social entrepreneurship' with too close a relationship to cost efficiency, and advised to rather concentrate on high quality, good access and affordability of social services as well as inclusion of voluntarism and existing welfare organizations (Birkhölzer et al. 2015: 10, citing Bundesarbeitsgemeinschaft der Freien Wohlfahrtspflege (BAGWF)).

Furthermore, Birkhölzer (2015: 23) highlights that for the *Ashoka*-style SE, the role and the distribution of profits is unclear and the movement disregards participatory governance (Birkhölzer 2015: 23). This line of critique is, of course, strongly linked to the *EMES* perspective on SE – sometimes differentiating between an 'American'-style social entrepreneurship and a 'European' style of social enterprise (e.g., Hulgard 2010; Defourny & Nyssens 2010, as discussed in Chapter 1). This perspective upholds that SE should include a 'governance' dimension, acknowledging ideas of democratic organisation, participation, ownership, decision-making, etc. as important and necessary features for organisations pursuing social goals. There is, arguably, also an overlap between academics in the *EMES* tradition and practitioners of the third sector and social enterprise or economy movements (using Birkhölzer's (2015) terms) – some academics often being linked to these, e.g., in Germany the *Wohlfahrtsverbände*.

All in all, there was considerable criticism of the early and dominant version of SE in Germany – that was promoted mainly by *Ashoka* and a few others – in particular by representatives of the third sector and 'older' social economy movements and by academics related to these. Birkhölzer, nonetheless, attempts a slight differentiation that suggests that social entrepreneurs in Germany do not compose a homogeneous movement, with 'some of them' differing from the dominant version of SE:

> Most of them seem to be based on the concept of (US-American) philanthropic entrepreneurship, with a strong focus on market activities, independence from the state, and co-operation with the traditional corporate sector;

> they also try to attract private investment by adopting a more market-oriented language and attitude. Some of them seem to be real 'hybrids' combining for-private-profit and not-for-private-profit logics (Birkhölzer 2015: 22).

This recalls the empirical studies mentioned in Chapter 1 (for other contexts, mostly for the UK), such as Parkinson & Howorth (2008), Teasdale (2012) or Dey & Teasdale (2016), who have pointed to different goals around SE between government and SE practitioners, or Kay et al. (2016), who write about different 'camps' of SE. Birkhölzer (2015) points to a certain diversity of the SE movement in Germany here, stressing that there may be different groups of SE practitioners – a fact, which often seems ignored in the early critique of the SE movement. This critique of the critique will be further explored in the concluding section to this chapter (2.6). First, however, the more general political and socio-economic environment of Germany of the time when SE emerged needs to be addressed, since I argue that part of the critique of the SE movement is related to wider political developments and the socio-economic context in general.

2.5 The Political and Socio-Economic Context in Germany During the Emergence of Social Entrepreneurship

The political and socio-economic context of the time, especially during the time of the emergence of SE in Germany, and how it relates to (or has been related to) SE is crucial for understanding the SE discourse in Germany. In addition, I have argued in 2.4 that the political and socio-economic context is important for better understanding the critique that the early SE movement received in Germany, in particular from a social science perspective and by actors related to the third sector and the social economy tradition. Of course, covering the political and socio-economic history of a country over several years in only one section is a near impossible task. I shall focus only on a few key aspects of the political and socio-economic context in Germany of the late 1990s and early 2000s, which have particular relevance for SE – and for understanding the critique of SE. More specifically, this includes aspects that have previously been raised in literature discussing SE, as well as aspects that are relevant to the newspaper articles that have been analysed in the empirical part of this book (see Chapters 3–7), in particular a few characteristics of the German welfare state and the *Agenda 2010*, the largest labour and social security reform in Germany in recent history. The SE movement in Germany was introduced in this political and socio-economic context, which is why its reception needs to be understood against this background. I focus here on the late 1990s and early 2000s.

First, concerning the socio-economic and institutional context, relying on Esping-Andersen's (1990) typology of *welfare capitalism*, Grohs et al. (2016: 2571) describe Germany as: "the paradigmatic case of a 'conservative welfare state regime' (...), the provision of social welfare in Germany takes place within deeply rooted traditions of corporatist governance." The *Wohlfahrtsverbände*, mentioned in 2.4, have a central role in the German welfare system, providing the lion's share of social services in Germany; their position is, in part, secured by law, by the so-called 'subsidiarity principle' (Grohs et al. 2016). Göler von Ravensburg et al. explain: "Welfare services are largely publicly financed and they are provided in a subsidiary way: the state outsources service delivery to more than 100,000 organisations, most of which are associations belonging to one of the six large welfare associations (*Wohlfahrtsverbände*)" (2021: 94). Since the 1990s, however, reforms have been introduced, opening some areas of welfare provision and institutions to private actors (including for-profit companies) and market-based instruments. In addition, new services that were developed during this time – against the background of demographic change, mainly in the area of care for the elderly – from the start were more often market-based and today are vastly shaped by (for-profit) private actors – much more so than other areas of welfare provision (e.g., child and youth care). Grohs et al. (2016: 2578) summarise: "welfare legislation (social care act 1995; social assistance act 1993; child and youth care act 1996), formally abandoned the old corporatist model of welfare production". However, they argue, that *de facto* the changes in the production and provision of welfare remain moderate, a view that they base on the fact that "the so-called *freigemeinnützigen* (non-profit) organizations continue to provide the majority of social services in Germany" (Grohs et al. 2016: 2578), despite tendencies towards privatization and marketization. Due to the 'closed' networks and corporate arrangements formed by the established actors, it remains extremely hard for new, private actors to enter these 'markets' (Grohs et al. 2016: 2579) – which is also an argument that the authors put forward for assuming that SE will not gain much relevance in Germany in the near future.

Nonetheless, Grohs et al. also acknowledge that "the porosity of these corporatist structures has increased over recent years" (2016: 2579). Others go much further, claiming that the German welfare state – and a few sectors and organisations in particular, such as hospitals – underwent a significant transformation. Beyond the newly created or opened markets, this includes the introduction of managerial tools and logics (following the idea of *New Public Management*) into *Wohlfahrtsverbände* and other organisations in the social field (Bode & Vogd 2016; Betzelt 2019; Bode & Turba 2022; Fehmel & Betzelt 2022). These analyses of the German welfare system turning towards neoliberalism thus, is also in accordance with Davies' (2014a; 2014b; 2017) understanding of neoliberal principles, as described in Chapter 1. Neoliberalism does not necessarily imply the creation of markets as such. While markets were established or strengthened in a few fields (as noted above), more importantly, the organising principles of competitiveness and economic calculation spread into many areas of the German welfare system and its institutions and organisations (Bode & Vogd 2016; Betzelt 2019; Bode & Turba 2022; Fehmel & Betzelt 2022).

This more general political environment of neoliberal reform, globally and in Germany, must be considered for an understanding of the time in which SE emerged (or was introduced) in Germany and for understanding the reception and critique of the SE term and phenomenon and its actors (Section 2.4). As explained in Chapter 1, neoliberalism was on the rise around the globe since the late 1970s, for example, through marketisation and liberalisation trends, a stronger focus on individual responsibility and entrepreneurialism. Grohs et al., too, note that "[t]he social entrepreneurship discourse in Germany has become more prominent at a time when the deeply rooted corporatist traditions of social provision have come under pressure for marketization" (2016: 2569). Often, the emergence of SE during this period is directly linked to neoliberal developments. For example, Birkhölzer (2015), citing Jähnke et al. (2011), explains the rise of SE as a result of ongoing cuts in public expenditure:

> the ongoing cuts in public expenditure gave rise to new philanthropic initiatives, and especially to a boom in the setting up of new foundations, funding initiatives and social sponsoring—and to the appearance of another model, during the last decade, under the headings of 'social entrepreneurship' and 'social businesses' (Birkhölzer 2015: 22).

As demonstrated in this quote thus, the SE movement or the emergence of SE was often seen as embedded in – or at least connected to – these wider developments under neoliberalism.

I argue that, to a large extent, this may also explain the critique and the very sceptical or even dismissive view of the (early) SE movement (by certain actors and perspectives) that was summarised in Section 2.4. The critique of SE (as summarised in Section 2.4) is voiced against the background of global developments of the specific historical, political and socio-economic era, that is global neoliberalism. Steyaert & Dey, too, describe that "social entrepreneurship (...) is a product of its time" (Steyaert & Dey 2019: 4). SE is an approach that matches this *zeitgeist*, as Steyaert & Dey explain:

> The introduction of social entrepreneurship into the academic canon signified a utopian spot in time, a moment of seemingly unbound possibility. Emerging already onto the scene in the 1980s, social entrepreneurship coincided with hot debates about the environment, migration, food safety, global warming, poverty and social exclusion. During that period, when the welfare state model was increasingly falling out of favour, and when the public sphere was no longer seen as a reliable force of either societal production or protection, people turned toward social entrepreneurship as a market-based form of organizing with primarily social/economic objectives (Steyaert & Dey 2019: 3–4).

Similarly, Dart sees SE linked to an environment of the "decline of the welfare-state ideology (...) and (...) pervasive faith in market and business-based approaches and solutions" (Dart 2004: 418). In this environment, "government-dependent social welfare organizations are considered less legitimate than initiatives that followed a more businesslike model framed as entrepreneurial generating revenue" (Dart 2004: 419). SE emerged during neoliberalism and is, therefore, part of neoliberalism – so the argument goes. In addition, SE itself has, or promotes, elements of the neoliberal society, as I have explained in Section 1.5 (A 'Systemic' Perspective: Social Entrepreneurship in Relationship to Neoliberalism). Beyond the global perspective, this applies to the national context and to the political and socio-economic developments of Germany at the time, where pressures for marketization intensified since the end of the 1990s (Grohs et al. 2016, Fehmel & Betzelt 2022).

In this light, another crucial momentum and set of events must be mentioned here: the labour and social security reforms in Germany under the Schröder governments.[12] In the late 1990s and early 2000s, Germany was

12 From 1998 to 2002, a coalition by the *SPD* and the *Green Party* formed the federal government in Germany, led by Gerhard Schröder. In 2002, Schröder's government (sup-

struggling with low growth rates and, above all, with high unemployment, rising during this time period from an already high 9.2 percent in 1998 to 11.1 percent in 2005 (Dustmann et al. 2014: 167). The shortcomings of the economy were mainly attributed to the general policy framework. As Schelkle (2007) explains, there was a broad consensus among economists of very different theoretical schools (e.g., including 'mainstream' neo-classical and post-Keynesian scholars) that the German economy was in a bad state and "that bad policies are to blame" (2007: 167).

In the late 1990s, the view that the German labour and social security laws needed reform was shared by large parts of the German society and international commentators alike. In international comparison, Germany was regarded as particularly hesitant and even 'unable' to conduct reform, due to a lack of political will and courage to undergo the necessary change (Heinze 1998; Hassel & Schiller 2010: 17). The majority public view prevailed that the high level of labour costs and excessive social benefits posed a problem; the economy was sometimes described as 'encrusted' (Zimmermann 2013; Seibring 2019) – and that it needed to be freed from these 'encrusted' structures and the ties of the welfare state in favour of more 'flexible' labour market and social security structures. A vivid image for this *zeitgeist* was provided by the British *Economist*, declaring Germany to be the 'sick man' of Europe (Dustmann et al. 2014; Spohr 2019). This image was then enthusiastically taken up by parts of the public, politicians and the media in Germany, in particular the powerful tabloid *BILD* (Butterwegge 2007; 2015). The imagery and rhetoric of the time was quite strong, calling to overcome Germany's '*Reformstau*' [reform backlog] (Butterwegge 2007: 173), and facilitated justifying the labour and social security reforms that were about to come. An illustrative example for this *zeitgeist* – and different actors jumping onto the bandwagon of portraying Germany as a failing country – is the story about so-called *Florida Rolf*. In August 2003, *BILD* introduced a week-long cover story about this person (*Florida Rolf*) – a German native, who was living in a house at the beach in the Miami area with benefits from the German social security system. The case of *Florida Rolf* should reveal the apparently bizarre state of the German welfare system and became a symbol for benefit abuse and 'parasitism'. Even though *Florida Rolf* was a marginal phenomenon, as other media outlets (e.g., Der Spiegel 2004)

ported by the same coalition) was able to enter a second term – until 2005, when Angela Merkel came into power as the leader of a coalition between the *CDU/CSU* and *SPD*.

were able to show, it was just what the Schröder government needed to launch the *Agenda 2010*.

High unemployment and public opinion thus, created both the pressure and the conditions for reform of the labour market and social security when Schröder came into power. The reform framework – under the name *Agenda 2010* – was introduced during the two governments headed by Gerhard Schröder: a coalition by the *Sozialdemokratische Partei Deutschlands* (SPD) and *Bündnis 90/Die Grünen* (first term: 1998–2002, second term: 2002–2005). In many ways, the Schröder era can be compared to Blair's *New Labour* in the UK. Schröder and parts of his cabinet were sympathetic to *New Labour*'s approach of the 'Third Way'. In 1999, Schröder and Blair published the joint Blair-Schröder paper on *The Way Forward for Europe's Social Democrats*. According to Schweiger, the Schröder's coalition was "substantially influenced by New Labour's 'Third Way' approach" (2010: 246). He further explains that the Schröder government, especially in the second term, harnessed the political climate for welfare reforms – labour reform in particular:

> In the case of New Labour and the SPD the political consensus (...) occurred during a limited period, at a time when New Labour's Third Way approach was able to successfully promote itself as the best practice model for economic growth and job creation in the EU on the basis of the stable post-1997 boom. This allowed Schröder to use the 2002 unemployment crisis to push through his own preference for the Third Way's 'welfare to work' approach by using expert advice which promoted the introduction of the principle into the German employment system (Schweiger, 2010: 246).

The reforms of the *Agenda 2010* thus, had the aim to re-shape labour (promotion) and social policy, strengthening the principles of 'activation', individual responsibility and 'welfare to work'. An expert commission, headed by Peter Hartz was invoked, which should work out the roadmap to reforming the German model. In the commission's proposals, the central aim was declared as restructuring labour promotion policy according to the idea of activating labour policy (Hartz et al. 2002: 19). The reform programme *Agenda 2010* was introduced in 2003, with '*Hartz IV*'[13], the reform of unemployment benefits and social assistance, that is often considered as the 'heart piece' (Hassel & Schiller

13 *Hartz IV* is the popular term for this policy, named after Peter Hartz, the chairman of the commission in charge of designing the reforms, *Hartz IV* being the fourth in a set of policies targeting labour market and social policy reform.

2010: 13) of the reform agenda in 2005. According to Hassel & Schiller (2010), this has changed Germany more fundamentally than any other reform in recent decades. *Hartz IV* has become the epitome of an unprecedented level of economic liberalization, but also of social cuts and fear of social decline in large parts of society, not only among the poorest strata but also and especially in the middle classes. Betzelt (2019) notes that the 'workfare' idea of *Hartz IV* represents a significant rupture in the German social security model under neoliberalism, shifting from a rights-based, emancipatory approach towards a more authoritarian approach (in the sense of demanding more from social service users and seeking to influence their behaviour under the threat of sanctions). Schweiger adds:

> The resulting *Agenda 2010* reform programme, in particular the substantial reduction of financial support for the unemployed under the *Hartz IV* labour market reforms reflected the principles which the Blair-Schröder paper had originally set out (...). Schröder himself explicitly conceded this in his political memoirs in 2006 (...). The incorporation of core principles of the Blair-Schröder paper into the red-green coalition's 2002 *Agenda 2010* was a manifestation of Schröder's deep-seated sympathies for *New Labour*'s 'Third Way' economic approach, especially the essential welfare-to-work principle (Schweiger 2010: 246)

Entrepreneurialism as a virtue and the ideal figure of the entrepreneur also had an important role in these reforms. Entrepreneurship and 'entrepreneurial spirit' were seen as important elements towards greater 'flexibility' of the labour market, which had become a political goal (see above). Entrepreneurship became a value as such, and different societal actors were now expected to act in an 'entrepreneurial' way – including the job agents in the newly established 'job centres' (Hartz et al. 2002). This saviour image of entrepreneurship also became enshrined in policy with the so-called '*Ich-AGs*' ('Me Inc.'), a programme introduced during the earlier *Hartz* reforms ('*Hartz II*') to encourage unemployed people to start their own businesses (Dörre 2011; Butterwegge 2015; Spohr 2019; Betzelt 2019).

Among others, for Zimmer & Bräuer (2014), these developments during the period of the late 1990s and early 2000s in Germany meant a favourable environment for SE – as testament to this, they bring the example that "chancellor Schröder supported by *McKinsey* and the *ProSieben Sat1 Media AG* founded the *startsocial* competition with which they awarded and supported emerging social entrepreneurs" (2014: 18) – the patronage of the competition was later taken up by chancellor Merkel. However, given the lack of SE-specific policy in Germany overall (as explained in Section 2.3), this seems a bit of an overstatement. Nonetheless, I argue that the critique of the early-style SE in Germany was propelled by the more general political and socio-economic context. The context of neoliberal labour and social security reform may to some extent explain why SE, too, which emerged during this time, was seen as a neoliberal phenomenon by most social science, third sector and social economy academics and actors.

2.6 Social Entrepreneurship in Germany: Once a Neoliberal Movement, always a Neoliberal Movement?

This chapter has demonstrated that under the non-translated term 'social entrepreneurship' a distinct movement can be identified in Germany, which has developed from the late 1990s and early 2000s, with its own set of actors and infrastructure. Judging from growing interest in academic publications and the media, this 'social entrepreneurship' term and movement is gaining popularity; while there have been occasional and rather timid attempts of policy support for SE before, it is only in the early 2020s that SE-specific policies are being increasingly discussed and developed. Furthermore, it has been noted that the early SE movement revolved mainly around *Ashoka* and a few other actors, such as the *Schwab Foundation* – and consequently has been interpreted mainly as an 'American' version of SE, and centred around the individual 'hero' entrepreneur. While this specific type of SE was applauded by some actors, who considered SE a welcome and 'changemaking' addition to the 'stiff' German context of welfare provision, commentators from social science perspectives, including practitioners and academics of third sector or social economy circles were quite sceptical or even dismissive of SE. A widespread view was or is that SE is linked to neoliberalism, being part of or promoting marketisation and liberalisation trends and a stronger focus on individual responsibility and entrepreneurialism. However, some offer a more ambivalent view, suggesting that the SE field and its actors are diverse and that – even in the early phase – the SE movement is, perhaps, less homogeneous than sometimes assumed. Birkhölzer (2015), for example, loosely hints that there might be different 'camps' in the SE movement.

Little has been written, however, about the heterogeneity of the German SE movement. Arguably, the literature that suggests that SE is (part of) a neoliberalization of the welfare state starting in the early 2000s that mainly come from a third sector and nonprofit studies perspective to some extent seem to disregard the diversity of the SE field. Some SE ventures, indeed, are active in the traditional areas of welfare provision, but others are not – including, for example, some of the most prominent members of *SEND*, such as *Ecosia*, a search engine provider that uses its revenues to plant trees, and competes with companies such as *Google* and not with institutions of the welfare state. Yet, the debate in academic literature almost exclusively revolves around SE and the welfare state and rarely about SE and the (capitalist) economy and (commercial) businesses. Perhaps, there is a tendency to try to explain niche phenomena – such as SE – as part of more general developments (i.e., neoliberalization), at the risk that this might overshadow some of the nuances of these phenomena. From a feminist perspective, McRobbie et al. (2019: 137, relying on the work of Kern & McLean 2017) have raised an interesting point here. They observe that some forms of women's self-employment and entrepreneurship may be interpreted as

> local practices which interrupt the 'juggernaut' narratives of neoliberalisation processes associated with male leftist figures such as David Harvey and Jamie Peck (...). This would be to suggest, paradoxically, forms of female-led social entrepreneurship as radical urban intervention (McRobbie et al. 2019: 137).

While the authors propose that the word 'entrepreneurship' might need to be replaced with "the idea of the making of livelihoods reconcilable with social care obligations" (ibid.), they argue that these practices could then "be seen as part of a spectrum of neighbourhood and community economic activities which might also dovetail into other forms of local commitments and activism" (ibid.). Focussing on individuals, Bandinelli (2017) offers a similar argument against prematurely classifying SE as a neoliberal movement (or as part of wider neoliberal developments). Highlighting the ambiguous nature of SE, Bandinelli argues that it is worth exploring what is going on at different levels, beneath the neoliberal framework:

> [S]ocial entrepreneurs (...) could be seen as eloquent expressions of a neoliberal world vision that wants the social sphere to be subjugated to the laws of

> the market. (...) But to dismiss the will and desire of social entrepreneurs as merely ideological could prevent us from reaching a deeper understanding of the phenomenon, ultimately leading to the tautological argument that neoliberal subjects act in a neoliberal way (Bandinelli 2017: 13).

Among others, Birkhölzer (2015), Bandinelli (2017) and McRobbie et al. (2019) thus, propose to take a closer look at the complex social and political phenomenon that is SE. Furthermore, there is a temporal dimension that must be taken into account here. I argue that little is known about SE as a political phenomenon and movement beyond the early phase, in which it has emerged or has been introduced in Germany (i.e., the late 1990s and early 2000s). The critical literature widely categorises the origins of SE as neoliberal – and there are many and good reasons for this, as I have explained throughout this chapter. However, the early phase might have shaped the impression and interpretation of SE in Germany a little too much, enshrining a certain (static) view of SE that risks ignoring (potential) developments in the SE movement that might have occurred later on. Yet, given the dynamic and ambiguous nature of the SE concept (see Chapter 1), it can be assumed that contestations and developments have been taking place.

Several observations support this view, hinting at developments in the SE discourse and movement since the late 1990s and early 2000s. As explained in Section 2.3, new actors have emerged in the SE field. By the late 2010s, *Ashoka* seems to have been replaced by *SEND* as the main organisation promoting SE in Germany (see Section 2.3). As *Ashoka* and other players (such as the *Schwab Foundation*) have lost their exceptionally dominant position in the SE field and discourse, it seems likely that the '*Ashoka*-style' version of SE that prevails in the initial phase in Germany has also lost ground to other versions and discourses of SE. Another interesting aspect is that the understanding of SE promoted by *SEND* is different, and more rooted in what is often described as the 'European' SE tradition. More precisely, *SEND*'s definition of SE includes a 'governance' dimension, i.e., elements of participatory governance, decision-making, accountability, etc. (as seen in Section 1.3). Before developing its own definition in 2019 – in an attempt to provide a definition that is tailored to the German SE scene and in particular to *SEND*'s members – *SEND* relied on the *European Commission's* (2014) definition for 'social enterprise', which in turn was strongly influenced by leading *EMES* researchers. Another observation worth mentioning is the 'Social Economy Berlin' programme funded by the Berlin Senate (see 1.3) – which obviously seeks to establish a link to the 'social economy' concept and tradition and includes actors of different 'generations' of social economy or social enterprise movements. Indeed, the programme is jointly executed by *SEND* and *TechNet*, a network and support organisation for the social economy that has been active since the 1980s. Karl Birkhölzer, who is also an important academic contributor to the third sector and the social economy and whose work I am considerably relying on in this chapter, is one of the founders of the organisation. *TechNet* is currently headed by Karl's daughter, Heike Birkhölzer (TechNet 2022).

These are only some observational examples indicating that multi-layered constructions and contestations of the meaning(s) of SE have been at play – and that, indeed, the German SE movement demonstrates 'conceptual confusion' and that it cannot be easily explained as a neoliberal phenomenon. The reviewed academic literature in Chapter 1 has also highlighted the ambiguous and dynamic nature of the SE concept. However, empirical studies targeted at the development of the SE phenomenon and movement in Germany, so far, are missing. Somewhat paradoxically, as the SE movement is gaining importance in Germany, (too) little attention is given to the (normative and political) contestations of meanings of and around SE. (Potential) developments of the SE concept and movement beyond the early phase of the late 1990s and early 2000s seem to occur widely unnoticed in academic research – or at least widely uncommented. I can only speculate on the reasons for this research gap. Perhaps, one factor may be that there are only few contributions from social science scholars, and that most research on SE (in Germany and internationally) currently comes from a business and management perspective – which does not primarily focus on this sort of questions around the normative and political contestations around SE. International research – such as the studies by Parkinson & Howorth (2008) or Teasdale (2012) for the UK – provide interesting findings and an analytical framework, but can only be of limited help to understand the detailed development of SE in Germany, as it is essential that SE is examined and understood according to and in relationship with the respective context (see 1.6). In addition, these earlier studies are not able to cover developments during the 2010s.

This is where this book makes a substantial contribution. The empirical analysis contributes to a better sociological making sense of the SE concept and phenomenon for the specific context of Germany (1999–2021) – and, in particular, help to better understand the concept of SE in Germany beyond the early phase. The following chapter (3) will explain how discourse analysis offers a way to analyse the normative and political constructions of SE, allowing to bridge the different levels where the meanings of SE are produced and contested as well as to analyse (potential) developments in the SE discourse(s) over time and then outline my methodological approach and empirical operationalization more specifically as well as to reflect on the choice of data (newspaper articles) and its implications.

Chapter 3: Grasping the Social Entrepreneurship Discourse(s) – Theoretical Framework and Methodology

3.1 Introduction: Empirically Investigating the Contested Concept of Social Entrepreneurship in Germany between 1999 and 2021

This book explores the contested concept of social entrepreneurship (SE) in Germany between 1999 and 2021 along four research themes: diversity and dominance, representation and relevance, development over time and notions of 'change' and politics. As I have explained in Chapter 1, descriptions and interpretations of the SE term and concept can be quite diverse, and are often intertwined with wider worldviews, narratives or visions about the economy and society, deriving from different normative underpinnings and political beliefs. SE seeks to advocate 'change' – but it often remains unclear, what exactly shall 'change' and how, and what sort of economy and society is ultimately envisioned by SE. Different actors see very different things in SE and pursue different goals with it. From Chapter 2, it is known that in the early phase, SE in Germany has mostly been interpreted as a neoliberal movement. However, there is a lack of academic literature – and in particular a lack of empirical sociological research – that investigates the German SE movement beyond the initial years. In addition, the SE scene has developed considerably in recent years, and has seen the emergence of new actors. Against this background, this book seeks to offer insights, contributing to a more differentiated sociological understanding of SE in the specific German context and to help better understand where the SE movement is currently standing (i.e., in the early 2020s) – when interest for SE in Germany is starting to grow.

In this chapter, I am going to explain how discourse analysis offers a suitable theoretical and methodological perspective to pursue the outlined research issues and to help making sense of SE in Germany. Discourse analysis allows to grasp a broad picture of the SE phenomenon – one that goes beyond single cases (of social enterprises or social entrepreneurs), doing justice to the heterogeneity in how SE is conceptualised, but also allowing to identify dominant accounts of (the representations of) SE. What is more, discourse analysis provides a framework for investigating the development of concepts over time. In addition, discourse analysis seems able to bridge the analysis of the complex constructions of meaning(s) of SE that have occurred and are occurring on different levels (simultaneously) (as described in Chapter 1). For understanding the SE concept in Germany – and in particular its development over the past two decades – the empirical approach that will be outlined in this chapter is novel and promises important insights.

In a nutshell, discourse analysis offers a theoretical and methodological perspective that helps to investigate and to untangle the complex interplay of language and social relations in constructing ideas. In the past few decades, the study of discourse has undeniably gained prominence in different academic disciplines (van Dijk 2007; Diaz-Bone et al. 2007; Keller 2011). Today, researchers can choose from a wide array of different approaches that sometimes have notable differences in terms of research design and methods. In the following section, I will first give a general introduction to the theoretical framework of *discourse*. Section 3.3 will then explain what it means to *analyse* discourse and focus, in particular, on *Critical Discourse Analysis*, mainly according to Fairclough (1992; 2010), who has developed his approach integrating social theory and linguistics and whose approach is used in sociological and linguistic studies alike. Fairclough's *Critical Discourse Analysis*, complemented with the approach proposed by Diaz-Bone (2006), serves as the principal methodological framework for the empirical research. Section 3.4 will then lay out the concrete operationalization for the empirical research, describing the compiling of the corpus of newspaper articles, the analysis of the corpus, ethical considerations and the presentation of the results. In this way, my empirical study grasps the representation of SE in newspapers, which I treat as a certain 'mainstream' view on SE – i.e., what a broader audience gets to learn about the SE concept. However, it must be taken into account that this methodological choice implies certain limitations for my research findings – namely, that my empirical analysis does not grasp an all-encompassing account of SE, but, instead, a mediated account of SE 'through the eyes of newspapers', as I will explain later in this chapter.

3.2 Discourse(s) as Systems of Thought around Specific Topics

The study of discourse is usually referred back to Foucault (1961; 1966; 1969; 1975). Foucault has analysed and revealed the formation of knowledge around different topics and ideas and even whole academic disciplines over certain (usually quite large) spans of time and coined this approach as the study of discourse. For example, Foucault has demonstrated how the idea of 'madness' – that did not exist in this sense in Western societies before the late Middle Ages – has been developed in a binary juxtaposition to 'rationality' and 'normality'. 'Madness' was criminalized and later pathologized, and over the years, societies have institutionalised this idea, e.g., though establishing psychiatric facilities (Foucault 1961). Based on Foucault's accounts of dissecting the genealogies and developments of different concepts, ideas and meanings, challenging deeply rooted or taken-for-granted assumptions and ways of viewing the world, a productive research perspective has emerged across different disciplines under the banners of 'discourse' and 'discourse analysis'. Today, discourses are researched across linguistics, cultural studies, sociology, media and communications, history, anthropology, political science, philosophy and social psychology (Mills 1997; Kerchner & Schneider 2006; van Dijk 2007; Diaz-Bone et al. 2007; Keller 2011).[1] The great variety of approaches to discourse analysis is also in part attributed to Foucault, who offered a broad research framework and perspective rather than a specific methodological approach, or even a 'toolbox'. Therefore, the research design and empirical operationalization of different empirical discourse analyses can vary considerably, even if most refer back to Foucault's work (Kerchner & Schneider 2006; Keller 2011). This is sometimes criticised as a lack of methodological coherence (e.g., Kendall 2007; Keller 2011), while others welcome the diversity and transdisciplinarity of discourse studies (e.g., van Dijk 2007).

The formation, development and negotiation of ideas is relevant for understanding past and contemporary societies, which is why *discourse* and *discourse analysis* have proven to be fruitful frameworks for social science research. *Discourse* refers to linguistic expressions ('text and talk'), but going beyond language itself, since "language users engaging in discourse accomplish social acts and participate in social interactions" (van Dijk 1997: 2). Van Dijk as well as

1 Foucault's body of work is recognised in different disciplines, and he has been described as philosopher, historian, social theorist, literary critic, sociologist or psychologist.

Fairclough and Wodak, arguably some of the most important scholars in the Anglophone tradition of discourse studies (and of *Critical Discourse Analysis* in particular), describe discourse itself as "social practice" (e.g., van Dijk 1997: 2; Fairclough & Wodak 1997: 258; Fairclough 2010: 92). The 'social practice' of discourse refers to a set of processes at the intersection of social relations and language. This includes processes of producing meaning and knowledge (around a particular topic), processes of building systems of thought (around a particular topic) or establishing "a framework through which we see the world" (Braham 2013: 58) as well as processes of constituting regimes of truth and falsity (around a particular topic). Mills (1997) explains discourses similar to this, as: "utterances which seem to be regulated in some way and which seem to have a coherence and a force to them in common" (1997: 7). This makes it possible "to talk about a discourse of femininity, a discourse of imperialism, and so on" (ibid.) – or, precisely: about a discourse of social entrepreneurship (in Germany).

Hall (1997) specifies this, explaining that discourse is not just about an idea or topic, but also about the whole system of thought around it. Discourse involves "a cluster (or formation) of ideas, images and practices, which provide ways of talking about, forms of knowledge and conduct associated with a particular topic, social activity or institutional site in society" (Hall 1997: 6). Braham further elaborates on this aspect of discourse – explaining that there are certain 'rules' that guide this production of knowledge:

> Foucault's (...) premise was that systems of thought and knowledge (epistemes or discursive formations in his terminology) were governed by rules that operated beneath the consciousness of individual subjects that determines the boundaries of thought in a given sphere and period. In his view, a discourse gave credibility to certain ideas and denied credibility to others, thus establishing what could be known and thought about a subject. For Foucault, discourse constituted the world by shaping the way knowledge was produced in particular historical circumstances (2013: 59–60).

Similar to this explanation, Diaz-Bone et al. (2007: 6) write of discourse as an 'ordered system', however, they also bring the attention to actors within a discourse. According to Diaz-Bone et al. "discourse is conceived of as a super-individual reality; as a kind of practice that belongs to collectives rather than individuals" (2007: 2). This is an important aspect of discourse, implying somewhat of a 'common' agreement or 'common' knowledge among a group of people about a certain idea or topic. Given that discourse is somewhat 'super-individual', this leaves the question of what role (individual) actors might have in the discourse. These are not necessarily aware of, or actively shaping, the rules of the discourse. As quoted above: discourses are *governed by rules that operate beneath the consciousness of individual subjects*. Diaz-Bone et al. (2007), too, emphasise that it is not "the intentionality of individuals in situations (although individuals still have to enact discourses and statements)" (Diaz-Bone et al. 2007: 6), which constitutes a discourse.

In quoting Braham, I want to emphasise the above introduced idea of discourses as common agreement:

> The power of discourses therefore resides in allowing or encouraging certain things to be thought, said, or acted out by constructing positions that are seen to be 'self evident', 'received wisdom', 'taken-for-granted' because they 'make sense' to us, or are 'what we expect'. Conversely, a discourse will tend to limit or prevent other things being thought, said, or done precisely because they do not satisfy these criteria (Braham 2013: 59).

Braham's quote, therefore, raises an important point: that within a discourse and its system of knowledge, some things (or utterances) are considered true and others false, constituting a "regime of truth" (2013: 59–60). Discourse "influences, regulates and constrains practices and meanings (therefore in order to think, people have to do so in terms established by the discourse)" (Braham 2013: 60). Hall explains this in a similar way: discourses "define what is and is not appropriate in our formulation of, and our practices in relation to, a particular subject or site of social activity; what knowledge is considered useful, relevant and 'true' in that context" (Hall 1997: 6).

In sum: "The simplest way to think of the concept of discourse is that it provides a framework through which we see the world" (Braham 2013: 58). Or, put in a different way:

> Discourses, as Said (1978) and Spivak (1987) note, are not innocent explanations of the world. They are, as Spivak emphasises, a way of worlding, of appropriating the world through knowledge. The strands of knowledge with which we engage in our attempt to describe and understand the world are produced in complex power relations in which different actors and institutions work to establish a dominant interpretation of 'reality'. (Diaz-Bone et al. 2007: 6).

This quote highlights two aspects: that discourse is about power relations and that discourse is dynamic or processual. Discourse is contested by different actors and may change over time. Jäger and Jäger (2007) have proposed an interesting formulation for this that suitably expresses the dynamic and contested nature: discourse is about 'battles over meaning' or 'battles over interpreting the world' (*Deutungskämpfe*) – and this is precisely a crucial aspect. As stated, for example, in the Introduction, one of my main research interests is to examine diversity and dominance, i.e., how the idea of SE is being constructed in Germany, what different understandings can be identified, but also what the dominant views on the SE concept are. Or, in Jäger and Jäger's terms: examining the 'battles' over giving meaning to or interpreting SE in Germany. As already explained in Chapter 1, Teasdale (2012) has demonstrated (for the UK) that SE is a concept over which such 'battles over meaning' or 'battles over interpreting the world' are fought and ongoing:

> The construction of social enterprise is ongoing, and fought by a range of actors promoting different languages and practices tied to different political beliefs. That is, social enterprise is politically contested by different actors around competing discourses (Teasdale 2012: 100).

The next sections will further elaborate how this particular discourse – or these discourses (in plural) – of SE in Germany may be analysed by applying a specific approach: *Critical Discourse Analysis*.

3.3 (Critical) Discourse Analysis: Researching Not Text, but 'Social Practice'

After diving into the theoretical framework of 'discourse', the question that should be answered next is how to investigate these 'battles over meaning', 'ways of worlding', or systems of thought and their rules around a particular topic – such as SE. How can discourse be analysed, and what does this entail?

Put simply, discourse analysis entails the analysis of linguistic expressions – i.e., 'text' (in a broad understanding of the term, which also includes, for example, spoken word or images). It needs to be noted, however, that for most social science approaches to discourse analysis – and certainly for my research – it is not primarily the linguistic expressions as such that shall be investigated, but precisely the 'social practice' that this text represents (as mentioned above). As Fairclough – one of the main discourse analysis theorists my research builds on, as I will explain shortly – puts it: discourse analysis "is not analysis of discourse 'in itself' as one might take it to be, but analysis of dialectical relations between discourse and other objects, elements or moments, as well as analysis of the 'internal relations' of discourse" (2010: 4).

I understand these 'internal relations' precisely as the set of processes that were explained above, namely: processes of producing meaning and knowledge, of building systems of thought and processes of constituting regimes of truth and falsity (around a particular topic). Or in the words of Jäger: processes of formation of meaning ("*Prozesse der Sinnbildung*", Jäger 1999: 12). These processes do not just occur 'naturally' or 'organically' – but, instead, at the interplay of the individual, society and language within discourse (Jäger 1999). Therefore, they are shaped by different agents; discourses and their production of knowledge and meaning are 'arenas' of political argument over which knowledge or meanings become valid in a specific social situation and time (Hirseland 2007). Diaz-Bone et al. describe this as "a socio-historic process in which the discourse as a field of knowledge and a system of rules emerges" (Diaz-Bone et al. 2007: 6). This also implies that in discourse analysis it is not possible to simply 'point towards' a certain (static or fixed) entity or object, as Fairclough notes (2010: 3). This gives discourse analysis a quite dynamic property, entailing an analysis of relations or processes that are in flux and constantly changing. Discourse analysis (in the social science perspective), therefore, explores how a society or group (or 'discursive community' in Jäger's term) reaches a 'common agreement' or 'super-individual reality' (around a specific topic), how and why specific ideas and systems of ideas come to be 'commonly agreed upon' (and others that do not). In sum, discourse analysis is the analysis of ideas and knowledge around a topic, how they are formed and (re-)produced as well as contested, which happens in interaction between different societal actors, who are at the same time producers and recipients of discourse (Keller 2011; Traue et al. 2014).

As noted in Fairclough's quote above, discourse analysis is also about researching the 'relations between discourse and other objects'. This means that a specific discourse (e.g., on social entrepreneurship) cannot be regarded or understood 'in isolation', but in relation to, for example, ideas of the state, of capitalism, or of entrepreneurship. Here, the 'dialectical' relationship of discourse needs to be taken into account (Fairclough 2010). Fairclough & Wodak explain this dialectical relationship as following:

> A dialectical relationship is a two-way relationship: the discursive event is shaped by situations, institutions and social structures, but it also shapes them. To point the same point in a different way, discourse is socially constitutive as well as socially shaped: it constitutes situations, objects of knowledge, and the social identities of and relationships between people and groups of people. It is constitutive both in the sense that it helps to sustain and reproduce the social status quo, and in the sense that it contributes to transforming it (1997: 258).

For my empirical analysis, this means that it needs to be investigated how SE is constructed, what is 'said' (in a broad sense) about SE – but also, in which way SE contributes to the understanding of other concepts, for example, notions of the state, capitalism or entrepreneurship, more generally – and how these notions, in turn, shape the understanding of SE.

As already indicated above, analysing discourse(s) concerns many research projects in different academic disciplines, which has resulted in a wide array of different types and methodologies of discourse analysis. One approach that foregrounds the 'social practice' of discourse is *Critical Discourse Analysis* (often capitalised and abbreviated 'CDA'). CDA places a very explicit focus on investigating 'social practice' – and not the language or text as such. In addition, CDA has been developed in a systematic and replicable way, while still allowing great flexibility for the specifics of each research project. This makes CDA a suitable methodological framework for investigating the SE discourse in Germany, as I will further address in the following paragraphs.

According to van Dijk (2007), CDA emerged in the end of the 1970s, originally introduced by Fowler et al. (1979), and developed, roughly at the same time and sometimes in cooperation, by Fairclough in the UK, Wodak in Austria and van Dijk in the Netherlands, who remain to be some of the most important authors in the English-speaking literature – perhaps for discourse analysis in general, and certainly for CDA (Keller 2011). Even though van Dijk, Wodak and Fairclough are originally linguists, their approaches to CDA are widely applied in the social sciences, since they strongly build on and draw upon (critical) social (science) theory. Keller (2011), a sociologist and one of the main German contributors to discourse analysis, also recognizes Wodak's and – especially – Fairclough's approach as being characterized by their primary focus on 'social practice' and for incorporating social theory into their approaches. Although originally a linguist, Fairclough stresses that "in referring to language use as discourse, I am signalling a wish to investigate it in a social-theoretically informed way, as a form of social practice" (Fairclough 2010: 92). According to Keller (2011), CDA views linguistic expression also as action; discourses (re-)produce and transform society. "Discourse is a practice not just of representing the world, but of signifying the world, constituting and constructing the world in meaning" (Fairclough 1992: 64).

Arguably, herein lie some of the distinctions between the different CDA scholars; van Dijk, Wodak and Fairclough each have coined their own versions of CDA, even though most differences are only nuances. The common ground between their approaches predominates, especially between those of Wodak and Faiclough.[2] Nonetheless, there are a few differences. It can be argued that van Dijk's research focus is closer to the core of linguistics, being primarily concerned with studying conversational interaction in social contexts (van Dijk 2007), rather than with the 'social practice' itself. In some of his work, van Dijk has also leaned into the psychological processes of the formation of language and ideas (Keller 2011), focusing on *cognitive* rather than *social* processes and relations. Certainly, the primary focus on 'social practice' is less explicit than in Wodak's and in Fairclough's work. In addition, as Wodak has outlined in an interview, the various approaches have different theoretical underpinnings: Fairclough bases his work strongly on Foucault, while Wodak relies more on the *Frankfurt School* (Kendall 2007). In terms of empirical research, Fairclough tends to research fewer discourse samples, while Wodak has also engaged in quite large sets of data, sometimes incorporating quantitative methods (e.g., in Baker et al. 2008). Arguably, Wodak (like van Dijk) is more interested in situating CDA within the discipline of linguistics, for example by combining CDA with corpus linguistics (e.g., in Baker et al. 2008; Wodak & Meyer 2001). Furthermore, the different schools of CDA sometimes choose quite different thematic fields or topics for research (Kendall 2007).

Today, CDA is applied to various empirical research problems, and by far not limited to the English-speaking world. Numerous empirical contributions can be found, for example, in the journals *Discourse & Society*, *Critical Approaches to Discourse Analysis Across Disciplines* (*CADAAD*), or in *Discourse Studies*. Perhaps, the most frequent research topics for CDA are studies on racism, nationalism, gender, or sexism (see, for example, the recent issues of *Discourse & Society*). Research problems related to the (political) economy – such as social en-

2 Wodak and Fairclough also share an institutional link, having both worked at *Lancaster University*.

trepreneurship – are less common.[3] Interestingly though, Fairclough himself has often addressed discourses related to topics of political economy (in a broad sense) in his empirical research. For example, in the extensive empirical account *New Labour, New Language?* (2000), which explores the discourse and the politics of the 'Third Way' and its leaders, or in his study from 1993: *Critical discourse analysis and the marketisation of public discourse: the universities*.

The specific perspective that researchers shed upon the object of study (often a situation of injustice) is also what makes CDA 'critical' – as understood by its theorists. Fairclough explains this 'critical' notion of CDA as following:

> By 'critical' discourse analysis I mean discourse analysis which aims to systematically explore often opaque relationships of causality and determination between (a) discursive practices, events and texts, and (b) wider social and cultural structures, relations and processes; to investigate how such practices, events and texts arise out of and are ideologically shaped by relations of power and struggles over power; and to explore how the opacity of these relationships between discourse and society is itself a factor securing power and hegemony (...). In referring to opacity, I am suggesting that such linkages between discourse, ideology and power may well be unclear to those involved, and more generally that our social practice is bound up with causes and effects which may not be at all apparent (Fairclough 2010: 93).

For this 'critical' stand, CDA has sometimes been questioned and viewed as somewhat opinionated. Jäger (1999: 8), for example, has voiced that, in his regard, Fairclough and Wodak would not (thoroughly enough) disclose their political stand. Proponents of CDA would argue from a 'position of truth', and not (thoroughly enough) reflect on their own ideological positions and assumptions, taking an unrealistic and somewhat 'superior' position as analysts (Jäger & Diaz-Bone 2006: 38). Fairclough and Wodak, however, have addressed this sort of criticism in different contributions, explaining their view on the relationship between ones ideological or political stand and scientific rigor. Fairclough & Wodak acknowledge that:

> CDA sees itself not as dispassionate and objective social science, but as engaged and committed. It is a form of intervention in social practice and social

3 A few interesting exceptions can be found in the edited volume by Diaz-Bone and Krell (2015).

> relationships: many analysts are politically active against racism, or as feminists, or within the peace movement, and so forth (Fairclough & Wodak 1997: 258–259).

However, the authors convincingly argue that this sort of involvement is nothing particular to CDA. Instead, "social science is inherently tied into politics and formulations of policy" (ibid.). On the contrary, they claim that CDA "openly declares the emancipatory interests that motivate it. The political interests and uses of social scientific research are usually less explicit" (ibid.). Ultimately, CDA researchers have to uphold methodological standards of "careful, rigorous and systematic analysis" (ibid.) and – perhaps even more explicitly so than in other approaches – disclose their individual or political stand. Wodak also highlights this argument in an interview, stating that CDA needs to be

> "'[r]etroductable' (*nachvollziehbar*) (...) [i.e.] that such analyses should be transparent so that any reader can trace and understand the detailed in-depth textual analysis. In any case, all criteria which are usually applied to social science research apply to CDA as well" (Kendall: 2007: 38).

I agree with this assessment when it comes to personal or political involvement and consider that for the researcher to reflect on their own position and personal and political involvement is nothing exclusive to CDA and certainly should be taken into account within all methodologies of (social) research.

This being said, I shall outline ('disclose') my own position regarding my empirical investigation regarding the SE discourse(s) in Germany. As I have explained in Chapter 1, normativity plays a central role in SE, being a 'value-loaded' concept. Furthermore, as Ranville & Barros (2021) have argued, this is only rarely acknowledged in research on SE. Normative positions are frequently (left) opaque (to use Fairclough's terminology). As addressed in the introduction, I have my own personal experience with the idea of SE – and certain 'hopes' that I associate with the SE movement. I was drawn to the SE concept, having understood SE as an idea of doing business differently, of imagining and experimenting with alternative economies that are more just and sustainable than current – i.e., profit maximising – business models within the capitalist economy. However, later on and especially during the research, I have learned that not everyone shared this view, and that SE was often regarded as part of the capitalist (neoliberal) business and economy – the sort of business and economy that SE (in my initial understanding) was seeking to overcome. For Germany, this even represents the dominant view – at least in the critical social science (informed) literature that comments on the early SE movement, as explained in Chapter 2. As stated in the Introduction, this 'irritation', i.e., this disconnect or even clash between my personal understanding of SE and how SE was often classified or interpreted in academic literature, was important for the starting point for this book. For the actual empirical research, however, I argue that this initial position does not represent a problem in the sense of a disproportionate 'involvement'. Ultimately, my 'irritation' and acknowledging the different understandings of SE and the different 'hopes' or 'fears' attributed to it, led me, above all, to wanting to understand, how it is possible to associate SE with such different political beliefs – which is primarily a scholarly interest.

Furthermore, I tried to ensure that my analysis would not be guided by my initial position or by any other single position. I made sure that the data (the corpus of newspaper articles) would be broad and balanced, covering a relatively high number of articles and different newspapers across the political spectrum. For the analysis, relying on Diaz-Bone (2006), I followed an approach that is strongly inductive, trying to navigate the material quite openly – instead of focussing on predetermined categories or particular aspects. These and more practicalities of my empirical operationalisation will be explained in detail in the next section.

3.4 Operationalising the Empirical Research

In the previous sections, I have introduced the concept of discourse as well as the framework of *(critical) discourse analysis*, and outlined reasons for why CDA, in particular according to Fairclough (1992; 2010), is a suitable approach for my empirical investigation of the SE discourse(s) in Germany. Arguably, Fairclough has the most explicit focus on social practice of the main CDA theorists and provides a framework that is systematic, while allowing flexibility for individual research problems. I will rely on the framework proposed by Fairclough, mainly based on the monograph *Discourse and Social Change* (1992), in particular, on Chapter Eight, *Doing Discourse Analysis* (1992: 225–240), where the author explains the "practicalities of doing discourse analysis" (Fairclough 1992: 225). It needs to be noted, though, that Fairclough highlights that his methodological propositions should not be regarded as a "blueprint" but rather as a "general guideline" (ibid.) that should be adopted individually to the respective research project, leaving considerable methodological flexibility and easily allowing to incorporate other methods of (qualitative) social research, to which I will come back to later.

In line with general guidelines for (qualitative) social research (e.g., Flick 2012; Przyborski & Wohlrab-Sahr 2014; Silverman 2015), the empirical research process consists of data gathering, then analysing the data and, lastly, presenting the results. This being said, Fairclough (1992: 225–240), too, proposes three main steps, with several sub-steps, namely:

I. Data
I.1 defining a project
I.2 the corpus
I.3 enhancing the corpus
I.4 (transcription)
I.5 coding and selecting samples within the corpus

II. Analysis
II.1 discourse practice
II.2 text
II.3 social practice

III. Results

The starting point for **data** – i.e., (I.1) **defining a project** – implies identifying the discursive arenas, in which the social practice is played out and constituted, and to clarify which discursive samples are good expressions or examples for the discourse(s) that the researcher intends to study. Based on these considerations, the (I.2) **the corpus** is compiled – i.e., the body of texts or set of "discourse samples" (Fairclough 1992: 226) that will be studied. Step I.3 ('**enhancing the corpus**') should make sure that the corpus is sound, in the sense of being able to provide meaningful results for the research problem at hand. I.4 ('**transcription**') only applies for research projects that analyse spoken word (e.g., gathered in interviews), which requires transcription. This step, therefore, could be excluded from my empirical operationalisation. The last step in terms of **data** (I.5), however, namely **coding and selecting samples within the corpus** was important for my research and, arguably, already feeds into the second major part of the empirical research: the **analysis** (II.). For this, Fairclough identifies three dimensions of studying discourse: **discourse practice**, **text** and **social practice**, while noting that these "three dimensions of analysis will inevitably overlap in practice" (Fairclough 1992: 231). Furthermore, Fairclough remarks that these propositions should be regarded as "very rough guidelines" (1992: 237). Indeed, in my research project, for the analysis, I will follow Fairclough's analysis rather loosely, focusing mainly on the dimension of social practice. I argue that some aspects of Fairclough's analysis are (too) strongly shaped by methods that derive from his background in linguistics, of which some are not relevant or suitable for my analysis. Instead, my analysis will be complemented with other approaches, mainly by Diaz-Bone (2006). As the third and last major step, Fairclough points to the (III) **results** of the discourse analysis, in which Fairclough discusses and reflects on selected aspects of (social) scientific results, and in which way findings could be (mis)used by different actors. Strictly speaking, I consider that these remarks are rather ethical and not necessarily methodological, and I will not discuss these further at this point.

In sum, *Critical Discourse Analysis* as proposed by Fairclough provides a useful general methodological framework, which can well be complemented with other approaches of social research and applied to my research on the SE discourse(s) in Germany between 1999 and 2021. In the following sub-sections, I will further outline the specific steps of operationalising the empirical research process.

3.4.1 What Data? Newspapers as Arenas of 'Common' Agreement and 'Everyday Text'

Where exactly may the SE discourse(s) in Germany be 'found'? Strictly speaking, the SE discourse or discourses would encompass all spoken word, all written text, all imagery, sound and video on SE (in Germany) that has ever been produced. As Fairclough puts it: "The order of discourse of some social domain is the totality of its discursive practices, and the relationships (...) between them" (2010: 93). The options for selecting discourse samples, therefore, seem infinite – CDA may be applied to all kinds of material, which for the researcher seems somewhat of a curse and a blessing at the same time. Naturally, however, analysing 'everything' is impossible – nor would this be necessary, given that the properties of a discourse – its rules and 'common sense' – should be inherent to different kinds of material ('text' in a broad sense). The orthodox discourse analyst might even claim that the choice of data was irrelevant, given that the properties of the SE discourse(s) should become apparent in any type of data and that the discourse (of SE) would predetermine or rule what can and what cannot be said about SE.

However, for a concrete empirical research project, a choice of data must be made. Following Fairclough's (1992) first steps of 'defining the project' and building the 'corpus', this implies to take an informed decision concerning which discursive 'arenas' or 'domains' to investigate, and which data or material to select as 'discourse samples' to study the SE discourse(s) in Germany. The discourse arena and samples should be able to provide a valid account of the object of study, i.e., representations and constructions of the SE concept and the wider narratives about the economy and society, which are intertwined with these. The empirical analysis is based on newspapers as discursive arenas and on newspaper articles as data or material to analyse, because these are suitable and relevant to explore my four research lines: 1) ***Diversity and dominance***: it is to be expected that newspapers (especially when looking at a large number of articles) offer different representations and explanations of SE – and in the analysis it can be identified what parts or aspects of SE are being presented as the dominant account of SE in German newspapers. 2) ***Representation and Relevance***: newspapers reach a wide audience, a large part of society, including different socio-demographic groups. To an extent, I take newspaper as a proxy for what (aspects about SE) receive attention from 'mainstream' society. 3) ***Development over time***: the very function of newspaper articles is to report on current affairs – they offer a chronical, an account of contemporary history. On a more technical-practical note, it is a favourable feature that each article is clearly assigned to a specific date, which makes newspaper articles very suitable to trace development over time. 4) ***Notions of 'change' and politics***: newspaper articles tell a story. Not all but many articles offer wider explanations of SE, a sensemaking of the SE phenomenon and the societal or political role that is ascribed to SE in Germany as well as the idea of economy and society that SE envisions.

In choosing newspaper articles as a base for my empirical analysis, I am following an established route in discourse analysis. For their practical empirical research, it is a popular choice for (critical) discourse analysts to look either to the media or to politics (see e.g., van Dijk 1997), and, more specifically, to newspaper articles or to political speeches in national parliaments. For the UK, previous empirical studies – including Parkinson & Howorth (2008), Teasdale (2012) and Mason (2012) – offer interesting examples for analysing SE discourse(s) (see also Chapter 1), mainly based on public policy documents. However, as I have explained in Chapters 1 and 2, before the early 2020s SE in Germany has not yet attracted significant attention or involvement of policymakers. Arguably, Germany represents a context, in which SE finds itself largely in a 'pre-policy-involvement'-stage. Therefore, focusing on policy documents is a less suitable option for Germany. On the other hand, selecting discourse samples from the media and from newspapers, more specifically, is a fruitful approach for the German context, as I will further explain in the following paragraphs.

In addition to the points made above, a simple yet effective argument for focusing on newspapers is that the (mass) media is an important arena for producing and shaping knowledge and even social relations. Fairclough (1995; 2000), among others, has pointed out the important role that the (mass) media plays in constituting discourses. In his monograph *Media Discourse*, Fairclough (1995) highlights "the power of the mass media (...) to shape governments and parties, (...) to influence knowledge, beliefs, values, social relations, social identities" (Fairclough 1995: 2). Arguably, this power of the mass media is particularly relevant when it comes to presenting 'new' topics, such as SE, to a wider audience – assuming that SE is a somewhat 'new' phenomenon, or at least one being presented as 'new' (see Chapters 1 and 2).

Moreover, (daily) newspapers have the function of informing a general public of current affairs in politics, the economy, society, culture, etc., and respectively include a broad variety of contemporary topics and news. They shape or even produce collective knowledge on these topics (Luhmann 2004; Karis 2010; Meyen 2013). This makes newspapers a popular source for empirical discourse analyses (see, for example, Kurtenbach 2018, or Hunter et al. 2019). In following this path, I am building on a strong research tradition in discourse analysis (Gredel 2018),[4] with the aim of capturing "everyday text" (Hunter et al. 2019: 626) – i.e., a non-specialist discourse, outside of the niche (or 'bubble', as it might be framed) of SE practitioners, support agencies and closely related actors.

My research interest is primarily concerned with 'common' knowledge or 'commonly accepted' knowledge – i.e., the perception of a 'general' society or a 'general' public rather than with a discourse that is representative for a niche

4 Focusing on mass media, and, more specifically, on newspaper articles is such an established practice that, e.g., Warnke criticises a "newspaper bias" (2013: 191) in discourse analysis.

or group of experts or the like. This is an important reason for concentrating on the mass media and newspapers as a source for selecting discourse samples, since it can be assumed that newspapers are playing an important part in introducing the SE concept to a broader audience and generating and establishing knowledge around it.[5] Many (readers) of the 'general' public may not be familiar with the term or concept of SE yet, and it is likely that they have found out or that they will find out about the SE term and concept only or first through the media. My book is concerned with what wide parts of society perceive and understand about SE, instead of a specialist discourse. I want to explicitly look outside or beyond the 'inner circle' of the support agencies, those who label themselves 'social entrepreneurs' and the actors, who are closely linked with the SE sector.

3.4.2 Reflections on the Choice of Data: Representations of SE in Newspapers as a Specific Part of the SE Discourse(s)

An orthodox discourse analyst might argue that material or data is irrelevant for analysing discourse. After all, the discourse (of SE) predetermines or rules what can and what cannot be said about SE – and the properties of the SE discourse(s) should become apparent in analysing any type of data. However, I do not support this view, following Fairclough (1992; 2010) and other authors, who have addressed the issue of 'discourse practice' – i.e., that different 'genres' or types of texts (such as newspapers) and the ways that these are produced are, indeed, relevant to empirical discourse analysis. Therefore, I argue that the choice of data does have an impact on the findings, and that it matters whether one analyses political speeches, newspaper articles, social media channels, transcribed interviews, or other types of data or text. So, what role does it play that I am basing my analysis on newspaper articles, and what can this type of data actually tell, and what can it not? Two main points should be considered here. First, my findings concern, strictly speaking, mainly representations of SE in the analysed newspapers – and not directly the SE phenomenon 'itself'. Second (and related to the first point made here), this means that my empirical analysis of newspapers only grasps certain parts, or a selection, of the SE discourse(s).

5 Of course, this shall be taken with caution, as newspapers do not reach *all* parts of society.

First, the representation of SE in (German) newspapers cannot be seen as an all-encompassing and balanced depiction of the SE field, covering the phenomenon in its entirety. Newspaper articles as data source provide insight on a specific perspective on SE – one that foregrounds the view of certain actors on SE – i.e., the view of journalists and editors. Instead of an all-encompassing account of SE, newspapers may provide one that journalists and editors find most interesting – and they may, perhaps, (over-) emphasise aspects of SE that (in their eyes) make interesting and marketable news stories. Furthermore, it should be noted that the representation of SE in newspapers is a perspective on SE that is mediated by a third party. It is rather an 'outside' view, instead of one that is promoted by 'inside' actors (who constitute the SE field), say social entrepreneurs or SE support agencies. This seems particularly relevant when it comes to the wider explanations of SE and to the narratives around it, i.e., when SE is embedded in a socio-economic or political narratives – as these narratives are curated by the journalists and editors, who are responsible for producing the news stories. The wider explanations of SE, the making sense of SE, to a large extent, is transmitted through the eyes of those producing the newspaper articles.

Here, it must be noted that newspapers are embedded in certain social and power relations that determine, which articles are produced, and how these are produced. It can be assumed that this might have an influence on the findings of my empirical research. It may be the case that the newspaper articles only represent the parts of SE that *can* be represented within the constraints of the social and power relations within neoliberal capitalism, in which the media are embedded (Fairclough 1995). As I have mentioned in Chapter 1, some authors (including Ridley-Duff & Bull 2011; Kay et al. 2016) have described two different 'camps' of SE: a 'radical' and a 'reformist' one. Following this thought, it could be the case that parts of SE that present a challenge or an alternative to neoliberal capitalism – namely, 'radical' versions of SE – are widely excluded from the media (newspaper) discourse, because they are beyond the limits of what can be said within the constraints of the neoliberal power structures. Newspapers, especially the more conservative outlets, might represent only a reformist version of SE, one that is more conforming to the current economic and social system.

These reflections on the role of newspapers as data source and what it means that my empirical analysis focuses on what newspapers represent about SE bring me to the other main point: the fact that the analysis of newspapers only grasps a part, a selection of the SE discourse(s). In sum, it can be assumed that the parts and aspects of the SE discourse(s) grasped by my analysis are restricted in the following ways, namely including:

- the part of SE discourse(s) that makes it into the news,
- the part of SE discourse(s) that journalists and editors find interesting – i.e., aspects of SE that make marketable news stories and/or that relate well to trending topics and current affairs,
- the part of SE discourse(s) that the media is able and willing to represent, possibly excluding more radical versions or aspects of SE.

In sum, my chosen research design and data base (newspaper articles) leads to certain limitations of the findings of my research that need to be taken into account. Strictly speaking, the empirical findings of my analysis are on certain *representations* of SE in newspapers – and not directly on the SE phenomenon and movement itself. Therefore, my empirical results mainly refer to an 'outside' view on SE. The data tells little about the 'inside' of the SE scene and its actors, its network(s) of practitioners, support organisations, etc. My research offers only marginal insight on the 'inside' view, on how the SE scene and its actors may try to construct a 'common agreement' or identity, nor does it explain the internal workings of the SE movement.

However, I argue that the mediatic representations, on which my empirical analysis is based, are a valid proxy for my research questions. As explained in the Introduction and in Chapter 3, my study is concerned with making sense of the SE phenomenon in Germany from a sociological perspective, in analysing different understandings of SE but also identifying dominant versions of SE, in particular aspects of the SE concept and wider narratives linked to it that receive attention from a broad(er) societal audience. It is, therefore, precisely this certain 'outside' view on SE that I am principally interested in capturing: i.e., what a broader (or 'mainstream') audience gets to perceive of the SE concept (which ideas 'make the news'), what ideas of and around SE reach out into wider society. I am mainly interested in the 'dominant', the main(stream) view, beyond the SE niche or 'bubble'.

Nonetheless, due to the points made in this sub-section, readers of this book must note that my findings are mainly on the main view on SE in the print media – and that they do not necessarily represent the dominant perspective in all parts of society, nor the main take on SE *within* the SE field, its practitioners and support organisations. People in the SE field might agree, but also disagree, with the media representation of SE. In order to gain a more encompassing picture of the SE phenomenon and movement in Germany, my research will need to combined and complemented with further research, as I will explore in Chapter 7.

3.4.3 Building the Corpus of Newspapers Articles

After explaining the rationale for conducting a media analysis – more specifically: an analysis of (generalist) (daily) newspapers – in order to grasp aspects of the SE discourse(s) in Germany, which are relevant to my four research themes (diversity and dominance, representation and relevance, development over time and notion of 'change' and politics), as well as reflecting on the limitations and implications of this choice of data, the next step of operationalising the empirical analysis consists in compiling a concrete corpus (Fairclough 1992; 2010) of newspaper articles. For compiling the corpus of newspaper articles, i.e., the data of my empirical analysis, I mainly used the *WISO* database, provided by *GBI-Genios Deutsche Wirtschaftsdatenbank GmbH*, a private company specialised on social science research. I gained access to *WISO* through the libraries of the *Berlin School of Economics and Law*, the *Free University Berlin* and the *Staatsbibliothek zu Berlin*. The licenses of different institutions vary, which means that certain newspapers may only be accessed in some libraries. Most of Germany's regional and national (daily and weekly) newspapers and magazines could already be accessed via the *WISO* database. However, for the corpus to encompass all the main newspapers, it was necessary to use two additional databases: the archive of the *Frankfurter Allgemeine Zeitung* (FAZ) and the archive of the *Süddeutsche Zeitung* (SZ). As a result, the corpus could be based on the most important newsprint media (see Table 2 for a complete overview of all the captured sources). In total, ca. 180 newspapers were covered, including the most-sold daily papers with national reach, i.e., *BILD*, *Süddeutsche Zeitung*, *Frankfurter Allgemeine Zeitung*, *Handelsblatt*, *Die Welt* and *taz.die tageszeitung* (IVW 2020), important weekly newspapers (*Zeit*, *Focus*, *Welt am Sonntag*), as well as many regional newspapers.[6]

---

6 Regional papers are quite important in Germany, their quantitative reach sometimes being higher than the reach of national papers (IVW 2021a; IVW 2021b). Collectively, more copies are sold of regional papers than of national papers (IVW 2021c).

Table 2: Overview of Newspapers Covered for Compiling the Corpus

Name of Newspaper	Available from (Date)
Aachener Nachrichten	03.03.2004
Aachener Zeitung	01.07.2003
Aar-Bote	02.01.1998
Alb Bote	01.02.2013
Aller-Zeitung	26.09.2015
Allgemeine Zeitung Mainz-Rheinhessen	02.01.1998
Anzeiger für Burgdorf & Uetze	26.09.2015
Anzeiger für Lehrte & Sehnde	26.09.2015
Badische Zeitung	15.08.2003
Bayerische Rundschau	01.09.2008
Bergedorfer Zeitung	22.12.2011
Bergische Morgenpost	25.02.2013
Berliner Kurier	24.09.1999
Berliner Morgenpost	01.03.1999
Berliner Zeitung	03.01.2000
Bersenbrücker Kreisblatt	03.07.2012
BILD	01.01.2014
BILD am Sonntag	01.01.1956
BILD International	02.07.2017
Börsen-Zeitung	03.01.1995
Bonner General-Anzeiger	02.01.1983
Bote vom Haßgau	27.08.2013
Bramscher Nachrichten	03.07.2012
Braunauer Warte am Inn	28.02.2013
Braunschweiger Zeitung	10.11.2020
Bürstädter Zeitung	02.10.2006

Name of Newspaper	Available from (Date)
B.Z.	01.09.2000
Calenberger Zeitung	26.09.2015
Christ und Welt	29.04.2015
Coburger Tageblatt	01.09.2008
Darmstädter Echo	01.09.1998
Deister-Anzeiger	26.09.2015
Döbelner Allgemeine Zeitung	01.10.2011
Dresden am Wochenende	27.01.2018
Dresdner Neueste Nachrichten	29.10.2011
Eichsfelder Tageblatt	26.09.2015
Ems-Zeitung	03.07.2012
EXPRESS	01.01.2000
F.A.Z. Frankfurter Allgemeine Zeitung	01.01.1993
Frankfurter Allgemeine Sonntagszeitung	01.01.1993
F.A.Z. Einspruch	27.11.2017
F.A.Z. Wirtschaftswissenschaft	02.01.2003
FOCUS	18.01.1993
FOCUS-MONEY	30.03.2000
Fränkischer Tag	01.08.2005
Frankfurter Neue Presse	27.06.1995
Frankfurter Rundschau	02.01.1995
Freie Presse	16.08.2011
Gelnhäuser Tageblatt	01.07.2004
Gießener Anzeiger	01.07.2004
Gifhorner Rundschau	10.11.2020
Göttinger Tageblatt	26.09.2015
Haller Tagblatt	01.02.2013
Hamburger Abendblatt	19.01.1999
Hamburger Morgenpost	02.01.1999
Handelsblatt	02.01.1986

Name of Newspaper	**Available from (Date)**
HANDELSBLATT MAGAZIN	02.10.2014
Handelsblatt Morning Briefing	18.11.2015
Hannoversche Allgemeine Zeitung	11.02.2016
HarzKurier	10.11.2020
Heilbronner Stimme	02.06.2008
Hildesheimer Allgemeine Zeitung	23.10.2017
Hochheimer Zeitung	02.07.2004
Höchster Kreisblatt	25.02.2013
Hofheimer Zeitung	11.04.2003
Hohenloher Tagblatt	01.02.2013
Hohenzollerische Zeitung	01.02.2013
Idsteiner Zeitung	02.01.1998
Jüdische Allgemeine	27.05.2010
Kieler Nachrichten	24.08.2017
Kirner Zeitung	19.09.2013
DIE KITZINGER	01.10.2010
Kölner Stadt-Anzeiger	30.10.2000
Kölnische Rundschau	02.01.2002
Kreis-Anzeiger	01.07.2004
kulturSPIEGEL	01.01.2003
Lampertheimer Zeitung	30.06.2007
Landshuter Zeitung	23.07.2014
Lausitzer Rundschau – Elbe-Elster-Rundschau	01.05.1997
Lauterbacher Anzeiger	01.07.2004
Le Monde diplomatique	13.02.2015
Leine-Zeitung Ausgabe Garbsen/Seelze	10.06.2016
Leine-Zeitung Ausgabe Neustadt/Wunstorf	10.06.2016
Leipziger Volkszeitung	02.01.1997
Lingener Tagespost	03.07.2012
Lübecker Nachrichten	07.06.2016

Name of Newspaper	Available from (Date)
Märkische Allgemeine	02.01.2006
Magdeburger General-Anzeiger	27.01.2016
Magdeburger Volksstimme	22.01.2016
Main-Post	14.08.1997
Main-Spitze	02.01.1998
Main-Taunus-Kurier	02.01.2002
Meller Kreisblatt	03.07.2012
Meppener Tagespost	03.07.2012
Metzinger Uracher Volksblatt	01.02.2013
Mittelbayerische Zeitung	29.10.2014
Mitteldeutsche Zeitung	17.03.1990
Münchner Abendzeitung	01.03.2005
Münchner Merkur	07.01.2016
Nahe-Zeitung	19.09.2013
Nassauische Neue Presse	25.02.2013
Neue Osnabrücker Zeitung	03.07.2012
Neue Presse	26.09.2015
Neue Ruhr/Neue Rhein Zeitung	10.11.2020
Neue Westfälische	02.01.2003
Neue Württembergische Zeitung	28.09.2007
Neuß-Grevenbroicher Zeitung	25.02.2013
Nordbayerischer Kurier	20.06.2015
Norddeutsche Neueste Nachrichten	22.11.2012
Nordhannoversche Zeitung	26.09.2015
Nordkurier	05.08.1999
Nordwest Zeitung	01.04.1946
Nordwest-Zeitung 1946 – 2016	01.04.1946
Nürnberger Nachrichten	21.11.1989
Nürnberger Zeitung	18.06.2002
Oberhessische Zeitung	01.02.2007

Name of Newspaper	Available from (Date)
Öffentlicher Anzeiger	19.09.2013
Oschatzer Allgemeine Zeitung	01.10.2011
Osterländer Volkszeitung	25.02.2013
Ostsee-Zeitung	07.06.2016
Ostthüringer Zeitung	03.01.2000
Passauer Neue Presse	01.10.1996
Peiner Allgemeine Zeitung	26.09.2015
Potsdamer Neueste Nachrichten	03.01.2005
Der Prignitzer	01.09.2012
Reutlinger General-Anzeiger	08.10.2007
Reutlinger Nachrichten	01.02.2013
Rhein-Hunsrück-Zeitung	19.09.2013
Rheinische Post	01.10.2001
Rhein-Lahn-Zeitung	19.09.2013
Rhein-Main-Zeitung	01.01.1993
Rhein-Zeitung	02.01.1997
Rieder Volkszeitung	28.02.2013
Rüsselsheimer Echo	01.08.2015
Rundschau für den schwäbischen Wald	01.02.2013
Saale Zeitung	01.10.2010
Saarbrücker Zeitung	02.01.1993
Sächsische Zeitung	01.10.1996
Salzgitter-Zeitung	10.11.2020
Schwäbische Zeitung	18.07.2011
Schweinfurter Tagblatt	27.08.2013
Schweriner Volkszeitung	01.09.2004
Segeberger Zeitung	24.08.2017
Solinger Morgenpost	25.02.2013
DER SPIEGEL	04.01.1993
SPIEGEL ONLINE	01.03.2002

Name of Newspaper	Available from (Date)
SPIEGEL special	01.10.2003
SPIEGEL Bestseller	12.10.2019
Stern	01.01.1996
Straubinger Tagblatt	24.07.2014
Süddeutsche Zeitung	06.10.1945
Südkurier	01.03.1999
SÜDWEST PRESSE	28.09.2007
Der Tagesspiegel	01.10.1993
Der Tagesspiegel Berliner Köpfe	01.02.2008
Taunus Zeitung	25.02.2013
taz. die tageszeitung	30.05.1988
Thüringer Allgemeine	03.01.2000
Thüringische Landeszeitung	03.01.2000
Torgauer Zeitung	01.10.2011
Trierischer Volksfreund	25.11.1997
uniSPIEGEL	01.05.2003
Usinger Anzeiger	01.07.2004
Volksblatt Würzburg	27.08.2013
Volkszeitung Schweinfurt	27.08.2013
DIE WELT	01.03.1999
WELT am SONNTAG	12.01.1997
WELT KOMPAKT	02.01.2008
WELT ONLINE	01.01.2009
Westdeutsche Allgemeine Zeitung	02.11.2020
Westdeutsche Zeitung	17.10.2008
Westerwälder Zeitung	19.09.2013
Westfälische Rundschau	02.11.2020
Westfalen-Blatt	29.04.2010
Westfalenpost	02.11.2020
Wiesbadener Kurier	02.06.1998

Name of Newspaper	Available from (Date)
Wiesbadener Tagblatt	02.01.1998
Wirtschaftszeitung	17.10.2014
Wittlager Kreisblatt	03.07.2012
Wolfenbütteler Zeitung	10.11.2020
Wolfsburger Allgemeine Zeitung	26.09.2015
Wolfsburger Nachrichten	10.11.2020
Wormser Zeitung	02.01.1998
DIE ZEIT	30.12.1994

Overall, this ensures that the corpus could be compiled on the basis of a broad scope of newspapers – both in terms of regional as well as quantitative reach (or circulation). All regions are covered: North, South, East and West Germany. In addition, the political spectrum of the news sources has been taken into account: it was made sure that the data basis contains more conservative papers, like the *Frankfurter Allgemeine Zeitung*, and more a left-leaning papers, such as *taz.die tageszeitung*. The data basis, too, includes both 'tabloid' and 'quality' newspapers. Most importantly, I have included the so-called *Leitmedien*, which are considered to be the most influential in shaping public opinion (Meyen 2013).[7] According to Meyen (2013: 41), these are: *Der Spiegel*, *Frankfurter Allgemeine Zeitung*, *Süddeutsche Zeitung* and *Die Zeit*.

3.4.4 Search Criteria

All three utilised databases (*WISO*, archives of *FAZ* and *SZ*) allow to conduct full-text searches within the accessed news articles. Therefore, I undertook a Boolean full-text search for the term 'social entrepreneurship' (i.e., as a fixed word combination) to identify articles that contain the terms 'social entrepreneurship' within the text (not just in the headlines). The Boolean search ensures that only articles appear that contain both words and in this particular order, excluding articles that contain only either the words 'entrepreneurship'

7 There does not seem to be an equivalent English term to '*Leitmedien*'; it roughly refers to: opinion-shaping broadsheet newspapers.

or 'social' or both words scattered across the text, which unlikely cover my research topic.

As I have explained in Chapter 2, searching for the English, non-translated term 'social entrepreneurship' in a German language context might, at first, seem unusual. To justify this approach, I rely on previous academic literature, in particular on Birkhölzer (2015), who has explained that 'social entrepreneurship' refers to a specific social economy or social enterprise movement of a specific time in history that can be differentiated from other social economy movements (as explained in Chapter 2). Following this view, I argue that searching for 'social entrepreneurship' in a German language context not only makes sense with regards to my particular research object – even more so, I argue that it is necessary, since any translation of 'social entrepreneurship' would be unprecise – and bare the risk of not capturing the social practice that should be studied. The specific ('social economy') phenomenon and movement that I am addressing in this book is terminologically linked to the English term 'social entrepreneurship' – therefore, possible translations of the term (such as 'Sozialunternehmertum') are not or less suitable for capturing my object of study.

In Chapters 1 and 2, I have also explained that some terms are used more or less interchangeably with 'social entrepreneurship'. In the German context, the main other term to consider is 'social business' (Birkhölzer 2015: 22–23). Hence, I have also searched the mentioned databases for articles on 'social business' and scanned over 600 articles containing the term. However, these articles were not included in the corpus for the following reasons: First, because the search results for articles on 'social entrepreneurship' provided a sufficiently sound basis for a qualitative analysis. Second, because the cursory overview of the search results for 'social business' showed that articles on 'social business' are very often related to a specific social entrepreneur: Muhammad Yunus. The articles on 'social business', therefore, portray a quite narrow account of the phenomenon that the terms 'social entrepreneurship' and 'social business' are supposed to refer to. Including these articles would then bare the risk of overemphasising particular aspects of the SE phenomenon or movement. Most importantly, I argue that in Germany, the term 'social entrepreneurship' is more usual and more relevant to refer to the movement as a whole. This can also be observed when it comes to the main actors in the German SE field, including the *Social Entrepreneurship Netzwerk Deutschland* (which carries the term in its name). In sum, the articles that include the term 'social entrepreneurship' are best suited to represent my research object and grasp it in a more precise and encompassing way than 'social business'.

Through the search in the three databases, it was found that the term 'social entrepreneurship' appears for the first time in 1999, therefore marking the possible starting point for my empirical analysis. This, of course, needs to be regarded carefully, since I cannot fully exclude that there might have been articles in the German press mentioning the term before this. As previously mentioned, the databases (*WISO*, *FAZ* archive and *SZ* archive) do not cover *all* newspapers before 1999. Therefore, it cannot be completely excluded that there might have been articles containing the term 'social entrepreneurship' before 1999. Nonetheless, this seems unlikely, given that the term is rather young and given that the databases (*WISO*, *FAZ* archive and *SZ* archive) cover the main newspapers long before 1999 (see Table 2), including the four *Leitmedien*. 2021 marks the end date of my corpus and research time frame for two reasons. First, 2021 is an interesting year for contextualising and situating my research. Even though this is too soon to tell, 2021 could mark the end of SE being in a stage of 'pre policy-involvement'. As I have argued in the introduction and in Chapter 2, at the time of writing, political interest in SE in Germany is growing. National (*Bundestag*) elections took place in September 2021, and the coalition agreement of the resulting federal government between *SPD*, *Bündnis 90/Die Grünen* and *FDP* (for 2021–2025) promises the most specific support for SE in Germany so far (Scheper 2021). Second, 2021 needs to mark the end of the analysis for practical reasons – simply to allow the research process to proceed to the writing-up of the results of the analysis.

3.4.5 Overview of Search Results and Selection of Articles that Constitute the Corpus

The search for 'social entrepreneurship' via *WISO* provided over 600 results for the time frame 1999–2021 plus over 40 results each in both the *FAZ* archive and in the *SZ* archive. During the search process, it could easily be noted that the number of yearly texts mentioning the term 'social entrepreneurship' in German newspapers has been increasing over time in the time period 1999–2021.

In order to compile a corpus of original articles that are relevant and meaningful to my research object, a total of about 700 search results were then filtered as following, excluding:

- Articles that were found twice or multiple times. The same article sometimes appears in several different (regional) newspapers with different regional reach, as the same story is sometimes purchased and published by various news outlets.
- Articles that were published in monthly magazines, in order to keep the sampling coherent and focused on newspapers (daily or weekly) that, in principle, have the same function (i.e., informing a general public about general current affairs). Monthly magazines are usually more specialised.
- Articles from online outlets. It was found that the texts published online were often the same or adapted versions of texts published in the respective newspapers' print editions. This should avoid repetition and that certain news stories would be overrepresented.
- Articles that are very short (generally under 200 words). It was found that these texts were mostly announcements (e.g., for an event), and not 'proper' (original) news stories, where ideas are fully developed and presented to the reader. These short texts, therefore, did not prove fruitful for my research of the SE discourse(s).
- Furthermore, 27 articles were excluded, based on a closer reading. Even though these articles included the term 'social entrepreneurship', they had little relevance and connection to my object of study. The context either remained unclear, or the term was mentioned completely incidentally, without developing ideas around SE.

These filtering steps, finally, resulted in a corpus of 349 original articles for the time period 1999–2021. Looking at the development over time, the increase of articles is also visible in the overview of the filtered results, as demonstrated in Graph 1, which was already included in Chapter 2. This might be an indication for confirming an assumption that is often found in literature on SE (see Chapters 1 and 2), namely that the SE term and phenomenon is getting more attention around the world in recent years. The increased attention in the German media certainly seems to reflect this.

The corpus of 349 articles includes a few different genres or types of text that are found in newspapers, e.g., news reports, opinion pieces or interviews. When this seems relevant for the analysis or presentation of results, I will address the specificity of the respective text types. For example, when someone is interviewed it might be relevant to briefly say who the interviewee is or to which organisation they are affiliated. But overall, since this is a sociological and not a linguistic analysis, and I am focussing on the 'social practice', not too much emphasis shall be given to the different 'genres' of newspaper articles. In order to maintain a clear overview during the analysis and presentation of the results, the 349 articles were archived, indicating year and newspaper. In addition, the articles were numerated chronologically, from 'A_1' being the first article (to appear in April of 1999) to 'A_349' (of December 2021), being the last article of the corpus.

3.4.6 Data Analysis and Identifying the Three Different Periods between 1999 and 2021

For the analysis of the corpus, I first gained a general overview of the articles by reading through all of them. Diaz-Bone (2006) proposes to engage in a naive reading of the text as someone, who (at best) knows nothing about the topic at hand. This should help the researcher to leave out previous knowledge and preconceived categories, in order to be able to explore terms, objects, argumentations, value statements, oppositions, etc. that emerge from the text (inductively). Of course, this approach is not entirely realistic, since it is impossible to 'forget' all background knowledge (on SE and the debates around it) when reading the texts. In addition, my research – just as any research project – is guided by specific research interests and questions, which inevitably bring a deductive element to the analysis. Nonetheless, I made an attempt to follow the idea of a naive reading and therefore delayed focussing on aspects such as the relationship between SE and the state, or about SE and capitalism and so on, which are close to my core research focus – i.e., how to make sense of SE as a movement and what sort of society and economy is envisioned by SE. Instead, I first focused on very general aspects, such as: 'what is said about SE?', or: 'how and why does SE appear in the article?' and so forth. I argue that following this approach also helps taking into account some of the ethical considerations that were raised earlier – in particular: not 'jumping' to particular aspects or themes around SE and making sure that the analysis captures an encompassing representation of SE in the corpus and allowing the researcher to identify aspects inductively that would otherwise, perhaps, be disregarded. In particular, this should have helped to challenge preconceived notions of SE, including certain 'hopes' that I might have associated with the SE phenomenon.

Following the 'open' reading and getting an overview of all the articles, I developed a set of 'heuristic questions' (Diaz-Bone 2006) to guide the next steps of the analysis. These were informed by the literature review but also formulated and refined continuously, integrating (inductive) elements of the open or naive reading. The main heuristic questions included:

- How is SE defined or explained?
- What examples are provided for SE (enterprises, entrepreneurs, organizations, activities)?
- What characterizes these examples of SE, what is said about their 'economic' and 'social' logics?
- Who are the actors of the SE field? Who appears and who 'speaks' about SE?
- In which fields is SE taking place?
- In which sector (area of society) is SE placed? How is the relationship to other institutions described?
- What is the need for SE and what sort of change shall SE bring about?

Based on the open reading and the heuristic questions, themes were identified that later developed into codes.[8] For closer analysis, the 349 articles were imported into the software *MAXQDA*, which allows coding large amounts of text – i.e., simplifying and segmenting the data into general, common denominators (e.g., Coffey & Atkinson 1996) – and organising the coded text passages. This involved a long process of close reading of the articles and coding of text passages, based on both inductively generated codes (see above) as well as deductively generated codes (close to the main research topics and questions). There is a cyclical relationship between these two types of codes, with both groups informing each other.

During the coding of text passages, the codes and the code structure (code tree) were constantly developed and adapted. From the codes – which in my understanding are rather transitory, assisting the process of the analysis (e.g., Coffey & Atkinson 1996) – the main categories and themes were developed, establishing the main findings of the analysis. For this, I identified commonalities, differences, patterns and structures in the material, sometimes paraphrasing selected text passages to assist the process. The software programmes *MAXQDA* and *Microsoft Excel* helped to organise the material in this process. While my analysis is qualitative, in a few instances, when this seemed possible and plausible (i.e., when segments of data could be reduced to the extent of

8 This, to an extent, was a circular process. Developing and refining the codes sometimes resulted in adjusting and refining the heuristic questions.

becoming quantifiable), I also counted selected aspects in the corpus. For example, I counted, in how many articles certain actors (such as *Ashoka*) are mentioned. The reader should note, however, that all numbers that are included in the results Chapters (4–6) are indicative or illustrative.

As said earlier in this chapter, *discourse* and *discourse analysis* often include a temporal element (sometimes having been described as 'history of ideas'). This is also an important element of Foucault's work, who has analysed developments over several centuries (e.g., the concept of 'madness'). Developments are of central interest, discourse analysts explore how ideas and concepts develop over time – what might changes, what might emerge, and so on. For my analysis of SE discourse(s) between 1999 and 2021, I, therefore, also focused on temporal aspects, asking whether I could identify developments over time, and whether the understandings of SE and/or the wider ideas and political beliefs associated with SE change.

This approach proved successful. In the analysis, I was able to identify three periods within the analysed time frame: a first period from 1999–2008, a second period from 2009–2014 and a third period from 2015–2021. This periodisation is based on the analysis and identification of commonalities, differences, patterns and structures in the material, and represents the central contribution of my book. It was found that each period has certain distinctive features that distinguish it from other periods – and that changes in the media representations of SE became apparent in two instances: around 2008–2009 (marking the shift from the first to the second period) and around 2014–2015 (marking the shift from the second to the third period). The most relevant categories that allowed to establish this periodisation are included in the following table:

Table 3: From Data to Three Periods

	Time Period		
Category	**1999–2008**	**2009–2014**	**2015–2021**
SE is frequently defined or explained through…	the person (the social entrepreneur)	the organisation (SE as business)	the organisation (business – however, a specific phase or process within business, namely: entrepreneurship/ founding)
Examples of SE mainly come from the fields of…	work integration & education	poverty reduction and development, sustainable production and goods & education	sustainable production and goods, environmental or climate protection, technology & work integration
Derived from these fields, the main sector(s), in which SE is taking place, is/ are…	the traditional 'social' (nonprofit) and public sector	the economy	the economy
Important actors	*Ashoka* and the *Schwab Foundation* have a prominent (almost exclusive) role in the media representation	business schools and universities become more important	Several different actors start to engage with SE, the *Social Entrepreneurship Netzwerk Deutschland* (*SEND*) is founded (and appears prominently in the media representation)
SE is mainly presented as an example or role model for…	traditional social and public institutions	traditional social and public institutions and (private) businesses	traditional social and public institutions and (private) businesses

	Time Period		
Category	**1999–2008**	**2009–2014**	**2015–2021**
Main target of reform addressed by SE	The traditional social sector and the state and their institutions and ways of functioning	Both the traditional social sector and the state as well as businesses and business logics in the private sector	Both the traditional social sector and the state as well as the private sector
References or links to broader political and social events/ circumstances	High unemployment, high costs for welfare	Financial crisis of 2008	The start-up culture and 'hype' on the one hand, deeper societal transformation on the other
(New) themes that emerge, or that become more dominant (only in the respective time period)	-	SE as work, SE as 'meaningful work' in particular, SE and business ethics.	SE is embedded in the context of start-ups, including tech companies, SE appears the political sphere (e.g., through media representation of policies targeting SE)
References to broader (geographical) models of economy/ economic development	the US model is presented as positive, as 'better' and as a role model for Germany	-	the German – or sometimes regional or local models (e.g., Berlin or Stuttgart) are presented as positive models, and sometimes as counter-models to the US or Silicon Valley

3.4.7 Ethical Considerations

My empirical research is mostly desk-based. It does not involve the interaction with vulnerable groups. Anyone can purchase or (via the respective databases) access the data that the research is based on, i.e., newspaper articles. As already argued in 3.3, the most important ethical aspects seem to revolve around my position in the SE discourse. To do the CDA approach justice, it is important to establish a sound research design as well as to conduct a thorough analysis that would ensure that my own (initial) position or perspective on SE (and 'hopes' or 'fears' associated with the SE movement) would not overshadow other perspectives. This ethical consideration is already acknowledged in the theoretical chapters, which presented various perspectives on the SE phenomenon. As explained in Chapter 1, this book does not settle on a specific definition of SE, which would inevitably establish a specific (normative) perspective and be contrary to my main research problem. In order to prevent that during the data gathering and during the analysis certain positions would be disproportionately represented, I compiled a broad and balanced corpus, covering a relatively high number of articles and different newspapers (e.g., across the political spectrum). The analysis, too, aimed to capture and present a balanced account of the various representations of SE as they were found in the newspaper articles, and refrain from prematurely focusing on particular aspects in the material or 'jumping' to early conclusions. As explained above, in following a widely inductive approach, approaching the material step by step and first engaging in a naive and open reading of the articles, 'slowing down' the process of analysis, I am confident that I was able to apply these principles throughout the empirical research process. Finally, these ethical considerations also fed into the presentation of the results – in which I intended to offer an encompassing picture of the wide range of results that would not overemphasise particular aspects. Therefore, the presentation of the results in Chapter 4 intentionally begins in a rather descriptive way, which leads me to the next subsection.

3.4.8 Presentation of the Results

The results of the data analysis will be presented in three chapters, according to the three periods that were identified in the analysis: Chapter 4 (1999–2008), Chapter 5 (2009–2014) and Chapter 6 (2015–2021). The chapters present the summarised findings of the empirical analysis and include particularly exemplary text excerpts from the newspaper articles. The text passages quoted from the newspaper articles are all translated into English by the author. The (translated) text excerpts from the articles are indented and in italics (even if the text is shorter than 3 full lines, which is usually the rule for indenting text), in order to mark a clear separation to the rest of the text. The news articles will be referenced according to their number in the corpus (chronologically). For example, in the short version, the seventh article in the corpus is referred to as: 'A_7' and in the detailed version as: 'A_7_Frankfurter Rundschau_31.03.2004'.

Each results chapter (4–6) has its own character and structure. Even though the analysis in principle was applied similarly to all articles and period, it is due to the strongly inductive approach that not all categories and themes receive the same attention in all three chapters. Being the first chapter that presents the findings of the data analysis, Chapter 4 will begin more descriptively than the subsequent Chapters (5 and 6). To some extent, this is to give Chapter 4 a somewhat double function in order to also reveal more about the process of data analysis (next to presenting the findings for 1999–2008). To avoid repetition, but also for more fluidity and in order to give more room for analytic aspects, Chapters 5 and 6 will dive faster into a more analytical presentation of the findings. In addition, due to the chronological sequence, Chapters 5 and 6 also allow to draw comparisons to earlier periods.

Chapter 4: Social Entrepreneurship Coming to the Aid of the 'Sick Man' (1999–2008)

4.1 Introduction

As explained in the previous chapter, through the process of analysing the data, three periods of the social entrepreneurship (SE) discourse(s) were identified – with the first period ranging from 1999–2008, to which this chapter is dedicated. The beginning of the first period is marked by the first article on 'social entrepreneurship' in the German press in 1999. The end of the period is marked mainly by what I call a 'sectoral shift'; until 2008, SE (as represented in the news articles) is principally conceptualised as part of the welfare-producing 'social' infrastructure; instead, from 2009, SE is increasingly understood as part of the economy, as will be explained in detail in Chapter 5. These beginning and end dates of the different periods, however, should be regarded as somewhat flexible. Furthermore, while one of the aims of my analysis was identifying certain main or 'dominant' aspects in the representations of SE, there is never a homogeneous view of SE. Contestations of SE are ongoing during all three periods, as should be taken into account when reading the results chapters.

In this first and early period, SE still plays a very marginal role in the German press, especially between 1999 and 2004 with (on average) only one article per year. In 2005, the number of articles considerably increases to seven articles per year (on average), but still remaining at a low level. Overall, the results that are presented in this chapter derive from the analysis of 35 articles published between 1999 and 2008. In Chapter 2 it was already noted that the early SE movement in Germany revolved mainly around *Ashoka* and a few other actors, such as the *Schwab Foundation* – and that SE has largely been interpreted as an 'American' version of SE. This version emphasises the individual entrepreneur and market-based solutions and business logics and establishes links to (business) elites. Although, several scholars recall the complexity of the SE phenomenon, suggesting that the SE field and its actors may be more diverse and ambiguous than sometimes assumed (Birkhölzer 2015; Bandinelli 2017; McRobbie et al. 2019). Moreover, academic literature has often connected SE to a more general context of neoliberalism, and explained SE as a result of marketisation and liberalisation trends. Chapter 2 has also explained specific aspects of the socio-economic and political context in Germany at the time. In the late 1990s and early 2000s, large parts of the public, politics and the media in Germany (and abroad) shared the view that Germany was the 'sick man' of Europe (Dustmann et al. 2014; Spohr 2019), mainly due to high unemployment rates.

Against this background, this chapter aims at complementing, contesting and expanding the existing literature on the origins of SE in Germany with empirical findings of the analysis of newspapers, which has captured certain representations of SE in the media (as explained in Chapter 3). The chapter begins with presenting the findings in a more descriptive way and focusing on how SE has been explained and described in the news articles. Gradually, the chapter moves towards more analytical aspects, reflecting on wider narratives that establish a relationship between SE and broader social and political developments.

4.2 Describing, Explaining, Defining Social Entrepreneurship

This section will focus on how SE is described in the analysed news articles of the early period (1999–2008). In the articles, SE is often presented as something 'new', a term or phenomenon that needs to be explained to the audience. However, the degree of detail of the different explanations varies greatly – and some articles do not really provide a systematic description of SE, explaining SE throughout the article. Other articles, instead, make an attempt to define the terms 'social entrepreneurship' or 'social entrepreneur', as, for example, in A_4:

> A social entrepreneur is someone who acts like an entrepreneur, but does not seek to create economic value but social value instead (A_4_Die Zeit_24.01.2002).

Overall, six main approaches to explaining SE could be identified for the 1999–2008 period, as the following table summarises:

Table 4: Approaches to Explaining 'Social Entrepreneurship' in the Newspaper Articles (1999–2008)

approach to explaining SE	**example (translation)**
1. SE as a mix or combination of two worlds	*a melange of entrepreneurship and philanthropy* (A_1_Die Zeit_08.04.1999)
2. SE as the creation of social value	*A social entrepreneur is someone who acts like an entrepreneur, but does not seek to create economic value but social value instead* (A_4_Die Zeit_24.01.2002)
3. SE as the solution to social (and sometimes ecological) problems	*People who "solve social problems with innovative ideas successfully, efficiently and in the long-run"* (A_9_Tagesspiegel_19.11.2005)
4. SE as social change	*People "employing entrepreneurial skills innovatively, in a pragmatic and long-term way, in order to achieve ground-breaking social change"* (A_7_Frankfurter Rundschau_31.03.2004)
5. Explaining SE through the sector	*entrepreneurs in the social field* (A_12_Südkurier_07.12.2005)
6. Explaining SE through the person/agent (the social entrepreneur)	*entrepreneurs with a social mission* (A_28_Welt am Sonntag_24.02.2008)

As can be observed in these examples, these different approaches to explaining SE are not mutually exclusive and might, in fact, be combined. The second example in the table illustrates this, explaining SE as the creation of social value, but also making use of the approach of explaining SE through the person or agent (the entrepreneur). In some explanations, even more than two approaches may be combined, such as in article A_10:

> Globally, the *Schwab Foundation for Social Entrepreneurship* has given awards to 84 'entrepreneurs in the social field'. On December 6th, the prize will be awarded in Germany for the first time. The award goes to people who have developed innovative solutions to social problems (A_10_Südkurier_02.12.2005).

This explanation of SE builds upon three approaches: explaining SE as problem-solving ("innovative solutions to social problems"), through the person and through the sector ("entrepreneurs in the social field").

Overall, for 1999–2008, the analysed data shows a predominance of the person-centred-approach to explaining SE, which is employed 25 times. The other approaches appear rather evenly, with the explanation of 'SE as solution to social problems' occurring slightly more often (10 times), against 'SE as the creation of social value' (7 times), 'SE as a mix or combination of two worlds' and 'Explaining SE through the sector' (both 5 times) and 'SE as social change' (4 times).[1] Furthermore, it could be noted that the explanations of SE become a bit more specific over time. The approach of explaining 'SE as a mix or combination of two worlds', which seems a bit vaguer than the other approaches, loses relevance. However, this gradual concretisation is not a linear process and, certainly, there is no common agreement in this time period about what SE is; there is no uniform way of describing SE, it remains a contested (and often vague) concept. The fact that SE "means different things to different people" (Dees 2001 [1998]: 1) when it comes to the level of conceptual or cognitive explanations of SE (see Section 1.2) is, therefore, also mirrored in the newspaper articles. Furthermore, it was found that the person-centred approach – i.e., understanding SE as an activity that revolves mainly around the social entrepreneur, or even equating the phenomenon (entrepreneurship) and the person (entrepreneur) – is predominant in the early period. This can be linked to the prominent role of *Ashoka* and the *Schwab Foundation* in the early SE discourse, as I will explore in the next section.

4.3 Three Groups of Actors and 'Speakers', and Social Entrepreneurship Coming to Germany

A few actors that appear in the news stories were already mentioned, e.g., social entrepreneurs, *Ashoka* and the *Schwab Foundation*. This section will now systematically address the actors that constitute the field of SE – as represented in the corpus for 1999–2008 – focusing on three groups: 1) the portrayed social

---

1 Mind that my analysis is mainly qualitative and when frequencies are mentioned, these are only indicative and illustrative.

entrepreneurs, 2) organizations and people of the wider 'ecosystem' (or support system) of SE and 3) the beneficiaries or target groups of SE.[2]

Social entrepreneurs are often portrayed in the analysed media articles, their stories are told and they serve as examples for explaining what SE is. Not all but many articles describe social entrepreneurs and their ventures. Moreover, the reader learns about the social entrepreneurs and their individual backgrounds. In A_1, for example, several social entrepreneurs are introduced: One of the portrayed social entrepreneurs used to a be a drug investigator, another a social worker, and two of them were managers in the food industry. In another article, A_7, the reader encounters a former *World Bank* officer, the former head of *Greenpeace Germany*, a nurse and a teacher. A_11 presents a (former) businessman; and A_23 a lawyer and education specialist.

The articles, therefore, provide information about the social entrepreneurs' professional backgrounds. With regards to different socio-demographic categories, however, it is more difficult to gain information on the portrayed social entrepreneurs. One article (A_33) places a focus on women and claims that women are not only drawn to 'social' professions but that women were also likely to start social enterprises. However, this claim does not match the representation of the social entrepreneurs in the analysed articles over the period 1999–2008. In total, 49 entrepreneurs or teams of entrepreneurs are introduced; of which 35 are (all) male and 10 (all) female; 4 are mixed teams, often (married) couples.[3] Overall, 42 individual entrepreneurs and 7 teams of entrepreneurs are presented in the news articles. Once more, this highlights the rather individualistic take on SE in the media representation. For other socio-demographic categories (such as class, race or sexual orientation, among others) it seems almost impossible to derive substantial information from the analysis. When assuming that class is linked to education, it can be noted that many of the portrayed entrepreneurs are degree-educated. It also stands out that many social entrepreneurs have had prestigious jobs previous to their SE engagement. Another aspect that certainly is relevant is dis/ability – not least

2 Social enterprises aim to achieve improvements for a specific target group, e.g., providing work for people with disabilities.

3 It should be noted that for this purpose I have assumed the gender identities of the entrepreneurs only based on their names. This, of course, must be taken with caution and might be rightfully criticised – not least due to a binary classification of gender identities (male/female).

because many social ventures aim to empower people with disabilities, as I will address later in the section.

Some social entrepreneurs appear in several articles, mostly social entrepreneurs that have won prestigious awards for their work. This includes international 'shooting star' Muhammad Yunus, the Nobel laureate and founder of the *Grameen Bank* (a pioneer in the microcredit movement). Yunus appears for the first time in A_20 (in January of 2007), and in total in 6 articles in the first period.[4] Andreas Heinecke, founder of *Dialog im Dunkeln*, an enterprise that organises exhibitions led by people with visual impairments and blind people, whose popularity might be specific to the German context, appears for the first time in A_9 (in 2005) and in total in 8 of the 35 analysed articles of the first period. Overall, the articles draw a quite favourable picture of the social entrepreneurs, generally representing them as competent, capable and committed. Their technical or professional skills are highlighted as well as their previous life and work experience, showing that they have a lot of experience and skills to offer and to apply to their ventures. This is also fostered by the award-culture of the young SE field: Organisations such as *Ashoka* organise competitions, seeking 'the best' social entrepreneurs with 'exceptional' talent and 'successful' ideas. In A_7, for example, Konstanze Frischen, head of *Ashoka Germany* is quoted, describing the social entrepreneurs that *Ashoka* is looking for, namely:

> People "employing entrepreneurial skills innovatively, in a pragmatic and long-term way, in order to achieve ground-breaking social change" (A_7, Frankfurter Rundschau_31.03.2004).

The strong focus of the media representation on 'star' social entrepreneurs such as Yunus and Heinecke further accentuates the idea of SE as a field for 'exceptional' individuals, mirroring the ideal figure of the entrepreneur in neoliberalism (Davies 2014a).

Moreover, social entrepreneurs are often quoted in the newspaper articles, sometimes in indirect or in direct speech. Through direct and indirect quotes, the social entrepreneurs are therefore given a voice, they are able to 'speak'. As said above, the presentation of the social entrepreneurs is generally favourable,

4 As I have noted in the previous chapter, the presence of Yunus is even much more striking in articles containing the term 'social business'.

they are mainly given positive attributes and are portrayed as figures of expertise and authority. Their utterances and statements contribute to shape the presentation of the situation and of the social or environmental problems that need to be addressed and that are addressed by their social enterprises. An example for this can be found in A_11, reporting on Moritz Lehmkuhl's social enterprise *Climate Partner* that deals with CO_2 offsetting. The entrepreneur is quoted several times across the text – e.g., at the beginning, establishing the 'social problem' (or in this case environmental) and, therefore, the framework in which his social enterprise operates:

> "On average, every German emits 10.3 tons of CO_2 per year," says the founder of *Climate Partner* (A_11_Süddeutsche Zeitung_06.12.2005).

Elsewhere, the entrepreneur is quoted, explaining what his enterprise does and describing an order of a client (the company *Averatec*):

> The notebook manufacturer *Averatec* gave its customers one ton of the greenhouse gas CO_2 for every computer. "That corresponds at least to the volume of a 25-by-10-meter swimming pool," says Lehmkuhl (A_11_Süddeutsche Zeitung_06.12.2005).

Here, the social entrepreneur is allowed to comment on the impact of his own enterprise, drawing a comparison between the volume of the CO_2 and a swimming pool, which is an accessible image for the reader, and in turn, establishes legitimacy for his project. While this is still mediated by those involved in producing the stories (journalists, editors, etc.), social entrepreneurs play an important part in the analysed articles in shaping what the readers get to perceive as 'social entrepreneurship'.

However, an even more powerful role can be ascribed to the second group of actors: organizations and people of the wider support or ecosystem of SE. This can be observed in the following passage of A_23, staging a social entrepreneur (Björn Czinczoll), who has received an award by the *Schwab Foundation* – and who, as a result, is invited to the *World Economic Forum* – and two representatives of this second group of actors, Klaus Schwab (President of the *Schwab Foundation*) and André Habisch (an academic):

> Björn Czinczoll would never have dreamed of being able to chat with the most powerful business leaders for setting up needs-based nursery schools

> for working parents. A year ago, the lawyer took part in the competition to become the 'Social Entrepreneur of 2006' (...). Björn Czinczoll won and was allowed to participate in the exclusive *World Economic Forum* in Davos. "In Germany there is a lack of impetus to implement new social ideas," says Klaus Schwab, founder of the *World Economic Forum*. "These social entrepreneurs are showing new ways." Their approaches are always also related to solving regulatory problems, adds André Habisch, head of the *Center for Corporate Citizenship* at the *Catholic University of Eichstätt*. Until now, the social sector has been left to the state and been delegated to the welfare associations. Now, it is time to rethink this (A_23_Berliner Morgenpost_21.10.2007).

While the social entrepreneur (Björn Czinczoll) appears quite prominently in the article (he is also described more in detail elsewhere), when it comes to conceptualising the SE phenomenon, i.e., providing a more abstract explanation of SE and embedding the concept in wider social structures, others are brought into the picture and even quoted directly: the head of the *Schwab Foundation* (Klaus Schwab), and an academic (André Habisch).

In fact, the examined media articles give this second group of actors a quite articulate and powerful role. Above all, this includes *Ashoka* and the *Schwab Foundation* and the people associated with these two organizations. In the period 1999–2008 overall, *Ashoka* (and/or its representatives) appears in 14 of the 35 articles and the *Schwab Foundation* in 13 articles. *Ashoka* (here referring to the American branch) is present in the corpus from the very first article (A_1). As mentioned in Chapter 2, *Ashoka* opens an office in Germany a few years later: in late 2003. Shortly after this, *Ashoka Germany* is introduced in the press – more precisely, in A_7_Frankfurter Rundschau_31.03.2004. Following suit, A_8 introduces the *Schwab Foundation* and announces its 'Social Entrepreneur of the Year' award, which in Germany is awarded for the first time in 2005 (A_8_Ostthüringer Zeitung_02.11.2005).

Without doubt, the remarkable increase of yearly articles in 2005 from, on average, one yearly article to seven – as mentioned in the introduction to this chapter – is linked to *Ashoka* and the *Schwab Foundation* initiating activities in Germany, the press taking notice of these organisations, and these organisations successfully engaging in public relations. Moreover, *Ashoka* and the *Schwab Foundation* 'coming to Germany' also marks an important shift in the geography or geographical focal point of SE in the corpus as I will explain in the following paragraphs.

Before 2004, all specific examples for SE that are introduced in the newspaper articles are from outside of Germany, often from the US. From 2004 onwards, and with the first article on *Ashoka Germany*, it is transmitted to the reader that SE is a phenomenon that takes place in Germany, too. A_7 even explicitly addresses aspects of the geography of SE, paraphrasing (Konstanze) Frischen, one of the two the managing directors of *Ashoka Germany*:

> The two managing directors often hear the argument that the type of people that *Ashoka* promotes all over the world doesn't exist in Germany. Then Frischen mentions people like Peter Eigen. Ten years ago, the former *World Bank* employee founded *Transparency International*, an organization with the aim to fight global corruption. Eigen started in a small one-room office. Today, *Transparency* has a wide network with branches in 90 countries. Thilo Bode, the former head of *Greenpeace Germany*, is another good example of a 'socially oriented' entrepreneur. Recently, Bode has launched the independent consumer protection organization *Foodwatch* (A_7_Frankfurter Rundschau_31.03.2004).

'German' examples for SE are provided here, in order to demonstrate that SE *does* exist in Germany. However, this does not mean that the international orientation of SE completely disappears – the same article (A_7) includes examples of SE from Brazil, South Africa, or Poland. In addition, the article assumes and emphasises that Germany is still struggling to accommodate this 'new' phenomenon, often picturing the US as a role model:

> The Germans, believes Frischen, still have to slowly get used to the idea that success-oriented entrepreneurial spirit and social engagement can very well go hand in hand. "In Germany this is – other than in the USA and in England – a radically new approach, because here, in our minds, we often still have the idea of the cold, heartless capitalist" (A_7_Frankfurter Rundschau_31.03.2004).

Very emblematic for this view is also the opening quote of A_7, again by Konstanze Frischen: "*Deutschland ist reif für Ashoka*" (Germany is 'ripe' [ready] for Ashoka). This opening has the effect of creating momentum for SE: finally, Germany, too, is 'waking up'. In the concluding section to this chapter (4.7), I will further elaborate on this idea of a backwards Germany 'finally' following international examples.

More generally, these quotes from A_7 show that representatives of support or umbrella organisations, such as *Ashoka Germany*, have a strong voice in explaining SE and constructing knowledge around SE in the media representation (through indirect or direct quotes). What is more, some articles are even written by the leading figures of these support agencies, as guest contributions or opinion pieces. For example, A_5 is (co-) written by Klaus Schwab (President of the *Schwab Foundation*), A_24 is authored by Konstanze Frischen (Managing Director *of Ashoka Germany*). Again, this emphasises the central role of these two organizations in the early SE discourse. In addition, this stands in contrast to the first group of actors (social entrepreneurs), who in the period 1999–2008 are not given the same degree of power or voice – i.e., the opportunity to themselves write about SE as (guest) authors of entire articles.

With regards to actors that appear in the newspaper articles as the wider support and ecosystem of SE in the early period (beyond *Ashoka* and the *Schwab Foundation*), it was a remarkable finding of my analysis that these primarily consist of wealthy individuals, foundations, corporations, universities and research institutes. The following overview lists all actors (organizations and individuals, apart from social enterprises, social entrepreneurs and 'beneficiaries') that I have identified in a selection of 11 articles for the first period:[5]

- In A_1: private companies (*Boeing* and *Microsoft*, as customers of a social enterprise), research institutions (*Kauffmann Center for Entrepreneurial Leadership*, *National Center for Social Entrepreneurs*, universities in Seattle), local administration (Seattle city administration), foundations (*Roberts Foundation*), associations (*Evergreen Society*), the *World Economic Forum*, *Ashoka*, *McKinsey* (as former employer of William Drayton, founder of *Ashoka*).
- In A_5: the *Schwab Foundation*, the *World Economic Forum*.
- In A_7: *Ashoka*, *McKinsey* (as former employer of William Drayton, founder of *Ashoka*, and as sponsor of *Ashoka*), supporters of Ashoka (PR agency *Hill & Knowlton* as well as law firms *Clifford Chance*, *Latham & Watkins* and *Hogan & Hartson*).
- In A_11: private companies and one NGO (*Allianz*, *World Wide Fund for Nature*, *Hansbeton*, *Neckarmann*, *Averatec*, *Deutsche Post*, *Playboy*, *Sixt*, as

5 The 11 articles included here are: A_1, A_5, A_7, A_11, A_14, A_23, A_24, A_27, A_29, A_30, A_33. These are particularly relevant, as they address and discuss the SE phenomenon in great detail. The selected articles cover different perspectives on SE within the corpus.

customers of a social enterprise), local administration (Munich city administration, as partner in planning), the *Schwab Foundation* (as host of the award, together with the *Boston Consulting Group* and *Capital* magazine).

- In A_14: *Ashoka*, prominent families of entrepreneurs (the owners of *C&A*: Brenninkmeyer, the Breuninger family and *Deutsche Bank*, as supporters of *Ashoka*), foundations (*Breuninger Foundation*, *Schwab Foundation*), wealthy individuals (Swiss entrepreneur Stefan Schmidheiny and Pierre Omidyar, founder of *Ebay*), a bank (*UBS*, as the sponsor of an SE competition).
- In A_23: the *Schwab Foundation* (as host of the award together with the *Boston Consulting Group* and *Capital* magazine, research institutions and academics (André Habisch, head of the *Center for Corporate Citizenship* at the *Catholic University Eichstätt*, Ann-Kristin Achleitner, Professor of Entrepreneurial Finance at *TU München*, *Saïd Business School* in Oxford and its *Skoll Centre for SocialEntrepreneurship*, established with a donation of the first president of *Ebay*, Jeffrey Skoll, *Instituto de Empresa* in Madrid), *Ashoka*.
- In A_24: *Ashoka*, a social investment fund (*Acumen*), a research institution (*Johns Hopkins University*).
- In A_27: the *World Economic Forum*, the *Clinton Global Initiative Meeting*, entrepreneurs (Susanne Klatten or Michael Hilti) and companies (*Allianz* and *Bertelsmann*), the alternative nobel prize (2003 for *Sekem*), the Nobel Prize (2006 for Yunus), an academic and a research institution (Johanna Mair, Professor of Strategic Management at *IESE Business School*).[6]
- In A_29: foundations (*Schwab Foundation*, *Skoll Foundation*, Ashoka), former politicians (Bill Clinton, Al Gore) business tycoons [sic!] (Bill Gates and George Soros), scientists (Muhammad Yunus), managers (former *Microsoft* employee John Wood or *Ebay* founder Jeff Skoll), artists (Bob Geldof, Bono or Mia Farrow), *Clinton Global Initiative*, the *Bill and Melinda Gates Foundation*, an academic and a research institution (Tine Stein, political scientist at *Wissenschaftszentrum Berlin* (WZB).[7]
- In A_30: *Ashoka*, *Schwab Foundation*, the *Boston Consulting Group*, research institutions (*Witten-Herdecke University*, *TU München*, *Zeppelin Universität*, 'Top-Business-Schools' in the USA as a reference, Ann-Kristin Achleitner, Professor of Entrepreneurial Finance at *TU München*), a venture capital fund and other financiers (*Bonventure*, *Forum for Active Philanthropy*, *National Lottery* (UK).

---

6 The academic appearing in the article (Johanna Mair) is also its author.

7 Tine Stein is also the author of the article.

- In A_33: a priest (Nick Francis), a social-ecological bank (*GLS Gemeinschaftsbank*).

This overview clearly shows that the field of support, the wider ecosystem of SE – as it is presented to the reader in the articles – mainly includes wealthy individuals, foundations, corporations, universities and research institutes. This highlights the SE field's links to global elites, foundations and multinational companies – in other words: to members of the capitalist elite or establishment. This has been addressed in Chapter 2 and noted, especially, in the critical reception of SE, e.g., by Voß (2015). SE being associated with the capitalist elite (and some names that could, arguably, be seen as its main flagships, such as *McKinsey* or *Deutsche Bank*) might explain the resistance to SE in large parts of social science and social economy circles. Whether or not these actors actually are the main actors around SE in Germany in the first period cannot be answered here for sure. Yet, this is the picture that the media representation (and my empirical analysis of it) shows.

Occasionally, public (local) administrations appear, too, but their position is not very prominent. People associated to universities have a slightly more significant role, as for example in the excerpt above, where an academic (Habisch) is quoted when it comes to making sense of SE as a phenomenon. In fact, some articles are written by academics (e.g., A_27 and A_29). However, it stands out that the academic institutions appearing in the articles are often expensive, 'elite' (international) business schools (such as IE Madrid or Oxford's *Saïd Business School*), and not the standard public universities that predominate in Germany.[8] Private universities such as *Witten-Herdecke* or *Zeppelin*, which were (and still are) very marginal in Germany, are definitely over-represented in the newspapers. The academics appearing in (or writing) the news articles (Johanna Mair or Ann-Kristin Achleitner) are some of those who have first published on SE in Germany, too. In the case of Achleitner, there are undeniably strong links to the corporate world. Next to her professorship of entrepreneurial finance at the *TU Munich*, Achleitner is a board member of

8 Taking 2000 as a year of reference within the first period, only approximately 25.000 of 1.799.000 students in Germany were enrolled at private universities, i.e., less than 2% (Statistisches Bundesamt 2018: 16).

several large companies, which, once more, accentuates the links between SE and business elites in the early period.[9]

Finally, I shall address the third main group of actors in this section: the target group(s) or beneficiaries of SE. As I have indicated above, not all but many forms of SE aim at improving or achieving something for a specific group of people or community, one that is viewed as 'disadvantaged' by mainstream society, as, for example, work integration for disabled people. These beneficiaries or target groups of SE also appear in the analysed newspaper articles. However, it could be noted that the representation of this group of actors is much less frequent and also lacking depth in comparison with the other actors mentioned above. When representatives of this third group appear, they often are depicted in a rather superficial way, as the following passage from A_1 illustrates, starring a social entrepreneur (David) and a beneficiary (Maria):

> One day, he [David] quit his job as a drug investigator: "It was frustrating. As soon as the junkies and dealers got out of jail, it all started again. After my time as a policeman, I had a business, but that didn't satisfy me either. And at some point, I heard about *Pioneer Human Services*." Today the 53-year-old is leading the company. (...) Walking around in a suit and tie, the boss greets everybody. "Hi, Maria," David says to a lady in an office suit. "Our construction manager. She used to trade in cocaine." Most permanent employees are former clients. They have made it. Others fail early; more than a third of the clients are fired from the company because they do not come to work regularly or they repeatedly fail the drug test (A_1_Die Zeit_08.04.1999).

The contrast between the representation of the social entrepreneur (David) and of the beneficiary (Maria) is quite remarkable. The reader receives a fair amount of information about David, the entrepreneur: including age, former employment, background and motivation to work for a social enterprise (elsewhere in the article there is more information on David and his background). Maria, on the other hand, only appears with her first name; the reader only learns that she used to deal with drugs, but nothing else about her personal background, or her age, etc. Most extraordinarily, she is spoken to ("Hi, Maria"), but does not

9 Ann-Kristin Achleitner, who was one of the first academics writing on SE in Germany (see Achleitner et al. 2007; Achleitner et al. 2010) and who is a co-founder of the *Social Entrepreneurship Akademie* in Munich, also sits on the supervisory board of several major companies, and, indeed, had been named 'most influential woman in the German business-world' by the *Handelsblatt* (Kewes 2017).

respond (or it seems irrelevant to include her response to the reporter). Maria is not given an active or distinct voice; others speak about her. She is reduced to the role of former-drug-dealer-turned-worker, a 'successful case' of the social enterprise led by David – appearing as an object rather than an agent.

An exception to this could be found in A_30, telling the story of Betty Schätzchen, a hearing-impaired businesswoman:

> Betty Schätzchen wakes her students from meditation with a nudge on the knee. She explains them the next exercise in sign language. It is quiet in the room, muted light breaks on sky-blue and white walls. Betty Schätzchen teaches yoga for both deaf and hearing people. She is almost deaf herself – and she is an entrepreneur. "I turned a weakness into a strength," says the 26-year-old. After a bank apprenticeship, she went to Asia for several months, completed courses in Thai massage and yoga. Back in Germany, she dared to take the step into self-employment (A_30_Die Welt_15.03.2008).

The article then goes on presenting *Enterability*, a social enterprise that helps people with disabilities (like Betty Schätzchen) into entrepreneurship. While Betty Schätzchen is portrayed as the beneficiary and not as the social entrepreneur (in this article the social entrepreneur is the head of *Enterability*), we learn something about her background and about her as an individual. She is not merely reduced to the feature of being almost deaf. However, this degree of detail in describing a beneficiary as in A_30 is certainly an exception; it is the only article in the period 1999–2008, in which the reader gets substantial information on a beneficiary that goes beyond their (perceived) disadvantage or disability. Most importantly, I argue that this example, too, should be regarded carefully, since Betty Schätzchen is also an entrepreneur, i.e., her role is not totally clear-cut.[10]

In sum, it can be concluded that the beneficiaries themselves rarely have a distinct voice as agents or actors. Their role in explaining SE is very limited in the newspaper articles in the 1999–2008 period. I argue that there is a certain clash between this finding and the idea of SE as being exceptionally 'empowering', as often claimed about SE in the literature (see Chapter 1). Often, SE is associated with defying established hierarchies and establishing more egalitarian relationships – in contrast to hierarchical relationship between a

10 In addition – even though this might be a mere coincidence – Betty's last name, 'Schätzchen', which is repeated several times in the article, somewhat seems to question her standing as an entrepreneur.

'benevolent' and a 'beneficiary', as in traditional forms of charity. All in all, the media representation does not seem to provide evidence for this idea of 'empowerment'.

4.4 The Fields for Social Entrepreneurship, the Sectoral Positioning and Relationships to Established Institutions

It was already mentioned that the articles of the corpus (1999–2008) contain many examples for SE, which are used in order to explain and illustrate SE to the audience. In the analysis, I have identified all concrete examples or references for social entrepreneurship or social entrepreneurs – which go hand in hand, given that SE is often explained through the person (entrepreneurs). As noted elsewhere, SE is a heterogeneous phenomenon, occurring in various areas or fields. Through clustering the examples from the newspaper articles, the following fields were identified in the first period:

- work integration (for people with disabilities and/or special skills)
- education
- environmental or climate protection
- support of self-employment, entrepreneurship, or co-working
- poverty reduction and development (in the Global South)
- support of street children (in Germany)
- housing and homelessness
- health and health care
- fight against corruption/ transparency
- consumer protection
- sustainable production and goods (e.g., organic food)

First, this overview shows that, generally speaking, when it comes to the different fields of SE, the diversity of SE seems to be represented in the newspaper articles. In addition, the articles mirror that, from early on, the 'social' in SE can sometimes mean 'environmental': examples for social enterprises with environmental or climate protection causes appear in the first period (1999–2008), even in the second article of the corpus (A_2). However, environmental or climate topics are not too prevailing yet: in total occurring 4 times in the first period.

The overview also shows that the articles mainly include examples from what in Germany would traditionally be considered either as part of the public sector and/or of the third or 'social' sector, such as the field of 'education'. Overall, the most frequently represented fields in the 1999–2008 period are 'work integration' (with 16 examples from this field) and 'education' (with 11 examples).[11] As explained in Chapter 2, unemployment was a pressing issue in Germany at the time. The prevalence of (un)employment as a main topic, to some extent dominating public discourse in Germany (as I will address again in Section 4.7), might explain why there are so many examples for work integration in the first period. While it could be argued that work integration has an economic dimension – integration or inclusion at work parts from an understanding that everyone should have access to work, and to provide for themselves financially – the main focus lies on achieving an improvement for a certain ('disadvantaged') group of individuals. Work integration is not necessarily about changing the system of work, the *economic* system, but rather about allowing disadvantaged groups to join it, giving them the chance of participating in the economic realm of social life, which is why I categorise this as a traditionally 'social' field. Similar to this is the field of 'support of self-employment, entrepreneurship, or co-working'. The only field that – from a sectoral perspective – can clearly be seen as part of 'the economy' – is the area of 'sustainable production and goods', for which there was only one example in the 1999–2008 articles.

This brings me to addressing the 'sectoral' perspective or positioning of SE in the 1999–2008 articles. For this, I am parting from a perspective of asking: 'where does SE take place?' and 'as part of which sector or subsystem of society is SE presented in the articles?'. I argue that this is an important aspect of understanding SE as a political phenomenon, because different relationships between SE and other, existing and established societal institutions and actors derive from the conditions in a specific sector. SE is often juxtaposed and set into relation to established societal actors and institutions, such as the state, non-profit organisations, businesses or individuals. The way that these relationships are constructed comes with attributing certain features and roles to SE, but also to these other actors. In some instances, this also entails wider narratives or visions with regards to how society should be organised.

First, it was already noted that one approach to explaining SE is through the sector (see 4.2). For example, A_12 describes social entrepreneurs as 'en-

11 Several ventures or entrepreneurs are active in more than one field.

trepreneurs in the social field' (A_12_Südkurier_07.12.2005). This approach to explaining or defining SE entails a clear sectoral positioning: placing SE in the 'social field'. As seen in Chapter 1, some definitions of SE in academic literature do the same (e.g., Dees 2001 [1998]). A similar positioning can be found in A_22, where SE is explained as a phenomenon that is linked to social work, and therefore, too, occurring in the 'social' domain. Here, SE is described as

> a movement (...), which aims at making social work more efficient by means of entrepreneurial methods (A_22_Die Zeit_27.09.2007).

There are different perspectives in the articles of the early period; in some, SE is positioned within the economy. For example, A_5 writes about SE in the context of a:

> new economic philosophy [that consists of] four elements known from Anglo-Saxon economic theory: corporate attractivity, corporate integrity, corporate citizenship and social entrepreneurship (A_5_Frankfurter Allgemeine Zeitung_26.03.2003).

In several articles, the situating of SE is ambiguous. A_1, for example, at first discusses SE in the context of capitalism (i.e., the economy):

> Here (...) a mixture of entrepreneurship and philanthropy is emerging, one that could give capitalism a new face (A_1_Die Zeit_08.04.1999).

Then, elsewhere in the same article (A_1), SE is described as part of the 'social' sector – i.e., as a new form of social work:

> A new culture of social work is emerging here, a social capitalist one, if you will. (ibid.)

Overall, however, the most widespread positioning in the articles for the period 1999–2008 is within the 'traditional' social sector or fields. This is further emphasised by the specific examples for SE (such as work integration and education), as I have explained above.

Second, in the analysis I have put an emphasis on the relationships between SE and established societal institutions and what the emergence or existence of SE implies for them. Once more, the diversity of the SE phenomenon becomes apparent. The analysed media articles present SE as many different things in relation to more established institutions and actors. At times, SE is presented as a complement to the state and its institutions (A_1; A_27; A_29). Other times, as a vehicle to reform the economy (A_1; A_5, A_27). Some articles present SE as a business opportunity (A_21; A_27). Again others, as a reform of social work (A_1; A_22). A different perspective sees SE as a new form of philanthropy (A_14; A_19; A_24). Several articles combine various presentations or interpretations (in A_1; A_16; A_23; A_27). In other articles, SE is described as a process of learning that transcends actors and institutions beyond different subsystems or sectors (A_1; A_2).

In short, the analysed articles provide a vast variety of interpretations when it comes to the societal role or positioning of SE. The accounts of SE are diverse and ambiguous – sometimes within one and the same article (in which SE might be presented as giving capitalism a new face in one paragraph and as a new culture of social work in another), and most definitely considering the overall media representation of SE between 1999–2008. Thus, they very well mirror the "conceptual confusion" (Teasdale 2012: 101) around SE that can be found in the academic literature (see Chapter 1). Yet, there is a dominant perspective on SE in the first period – for which it is necessary to look beyond the overview and deeper into the wider narratives around SE, how they introduce the need for SE and the vision(s) for the economy or society that these are embedded in.

4.5 Why Social Entrepreneurship? The Need and Urgency for SE

As I have addressed in the previous section, the examined articles often present SE within wider narratives that establish a relationship between SE and society. These explanations are based on a certain problematisation, a 'vision' for society and what should 'change' about it. SE is then introduced as an idea that can contribute to this 'change'. The reason for SE – or even the 'need' in a more forceful way – is explained to the audience, creating urgency and justification for the SE phenomenon. Often, these narratives entail assumptions and statements about established societal institutions.

Once more, there is no single view – the reasons or the need for SE may be rooted in various narratives and strategies. The following table shows six rationales for SE that were identified in the news articles in the first period:[12]

Table 5: Overview: The Need for Social Entrepreneurship in the Media Representation (1999–2008)

rationale for SE, why SE is presented as necessary	**example, text passage from article**
SE as a result of state failure: the state is unable to cope with the tasks at hand	*When it comes to child care, there are a lot of problems. "There have to be private offers because the state system can no longer or doesn't want to shoulder everything. What the state has to offer is not enough and it is getting worse and worse" (A_18_Süddeutsche Zeitung_17.11.2006).*
SE as a result of the failure of both public institutions and businesses	*Social entrepreneurs are needed worldwide: In most countries and cultures, important social needs are still not taken seriously neither by existing political institutions, nor by companies or markets. This is where social entrepreneurs come in: They recognize these 'faults in the system' and develop innovative business models to meet the respective demands (...) (A_27_Handelsblatt_14.01.2008).*
SE is necessary due to the sheer amount and magnitude of the current challenges	*Nature itself is making sure that climate protection is becoming more important and relevant: Pictures in the news of flooded Bavarian villages and patrolling soldiers in a devastated New Orleans are the best advertisement for Climate Partner (A_11_Süddeutsche Zeitung_06.12.2005).*
SE as (necessary) reform of the social sector	*a movement that is described by the term 'social entrepreneurship', which aims at making social work more efficient by means of entrepreneurial methods (A_22_Die Zeit_27.09.2007).*
SE as (necessary) reform of the economic sector	*It used to be quite common for companies like Ford or Swarowski to get involved in social issues. Much of this tradition has been lost in the past few decades. Shareholder interests and profit maximization were increasingly at the centre of entrepreneurial activity. Against this, social entrepreneurship has established itself as a counter-movement (A_27_Handelsblatt_14.01.2008).*

12 Some of these quotes were already included in previous sections. This also demonstrates that *explaining* and *justifying* SE often comes together. Indeed, all descriptions of SE carry wider normative or political meaning(s), as demonstrated in section 1.2.

rationale for SE, why SE is presented as necessary	**example, text passage from article**
SE as a response to public discontent with the free-market economy	*Large sections of the population today have the impression that a deep gulf has opened up between the economy and society. At first glance, economic interests and social objectives appear to have become irreconcilable. (...)* *The market economy system itself is being called into question! (...) The only way to prevent further erosion is for business to take the initiative and present itself clearly and convincingly as part of society. It must develop a new philosophy of economics (...). This philosophy consists of four elements known from Anglo-Saxon economic theory: corporate attractivity, corporate integrity, corporate citizenship and social entrepreneurship (A_5_Frankfurter Allgemeine Zeitung_26.03.2003).*
SE is a necessary to achieve (economic) growth	*Companies [are] always [looking for] new growth markets. Market entry in developing countries, also known as business at the base of the pyramid, is a hot topic for many companies (A_27_Handelsblatt_14.01.2008).*

However, not all narratives are given the same attention in the media representation. 'State failure' is by far the most prevalent narrative in the articles in the 1999–2008 period. Most of the other rationales are marginal, with some only appearing once. The view that the state is unable to cope with the challenges of the contemporary world and that it needs the assistance of other (private) actors, is shared in different articles. For example, in A_1, in which it is argued that Germany's welfare state is ineffective and the US (model), on the other hand, is presented as a role model for Germany. A_3 even uses the terms 'failure of the state' to describe the (public) German education system, claiming that, in the future, it will just be impossible for the state to manage education alone:

> The first political experience of *Generation@* [sic] is the failure of the state in schools and universities. In the future, it will not be possible anymore that tasks such as equal opportunities, access to knowledge and learning only rely in the state's responsibility (A_3_Die Welt_30.06.2001).[13]

13 By 'Generation@', which is not an established term, the author is referring to a generation of students, who are growing up with the internet.

A similar view is promoted in A_23. A need for change (implementing 'new social ideas') is described here; however, this sort of reform cannot come from the traditional actors in the public or 'social' field – so the view presented in the article:

> "In Germany there is a lack of impetus to implement new social ideas" (...). Until now, the social sector has been left to the state and been delegated to the welfare associations. Now it is time to rethink this (A_23_Berliner Morgenpost_21.10.2007).

This is precisely where the new SE actors are able to step in, as another article (A_7) proposes:

> "Germany is ready for *Ashoka*" (...) In view of cuts in the social sector, job cuts and high unemployment, the conditions for the commitment of the non-profit organization are given here in Germany (A_7_Frankfurter Rundschau_31.03.2004).

As demonstrated in these quotes, the state-failure narrative is presented with a certain forcefulness. This becomes apparent especially in contrast to narratives that are related to the (reform of the) economy. A quote from A_5 (the article written by Klaus Schwab) helps to illustrate this contrast. Here, the author argues that

> The market economy system itself is being questioned! (...) The only way to prevent further erosion is for business to take the initiative and present itself clearly and convincingly as part of society. It must develop a new philosophy of economics (...) (A_5_Frankfurter Allgemeine Zeitung_26.03.2003).

This quote is interesting for two reasons: First, because it is not the market economy system *itself* that is being criticised – this is not the main 'problem' that is raised by the author. Instead, it is the *image* of the market economy system, its public acceptance that needs to be addressed. The (main) contribution that SE shall make here is restoring the image of the market economy – yet, without necessarily tackling structural change of the economic model. Second, Schwab's article postulates that business – or the economy as a system – has the ability to reform *itself*. There seems to be no need for external actors (let alone for regulation). This is a stark contrast to the 'solutions' to 'state failure' that are proposed in the quotes above – in which the state is declared unable to reform itself. Business *is* able to reform itself, but the state is not, and there is no other way than for other (external and mainly private) actors to step in – to come to the aid of the 'sick man', as the German economy and welfare state was often portrayed in the late 1990s and early 2000s, as I will further explore in the final two sections of this chapter.

4.6 Logics and Value Statements in and around Social Entrepreneurship

The narrative of a deficient or ineffective state and social sector is not only promoted in a direct and explicit way. It is also reinforced by certain assumptions and normative statements that appear in a more subtle or opaque way, e.g., in statements about entrepreneurs, managers or organisations, as will be addressed in this section. Before discussing the relationship between these statements to wider narratives about the public or 'social' sector, however, this section shall first address the logics of SE, especially those that derive from combining 'the economic' and 'the social' more generally.

By its very name and definition(s), social entrepreneurship combines (and blurs) 'the social' and 'the economic' (see Chapter 1). Beyond the terminology, this combination also entails a combination of different logics, ways of thinking and doing. An important focus of my analysis was how the media articles address the interaction of these two poles and how 'the social' and 'the economic' are organised within the portrayed SE ventures. In particular, I wanted to examine the hierarchies between social and economic goals, and the value statements that are attached to these.

First, I would like to emphasise that not all articles engage in a detailed discussion of what it means to combine these two different domains ('the social' and 'the economic'); sometimes, it is reported matter-of-factly that SE is a combination of the two. This is in line with rather simple explanations of 'SE as a mix or combination of two worlds', which I have mentioned in Section 4.2. It is sometimes merely said that social entrepreneurs are 'entrepreneurial' or that they 'act entrepreneurially', but this is rarely further specified – let alone critically discussed. In this way, the articles make the combination of 'social' and 'economic' domains within SE seem easy and unproblematic.

A slight differentiation or specification is sometimes made between goal and method, e.g., in A_33, where social entrepreneurs are described as joining:

> the methods of an entrepreneur with a do-gooder's intentions (A_33_Tagesspiegel_01.06.2008).

This combining of the 'social' and 'economic' domains is presented to the reader as an important innovation. In line with academic literature (see Chapter 1), the analysed news articles widely promote the view that SE is a 'new' phenomenon. However, most of the time, the details on what is actually supposed to be 'new' remain unclear. In particular, little attention is given to the structures that are expected to emerge when 'the social' and 'the economic' worlds meet, and in which ways and according to which principles, processes are actually done and organised.

Some articles address the role of (financial or economic) profits and the relationship between these profits and the 'social' orientation of the portrayed ventures. At times, this relationship is addressed in a rather functional manner, in the context of explaining funding structures or business models of the social enterprises. Only some articles discuss this as a moral issue, asking whether 'the social' and 'the economic' are compatible, or in conflict with each other. As always, there are different perspectives on the relationship between (financial or economic) profits and social aims within SE.

Mainly four different perspectives could be identified. First, profits and social aims are described as being mutually beneficial. A_2, for example, claims a 'win-win'-relationship between economic and social goals. In A_34, a social enterprise claims that hiring employees with disabilities improves the overall work atmosphere in the company and that it helps fostering a feeling of togetherness across different departments of the company. Following this view, the social cause may generate an economic (competitive) advantage against other businesses. Second, profits and social aims are presented as parallel or coexisting side by side. This perspective does not claim that financial and social gains are beneficial to each other, but neither that there is a clash between the two. Economic and social aims are presented as coexistent, and this coexistence is not questioned, nor discussed in detail. SE serves as an example (or even 'proof') that it (nowadays) seems possible to join the two different domains. For some articles, this even seems to be one of the main concerns or messages to the audience. For example, A_7 explains that – in spite of what the Germans [sic] believe –

> success-oriented entrepreneurial spirit and social commitment [can] very well go hand in hand (A_7_Frankfurter Rundschau_31.03.2004).

Very similar to this, A_14 explains that:

> "Ashoka shows how outdated the old dichotomy is: either someone is evil and makes a profit or they are good and charitable," says Frank Trümper, head of culture and society at *Deutsche Bank* (A_14_Die Welt_24.12.2005).

A third perspective sees profits and social aims as coexisting side by side (as in the second perspective), but a hierarchy is established between the two. This perspective only appears towards the end of the period (in articles from 2007 onwards). In most cases, it is emphasised that the social aim comes first (e.g., in A_24, A_27, A_33). In one case (A_25), however, the social aim is described as additional, i.e., secondary to (financial) profit. A fourth perspective, on the other hand, describes a conflict between profit (economic benefit) and social benefit. Articles that maintain this perspective delineate SE from economic or financial gain and emphasise that SE is about the social aim. They imply that there is a conflict between the economic and the social aims, or that there are trade-offs between the two. In the most explicit and detailed manner, this conflict is addressed in A_1. The reader learns about the history of a social enterprise, and that, in the past, there had been conflicts between social and economic logics, which were to some extent personified through different people working for the company. The article describes

> disputes between social workers and managers; the businessmen prevailed and bought semi-automatic ironing and folding machines. "Now the department was making a profit, but we had eliminated 20 jobs for the mentally disabled. In addition to the dozen healthy employees [sic], only 16 slightly disabled people now work in the laundry – that's very much on the edge of our social goals." (A_1_Die Zeit_ 08.04.1999).

Some articles indicate that there are different models of SE that differ based on their profit orientation. A_14 explains that *Ashoka's* fellows must work on a non-profit basis, while the *Schwab Foundation* allows contestants with profit-oriented ventures. In addition, several articles discuss the role of money or funding for social enterprises, but instead of 'profit' the discussion revolves around covering costs, e.g., addressing 'financial independence' ('*finanzielle Selbständigkeit*') in A_5, or 'financial sustainability' ('*finanzielle Nachhaltigkeit*') in A_27.

Overall, questions remain both regarding the different (competing) perspectives on the role and relationship of (financial) profits and social aims as well as on the 'newness' of SE. On the other hand, when it comes to value judgements in the articles for the 1999–2008 period – i.e., what is presented as positive or negative – there is a much clearer picture. The articles transmit a very optimistic take on SE. SE is almost always presented as bringing positive change for people and communities, or the economy and society as a whole. In most articles, SE has a clearly positive connotation; some accounts are overwhelmingly euphoric. Five articles give a merely factual, or a neutral or balanced account of SE. Only one article (A_11) includes criticism or doubts about the self-proclaimed positive impact of SE. Here, even the title of the article, which presents a CO_2 offsetting company, questions the social enterprise's beneficial impact as 'ecological sale of indulgences' ("*Ökologischer Ablasshandel*") (A_11_Süddeutsche Zeitung_06.12.2005). Other than this example, the articles simply assume and accept the beneficial impact of SE in a taken-for-granted fashion, almost as if it would not need further explanation.[14]

It appears that this assumed positive impact of SE derives mostly from two things. First, from the 'social' mission pursued by SE ventures. As explained in Chapter 1, 'social' in the context of SE is mainly understood as 'doing good', an assumption that is widely (and uncritically) reproduced in academic literature as well. The media representation, on the whole, reflects this assumption and the reader seemingly just has to accept this as fact. Second, almost by definition the approaches and methods of SE are described as 'innovative', 'effective' and 'efficient'. Social enterprises and social entrepreneurs seem to be able to achieve what others – other institutions or even entire fields, such as social work or international development – have been unable to achieve.

This brings me to further value statements in the early (1999–2008) period. It stands out that the media representation of the 'economic' world as such, of businesses and of entrepreneurs is very optimistic. The articles generally describe business and the private sector with positive attributes, highly valuing its skills and logics. The private (business) sector is presented as a role model for the 'social' sector, which apparently lacks the positive virtues of the business world. This is expressed, for example, in A_10, announcing the nomination of a local social enterprise (*Off Road Kids*) for the *Schwab Foundation*'s award:

14 Two articles were excluded from this classification, since they would not connect the term and concept of SE to any adjectives or descriptions that entail a clear value statement.

> The award [by the *Schwab Foundation*] goes to people who have developed innovative solutions to social problems. (...) With this award, the social field is finally taken out of the dirty corner. "It shows young people that this task is interesting. We [*Off Road Kids*] are like other companies, but our profit is the perspective for young people, not the money" (A_10_Südkurier_02.12.2005).

Here, the 'social' field is assumed to find itself in a 'dirty corner'. While it remains unclear what exactly this expression is supposed to mean, there is no doubt that it is a negative description, and one employing rather aggressive language. The journalist does not seem to see the need to explain or problematise this term. Including it suggests that (apparently) it can be widely assumed and accepted as 'common' knowledge that the traditional social sector finds itself in said 'dirty corner'.

The nominated social entrepreneur, on the other hand, is different than the traditional 'social' sector – instead, sharing the virtues of the private business world: *We are like other companies*. The economic, private or commercial sector is presented as superior, as an ideal that the social sector should aspire for – and SE is an instrument that can help to achieve this. SE offers 'salvation' for the social sector, which, as it is implied, finds itself in an inacceptable state, as deficient or dysfunctional (or 'dirty').

A_12 (published five days later than A_10) follows up on this – the founder of *Off Road Kids* has now won the award:

> "The title [awarded by the *Schwab Foundation*] helps enormously in making social professions attractive for young people with managerial skills." And it is exactly these people that are needed in social work (A_12_ Südkurier_07.12.2005).

Again, the argumentation implies that the traditional social sector and the field of social work are deficient. Yet, in this representation the focus lies on the individual level, arguing that social work lacks the 'right' people, i.e., *young people with managerial skills*. But, once more, the business world and entrepreneurship have the answers. Businesspeople, managers and entrepreneurs are presented as exuding efficiency, as highly skilled and applying a can-do attitude to tackling problems and 'getting things done'. Therefore, they may come to the rescue of the social sector. This (potential) introduction of managers and social entrepreneurs into the social sector is presented as a form of professionalisation, as, for example, in A_30, explaining that:

> the number of social entrepreneurs is increasing in Germany, too. More and more professionals are mingling with the benefactors. They are people who tackle social problems with entrepreneurial enthusiasm (A_30_Die Welt_15.03.2008).

This implies that there has been a lack of professionalism and of professionals (and of 'entrepreneurial enthusiasm') in the social sector before. In turn, adopting the talent and the techniques of business and management (behaving like entrepreneurs and managers) would mean a professionalisation. Similar to this, A_24 argues that

> the turn to the person and to entrepreneurship is particularly important in the social sector, which is often associated with alms and charity but not with strategic thinking and business concepts. Those who support social entrepreneurs do not hand out alms. They support talent with targeted means in order to see sweeping results (A_24_Frankfurter Allgemeine Zeitung_23.10.2007).

The article, therefore, also more explicitly addresses the *methods* of the business world, such as 'strategic thinking' and 'business concepts'. It is not only the amazingly skilled managers of the commercial sector that are required in the ailing 'social' sector, but also their methods. The ways of doing things of businesses are presented as an example to follow and may lead the social sector to achieve 'sweeping results'.

Furthermore, A_24 openly celebrates and calls for a 'turn to the person' and entrepreneurship in the social sector and thus, propagates the understanding and narrative of SE as a person-centred activity. Commercial entrepreneurs are introduced as role models for social entrepreneurs – for which A_16 provides another illustrative example, stating that:

> Social entrepreneurs "formulate excellent ideas to solve important problems, and they are neither willing nor able to sit back and relax until their ideas have spread throughout society" (...). Parallels to entrepreneurs in the economy cannot be denied. Similar to Henry Ford or Steve Jobs (*Apple*), who whirled entire industries upside down with their innovative products, social entrepreneurs are also creative visionaries (A_16_Frankfurter Rundschau_03.05.2006).

The figure of the entrepreneur is highly valued here. Regardless of the prefix 'social', entrepreneurs are described as 'creative visionaries', who are all (apparently by definition) untiring in the pursuit of their 'excellent ideas'. Clearly, these idealised and glorifying descriptions of entrepreneurship rely on the ideal figure of the entrepreneur in neoliberal theory, in particular on Schumpeter's "ideal vision of the heroic, creative entrepreneur" (Davies 2014a: 47). In this understanding, entrepreneurs are 'exceptional' and 'uncommon' individuals with a competitive spirit. However, the article fails to explain what it would mean for the social sector that these individuals *are neither willing nor able to sit back and relax until their ideas have spread throughout society* (A_16_Frankfurter Rundschau_03.05.2006). The same goes for the comparison with Henry Ford or Steve Jobs, who have *whirled entire industries upside down* (ibid.). But where would this leave the social sector and its existing structures and institutions? A question that is left unanswered.

In sum, it can be concluded that the media articles on SE in the first period (1999–2008) draw a quite negative picture of the traditional social sector. Business and (commercial) entrepreneurship, on the other hand, are understood as positive, their methods and techniques as superior and their people (managers and entrepreneurs) as more skilled and professional than those traditionally integrating the social sector. Business and (commercial) entrepreneurship and the private sector, more generally, are presented as role models. On occasion, the articles uncritically reproduce the ideal figure of the heroic entrepreneur, which is an important component of neoliberal ideology (Davies 2014a). SE then appears as a phenomenon that facilitates a transfer of knowledge, logics, methods, skills and people from the economic into the social realm, introducing management practices and techniques, business models and structures can be introduced. In the media representation of SE, this development is presented as positive and as a form of professionalisation of the social sector. This perspective on SE as the introduction of managerial and entrepreneurial logics into the public and social realms is the dominant feature of the first period, as I will elaborate in the following (concluding) section.

4.7 Business Virtues as a Cure for the 'Sick Man'?

This chapter has demonstrated that SE in the first period (1999–2008) is still quite marginal. SE is presented to the readership as 'new' and as a phenomenon that requires explanation. The news articles have different approaches to explaining SE, but most often, SE is explained through the person (the social entrepreneur). Arguably, the predominance of the person-centred view is related to *Ashoka* and the *Schwab Foundation*, who have a central role in the SE discourse in the first period, and who promote an award and competition culture that circles around individuals. In the analysed articles, social entrepreneurs are often described as 'exceptional' individuals with very favourable attributes. They are presented as skilled and as able to achieve what others for so long have been unable to achieve, which sometimes verges on heroization – an aspect about SE that has been criticized by Dart (2004), Nicholls (2010), Papi-Thornton (2016), among others. There is also a considerable parallel between the media representation of SE and the ideal figure of the entrepreneur in neoliberal theory and ideology (Davies 2014a).

Another interesting finding for the first period is that the circle of supporters, the extended ecosystem of SE in Germany (beyond *Ashoka* and the *Schwab Foundation*) not exclusively but largely includes business elites or people close to them – an aspect that has previously been raised by Voß (2015). It is striking that the articles mention these actors quite matter-of-factly, without really *addressing* these links between SE and the corporate world. The journalists do not really question or discuss these power relations and whether it is acceptable or not for actors and individuals like Klaus Schwab, *McKinsey* or *Deutsche Bank* to be involved in the SE movement. Arguably, (using Fairclough's words) these strong links to business elites and the corporate world may be seen as 'opaque' relations in the SE discourse. In addition, this explains that these links are part of the reasons why the early SE movement encountered such critical reactions in social science, third sector and social economy circles (see Chapter 2).

Overall, this chapter has demonstrated that, while there are different competing narratives about SE in the newspaper articles during the first period (1999–2008), a dominant perspective stands out: representing SE as a (re)form of welfare production and social infrastructure. SE is described as a phenomenon that occurs mainly in areas where the state and non-profit organisations are active. The specific examples for SE that are presented to the reader are mostly from these areas, such as work integration or education. The newspapers create a contrast between SE and the established institutions in the public and social realm. While public institutions, welfare associations and non-profit organisations are presented as inefficient or even deficient, SE appears as a (necessary) vehicle for reform and sometimes as the 'better' alternative.

The 'state failure' narrative is dominant in the first period – arguably, extended into large parts of the third, non-profit (or 'social') sector. Considering the corporatist structures of the German welfare system, a clear-cut distinction between the public and the third sector is difficult, anyhow (as explained in Chapter 2). In addition, these state failure narratives surrounding SE are sometimes linked to geography. While the traditional public and social sectors are associated with Germany, the modern and business-like SE scene is associated with the US. SE and the US are both depicted as role models for a backward Germany, which finds itself in need of reform.

The wider political and socio-economic context of Germany in the late 1990s and early 2000s, which was discussed in Chapter 2, needs to be taken into account here. In these years, unemployment was high and large parts of the German society and international commentators held the view that the German labour market and social security system needed reform (Heinze 1998; Hassel & Schiller 2010; Zimmermann 2013; Seibring 2019). A vivid image for this *zeitgeist* was provided by the British *Economist*, which was then taken up by others, including the German media, labelling Germany as the 'sick man' of Europe (e.g., Dustmann et al. 2014; Spohr 2019). As a result, the Schröder governments introduced the largest reform programme in recent German history: the *Agenda 2010*. This reform programme significantly transformed the labour market and welfare system, on the basis of marketisation, liberalisation and entrepreneurialism, and strengthening the principles of 'activation', 'individual responsibility' and 'welfare to work' (see Chapter 2).

Therefore, SE – or more precisely: how SE is presented in the media in the early period – is mainly embedded in (or part of) a wider discourse of welfare and labour reform, and may be interpreted as part of a global neoliberalisation. This is in line with the main view on SE in the social sciences, as Chapters 1 and 2 have demonstrated. Dart (2004), for example, has highlighted the (global) environment for SE as one of "decline of the welfare-state ideology (...) and (...) pervasive faith in market and business-based approaches and solutions" (Dart 2004: 418). Referring to the global neoliberal era, Steyaert & Dey (2019) have described "social entrepreneurship (...) [as] a product of its time" (Steyaert & Dey 2019: 4). While I have challenged this perspective for the specific German context in Chapter 2, arguing that there is little empirical evidence to substantiate it and that projecting findings from other contexts is problematic, the empirical findings presented in this chapter, indeed support this view. According to the empirical findings, the dominant perspective on SE in Germany in the first period (1999–2008) sees SE as a reform of the social infrastructure and related to (neoliberal) welfare and labour market reform. My analysis thus, provides empirical evidence for the specific context of Germany between 1999–2008, which is widely in line with previous literature (mainly focusing on other contexts).

Beyond the 'grand' or 'macro' narratives around state failure, or welfare and labour market reform, the empirical findings presented in this chapter also provide important insights into other levels. The pressure on the social work profession and on organisations in the social field, which are expected to adopt the techniques of business and management, were some of the main themes in the analysed articles. The dominant – and apparently 'commonly accepted' – view in the newspapers is that social work needs to become more efficient and to adopt business methods. The private (business) sector is presented in an overwhelmingly positive light – its virtues are praised as effective and efficient. On the whole, the newspapers suggest that business is able to offer the 'better' and 'more professional' solutions than the public or social sector. Private for-profit business serves as a role model for public and 'social' sector institutions – and SE is presented as a way for public and 'social' sector institutions to become more like businesses. A similar pattern could be observed on the individual level. Managerial skills are described as positive, or even 'necessary' attributes of individuals. People working in the social field should act and behave (more) like entrepreneurs and managers – and SE may help them to achieve this. Overall, the articles portray an extremely favourable view of entrepreneurship and of the figure of the entrepreneur.

These findings on organisations and individuals and on the value statements that are made regarding public and non-profit institutions and social workers on the one hand, and on private businesses, managers and entrepreneurs on the other hand, mirror various key aspects that have been addressed in critical literature on SE or on neoliberalism, more generally (see Chapters 1 and 2). SE in the first period appears linked to some of the core principles of neoliberalism, such as individual responsibility (Rose 1999; Hulgard 2010), a glorified figure of the heroic entrepreneur (Davies 2014a), or elevating economic rationality (Davies 2014a; Bruder 2021). Values and logics of the private sector are projected and applied onto social and public fields (Dart 2004; Dey 2010). This development can be described as 'economization', in the sense of a transfer of economic logics into social fields. Overall, the empirical findings for the first period, therefore, show and exemplify a connection between SE and neoliberalism in the specific context of Germany (1999–2008). In addition, they demonstrate the extent to which neoliberal logics have already permeated into different levels (organisations and individuals), beyond the 'grand' or 'macro' narratives around the state, welfare or the labour market – and they may help to shed light on some of the ongoing processes within this development.

Another interesting theme in the first period is legitimacy, and I argue that there is an interesting two-way relationship (or 'dialectical' in Fairclough's terms) concerning legitimacy between SE and capitalism at hand. Earlier, I have explained that SE in the first period appears as new and as little established. In the initial years, SE receives little media attention (see e.g., the very low number of articles per year), only few actors seem interested in SE and the concept is very weakly institutionalised. The newspaper articles seem to have the function of not only writing about SE, but also of creating legitimacy for the SE term, concept and phenomenon. First, this is done in a rather simple and direct way: depicting SE as positive *per se*. As described in the previous section, the representation of SE in the newspapers is overwhelmingly positive, with only one of 35 articles being primarily critical of SE. It is widely assumed that SE brings positive change to the world. The media articles, therefore, reproduce what I have noted in Chapter 1, i.e., that the 'social' in SE is almost always understood as 'good' for society and as morally legitimate (e.g., Cho 2006; Bruder 2021; Ranville & Barros 2021). Second, SE is able to gain legitimacy for resembling the private (businesses) sector. As I have already discussed in this section, according to the wider neoliberal framework, the (assumed) virtues of the private sector, including businesses as organisations and managers and entrepreneurs are *en vogue*. Or, as Dart has put it: "government-dependent social welfare organizations are considered less legitimate than initiatives that followed a more businesslike model framed as entrepreneurial generating revenue" (Dart 2004: 419). In acting (more) *like* business, SE earns legitimacy.

This is where I would like to highlight the dialectical relationship between SE and (neoliberal) capitalism. I argue that a process of mutually establishing legitimacy can be observed here. The articles create legitimacy for SE – but at the same time they provide legitimacy for *commercial* entrepreneurship and businesses. This occurs not only through the abstract praise of the (assumed) virtues of the private (business) sector (as explained above). Commercial entrepreneurs, businesses and business elites also gain legitimacy from their (direct) links to or from being associated with actors in the SE field. An illustrative example is A_7, in which *Ashoka*'s managing director (Frischen) explains:

> The Germans, believes Frischen, still have to slowly get used to the idea that success-oriented entrepreneurial spirit and social engagement can very well go hand in hand. "In Germany this is – other than in the USA and in England – a radically new approach, because here, in our minds, we often still have the idea of the cold, heartless capitalist" (A_7_Frankfurter Rundschau_31.03.2004).

Making use of the recurring *motif* of the overly sceptical and backwards Germans (see above), *Ashoka*'s Frischen pleas for overcoming the idea of the 'heartless capitalist' – suggesting that it is now possible to marry capitalism and 'doing good' – in the shape of SE. Ultimately, however, this is a direct promotion of (neoliberal) capitalism.

Similar to this, A_14 quotes an employee of *Deutsche Bank*, who applauds *Ashoka's* work:

> "*Ashoka* shows how outdated the old dichotomy is: either someone is evil and makes a profit or they are good and charitable," says Frank Trümper, head of culture and society at *Deutsche Bank* (A_14_Die Welt_24.12.2005).

This alliance between *Ashoka* and *Deutsche Bank* and the fact that the 'speaker', who is allowed to construct meaning around SE in this article, is no other than a *Deutsche Bank* representative is interesting in itself. What is more, similar than in the previous quote, Trümper declares that making profits and being 'good and charitable' can now go hand in hand – which in both cases is not questioned or problematised by the journalists. Making profits loses its (assumed) negative connotation – thanks to SE. In turn, SE obtains a legitimising function for (neoliberal) capitalism – and for the actors linked to it, such as *Deutsche Bank*.

Once more, it shall be noted that there is no single or homogeneous portrayal of SE, or of the 'wider' narratives around SE in the first period (1999–2008). As explained earlier in this chapter, some narratives, for example, embed SE into a critique of the economy (even if the critique is usually not a structural one). But a dominant version of SE was certainly identified: SE in the first period is mainly represented as person-centred activity, based on the ideal figure of the neoliberal entrepreneur and with the aim of reforming the social and welfare infrastructure, promoting the methods of the business world as superior. My empirical analysis, therefore, widely substantiates, exemplifies and expands previous perspectives on SE as a phenomenon that is linked to wider neoliberal developments – specifically for Germany and for 1999–2008. Around the years 2008–2009, a significant shift could be observed in the media representation of SE. This introduces the second period in the SE discourse, ranging from 2009 to 2014, as I will address in the following chapter (5).

Chapter 5: Social Entrepreneurship Becoming Part of the Economy (2009–2014)

5.1 Introduction

As explained in Chapter 3, the empirical analysis identified three different periods in the social entrepreneurship (SE) discourse(s) in Germany between 1999 and 2021 and this chapter will present the results of the empirical analysis for the second period, spanning from 2009 to 2014. In the media representation, SE is now increasingly understood as part of the economy, as taking place *in* the economy – which is an important difference to the first period, when SE was mainly seen as part of the welfare-producing 'social' infrastructure. For this second period, the findings are based on the analysis of 76 newspaper articles. In principle, the analysis followed the same guidelines for all periods (as described in Chapter 3). However, due to the strongly 'open' or inductive approach, each chapter follows its own structure, doing justice to the most relevant categories and themes of the respective period. The structure of this chapter thus, is not identical with the structure and sections of the previous chapter, in order to better focus on new themes and on changes and developments that may stand in contrast to the first period (1999–2008) and allowing me to present the results in dialogue with the previous chapter.

First, I will focus on the 'sectoral' perspective, arguing that, different to the first period, SE is now portrayed as a phenomenon that occurs mostly in the economy (see 5.2). I argue that this may be regarded as the main shift between the two periods, marking the beginning of the second period. Linked to this main shift, it was found that SE is more often embedded in a discussion of business ethics, as I will explain in Section 5.3. In addition, SE appears connected to the search for meaning or purpose in the work life, and becomes a career (option), especially for young people (5.4) Focusing on explanations, actors and value statements, Sections 5.5 to 5.7 will show that SE becoming part of the economy entails various multi-layered and ambiguous aspects. Finally, 5.8 discusses the links between SE and the political context, including the role of the financial crisis of 2008.

5.2 Social Entrepreneurship as Business and Economy

As I have explained in the previous chapter (4), SE in the first period (1999–2008) was mainly presented as a phenomenon that is situated in the areas of the state and non-profit organisations and, therefore, mainly as part (and reform) of the social infrastructure and welfare production. In the second period (2009–2014), however, the analysed articles position SE mostly within the economy. A_50 is an example for this positioning, more precisely, describing SE as part of

> [the] socially and ecologically sustainable economy (...) [and] the already existing scene of ethical business (A_50_taz_20.03.2010).

A similar situating is found in A_37, where SE is explained as a topic '*of* the economy':

> Social Entrepreneurship, or SE for short, has (...) become the 'it' topic of the economy. Its image has long left the dirty corner of hopeless idealists and self-proclaimed do-gooders (A_37_Süddeutsche Zeitung_24.07.2009).

Interestingly, the positioning here is contrasted with 'the dirty corner of hopeless idealists and self-proclaimed do-gooders' – most probably referring to people working in traditional social fields (or activists). This derogatory language about the social sector strongly reminds of the first period. However, the sectoral positioning of SE is different in this article, given that SE has left the social sector for the economy, so the argument goes.

Supporting this view is that SE organisations are now more often explicitly described as businesses, as for example in A_44. Drawing on scientific authority (by referencing 'researchers'), the article explains that:

> researchers agree that social enterprises are primarily companies and not charitable organisations (A_44_Handelsblatt_12.11.2009).

This situating of SE within the economy can also be observed in the relations that are drawn between social entrepreneurs or enterprises and other actors or institutions. In Chapter 4, I have demonstrated that, in the early period (1999–2008), narratives of SE often included state institutions and non-profit organisations. Instead, SE is now more often being compared to traditional companies (private sector businesses), as in A_44, where it is claimed that:

> [s]ocial entrepreneurs initially face greater challenges than traditional company founders (A_44_Handelsblatt_12.11.2009).

A similar account was found in A_70, explaining that in the SE field,

> companies make a larger proportion of advance payments than in conventional sectors (A_70_Die Welt_01.10.2011).

These articles, therefore, contrast the (business) practices of social enterprises against the business practices of commercial enterprises.

As in the first period, it should be noted that there is no uniform view of SE in the media representation in the second period (2009–2014). The dominant perspective of the first period – i.e., SE as a reform of the social infrastructure – does not completely disappear. For example, A_65 still expresses this narrative quite vividly, explaining the need for SE as following:

> There is no question today that social entrepreneurs are a great complement to government provision systems, welfare associations, self-help groups, or initiatives that are built on donations and compassion. They overcome things that until now have often prevented social change: poor management, political dependencies, a lack of professionalism and, above all, the lamenting about the evils and injustices in the world (A_65_Die Zeit_28.04.2011).

This example, therefore, is holding on to the image of a deficient state and social sector that was so emblematic for the first period (1999–2008). However, this narrative definitely loses relevance in the second period, with this article (A_65) being an exception instead of the dominant perspective. Furthermore, even in this example (which is the most explicit for this perspective in the second period), SE is presented as a *complement* to existing institutions of social welfare – and not as a *replacement* of these institutions. The tone is less dismissive of the state and of the actors and institutions of the 'social' sector, as compared to the first period.

These more moderate narratives may also come with descriptions of SE that are more down-to-earth, acknowledging that SE may not be the messianic solution to everything. In turn, different approaches and actors may have different strengths – and SE may be appropriate in some but not in all situations or fields. This is, for example, expressed in A_94:

> one [needs] to move away from the idea that social enterprises can solve every societal problem without requiring taxes or donations. After all, none of these companies function without income. "With a project for victims of abuse, however, you wouldn't want the abused to pay for themselves. Something like this can only be organized on an entrepreneurial basis if the state pays for the social services," says Beckmann. Things such as short-term emergencies after natural disasters, too, can only be bridged with donations (A_94_Welt am Sonntag_28.04.2013).

Moreover, an idea of partnership between social enterprises and established institutions and actors (such as the state) is introduced here. This idea of partnership – sometimes including public institutions and sometimes private companies – was found in several articles in the second period (including A_37, A_51, A_52, A_72, A_79, A_81, A_86). Article A_79, for example, portrays a social entrepreneur (Dopstadt), who collaborates with different actors – both private companies and non-profit organisations:

> Dopstadt (...) convinces companies to offer donations that non-profit organizations can then apply for: an electricity supplier donated a solar system, a newspaper publisher donated professional CD recordings and the evangelical magazine *Chrismon* several gifts of money (A_79_Frankfurter Allgemeine Zeitung_12.05.2012).

An emphasis on partnerships was often found in articles on social enterprises in the field of (international) development. A_71 provides a good example for this, telling the story of a former development aid professional turned social entrepreneur (Collenberg):

> For (...) Collenberg it was clear early on that he would dedicate his career to development (aid). However, he did not find the right answers in the German development aid system. (...) The more experience he gained, the

> stronger his conviction became that for an initiative to be self-sustaining in the long-term, ultimately only a locally managed company with an international network would work successfully (A_71_Frankfurter Allgemeine Zeitung_07.10.2011).

The article goes on, explaining how Yunus's *Grameen Bank* as well as *Sekem* (another internationally known social enterprise) have served as role models for Collenberg's social enterprise *Kaite*, which consists of a company and a trust, complementing each other. About *Kaite*, the article then describes:

> Ideally, the company should earn enough money to (...) finance the accompanying social tasks. However, this still exceeds the financial capabilities of the company. The trust is therefore dependent on donations from the German *Kaite Association* and on funds from international project partners such as the *United Nations Development Program* (UNDP) or the German development aid program. In cooperation with the Weltfriedensdienst, it was possible to secure a project commitment of almost half a million euros by the *Ministry for Development Cooperation* (BMZ). Collenberg invests a lot of time and effort in this project acquisition. But the effort is worth it, because "collaborating with good international partners is immensely important for companies and trusts, since the partners have different requirements, which oblige us to critically analyse our position time and time again, and which help us to move forward," emphasises Collenberg (A_71_Frankfurter Allgemeine Zeitung_07.10.2011).

So, while Collenberg, the social entrepreneur, expresses his (personal) discontent with established forms of development and he certainly celebrates the 'new' and 'different' SE approach, represented by *Sekem* and the *Grameen Bank*, the way forward for him does not lie in a complete replacement or dismantling of the existing (development) field and its institutions. Instead, Collenberg's SE project functions in partnership with established actors (such as *UNDP* and *BMZ*), and they are described as necessary. As noted above, this is a different rhetoric as in the first period, when established institutions and actors (of the state and the 'social' field) were often depicted as entirely incompetent.

Moreover, it was found that (international) development as a field or area of SE is quite prominent in the second period, which brings me to the findings on specific examples and fields for SE that are portrayed in the media articles. As for the first period, all examples and references for SE or social entrepreneurs were identified and clustered into fields of action or areas of work. The identified fields further substantiate the sectoral shift between the first and the second period, showing that SE is now being increasingly presented as part of the economy.

For the second period (2009–2014), the most frequently occurring examples and references for SE are from the fields of 'poverty reduction and development' as well as from 'sustainable production and goods', both occurring 19 times in the articles. These fields are usually considered to belong to the economy – as compared to fields of the traditionally public or social realm, such as 'education'. 'Poverty reduction and development' usually refers to activities in the Global South. The microcredit concept and in particular Yunus and the *Grameen Bank* have a prominent role here.[1] 'Sustainable production and goods' includes cooperatives and ventures around organic farming, food, fair trade, or sustainable clothing, among others. However, social enterprises that address work integration (e.g., for people with disabilities) or education, which were the most frequently represented fields in the first period, do not disappear: across the articles, there are 10 examples for work integration and 14 for education. Nonetheless, the rise of the field of sustainable goods and production to 19 examples is quite remarkable, since only one example from this field was included in the articles of the 1999–2008 period. Other fields of action for SE (but with less examples) are: health, support of self-employment or entrepreneurship, family and youth support, etc. Interesting, too, are a (few) 'historic' examples of SE that are referenced in the articles. In A_105, for example, a comparison of SE is drawn to Carl Mez and Max Gütermann, two German entrepreneurs during the industrial revolution with a pronounced social responsibility agenda. In sum, the specific examples and portrayed fields of action in the media representation mainly position SE as part of the economy. This sectoral shift between the first and the second period comes with various key developments, which I will address in the following sections.

1 As I have addressed in the previous chapter, Yunus was already a reference in several articles in the first period. The media attention for Yunus and the *Grameen Bank* is particularly high in the years after having received the Nobel Peace Prize in 2006.

5.3 Social Entrepreneurship as Business Ethics and Reform of the Business School

An important finding for the second period is that SE often occurs within wider narratives that are concerned with business ethics. As I have explained in Chapter 4, even in the first period, SE was sometimes embedded in a discussion around business ethics, but this perspective was rather marginal. In the second period, instead, this is a main narrative – which may not come as a surprise, considering the wider political and social-economic context. In 2008, the financial and economic system was experiencing one of the most severe crises in recent history, in turn causing discontent with the global model of financial capitalism (e.g., Hart et al. 2010; Castells et al. 2012; Aigner et al. 2018), as I will further address in Section 5.8. Several articles (A_36, A_48, A_50, A_55, A_59, A_66, A_91, A_103) establish a direct link to the financial and economic crisis of 2008 and argue that the crisis and the need or demand for business ethics is the very reason for the existence of SE, or for why it is gaining popularity. For example, in A_36 it is argued that there is a direct causality between the crisis and the raise of SE:

> The economic crisis is causing that social entrepreneurship is gaining relevance. More and more MBA students question the previous economic models of profit maximization. "Many want to build careers in a more socially responsible way" (A_36_ Handelsblatt_06.03.2009).

A very similar explanation is offered in A_103:

> In recent years, the idealism of SE has found a lot of support and has gained popularity, above all as a result of the developments triggered by the financial crisis (A_103_Aachener Zeitung_02.04.2014).

Sometimes, the articles include quite fundamental and substantial critique of the economy or the economic system, as in A_68:

> Social entrepreneurship is a hot topic. It meets the spirit of the time, which is looking for alternatives to the capitalist market economy, for beacons of an alternative way of doing things (A_68_Süddeutsche Zeitung_28.05.2011).

This idea of SE as an 'alternative' is also voiced in A_76, where SE is framed as an:

> alternative to the classical economy, as a 'grassroots movement' striving for a 'new we-culture' (A_76_Süddeutsche Zeitung_21.01.2012).

Similarly, A_108 claims that SE is proposing a different way of organising the economy, as being part of or leading towards an:

> economy of the future [which] will rely on cooperation instead of competition (A_108_Frankfurter Rundschau_24.10.2014).

However, these perspectives that offer a systemic critique of the current economic (capitalist) model, presenting SE as an alternative to it, remain the exception. In most articles, the critique of the current economic model (capitalism) is rather moderate. Most importantly, even if the crisis is alluded to and even if the need for some sort of reform of business and the economy is expressed, the critique remains mostly on an individual – not on a systemic – level, as I will explain in the following paragraphs.

It was found that when SE appears in business ethics narratives, most of the time, SE appears linked to business education, in particular to MBA (Master of Business Administration) degrees – such as in the quote from A_36 that was already included above. The reform that SE represents in these instances, therefore, is primarily a reform of the business school and of business education. This includes the way that business professionals are trained, but not necessarily the foundations or structures of the economic model as such. This is nicely presented in A_48, quoting a high-ranking businessperson (Sattelberger) who is also described as an 'MBA critic':[2]

> Since the beginning of the financial crisis, MBA education has stood in the pillory. MBA critic Sattelberger even considers misguided education as "a very important intellectual catalyst" of the crisis. After all, many of the responsible financial managers have an MBA degree (A_48_Die Zeit_11.03.2010).

---

2 Interestingly, Thomas Sattelberger, who at the time was a member of the board of directors at *Deutsche Telekom*, went into politics as a member of the German *Bundestag* for the liberal party *FDP* in 2017. He later became one of the main high-ranking politicians advocating for social entrepreneurship and social innovation.

After outlining the problem (the state of MBA education) and arguing that for a 'new generation' of students, money is not the main focus and that they have other priorities, a current MBA student (Corinna Thomassik) is quoted as following:

> Corinna Thomassik can confirm that. "Many are concerned about the social value that their future job should have," observes the 28-year-old, who began her MBA studies at *Saïd Business School* in September. She, too, decided to go to Oxford because there she could intensively study social entrepreneurship (A_48_Die Zeit_11.03.2010).

SE – in this perspective – is presented as a reform of business education, which is considered to be under pressure. SE offers a way out for business schools and for MBA students and graduates, it allows the MBA system to remain current and to adapt to the changed (post-crisis) circumstances. A_61 focuses on a specific business school: the *European Business School*.[3] The article is titled:

> 'Noble – and good. The European Business School wants to change its image' (A_61_Die Zeit_30.12.2010)

and then describes how the school wants to overcome its image. The article addresses the school's allegedly elitist student body and a recent incident of students engaging in excessive drinking that apparently had made it into the news. Once more, a reference to the crisis of 2008 is made, with the argument that something needs to change in the business education system, which relies too heavily on returns on investment and shareholder value. The title, however, seems quite revealing, foregrounding the *image* of the business school. Arguably, the question remains, whether the proposed reform of business education – e.g., by integrating SE into the curriculum – is only aiming for a cosmetic image change or whether there is a more substantial concern about structural reform as well.

---

3 The *European Business School* (EBS) was the first business school in Germany established after the US role models, i.e., private, expensive, and pursuing the aim of educating a future business elite.

5.4 The Search for 'Purpose' in Work - Social Entrepreneurship Becoming a Career (Option)

To some extent linked to the narrative around business ethics and business education, another important theme develops in the second period, namely: SE related to the search for meaning or purpose in the work life. The newspaper articles in the second period (2009–2014) often present 'purposeful' or 'meaningful' work as the reason for why SE exists – as the 'need' or justification for the SE phenomenon. It is often argued, such as in A_91, that a widespread public discontent with the economic model has catalysed a quest for meaning – and that SE opens up a perspective for finding such meaning or purpose in work:

> It's big words that social entrepreneurs play with in their company names and on their websites. Quite as big as the promise of social entrepreneurship itself (...). This idea has become increasingly popular over the past ten years, reinforced by the financial crisis, which is causing young people in particular to look for meaningful jobs (A_91_Die Zeit_27.12.2012).

The claim that the quest for 'meaningful jobs' can be attributed especially to 'young people' and students in particular is a recurring theme. In A_79, an academic (Beckmann) explains this as following:

> Beckmann sees the reason for this rush [on SE] in a change in values: "Today, students define careers differently," says the researcher, "more and more well-trained graduates are primarily concerned with doing something meaningful in their jobs." (A_79_Frankfurter Allgemeine Zeitung_12.05.2012).

Providing a similar narrative, focusing on students and their career expectations, the head of *Ashoka Germany* is quoted in A_55:

> "Many students ask themselves: What type of career do I want to pursue?" says Felix Oldenburg, Managing Director of *Ashoka Germany*. The global organization has been supporting social entrepreneurs since 1980. "The prospect of changing the world with economic concepts and still earning money at the same time is like the Holy Grail." (A_55_Die Zeit_30.09.2010).

Focusing on a different demographic (not students) is article A_102, unfolding the story of a former (music) manager, who has started his own social enterprise (selling cakes in cafés while employing a work integration model). The article initiates a debate around work, asking the question –

> But how does someone end up giving up a well-paid dream job and trying something completely new? (A_102_Frankfurter Neue Presse_25.03.2014).

– to then reveal:

> "Working in the music industry was great," the ex-manager recalls. "But there came a point in time when I wanted to do something more substantial." (...) Those who are searching for meaning are mostly between their early 30s and mid-50s, says Scheidt. "Then you realize that not only life but also professional life is finite." 'Social entrepreneurship' is the keyword (ibid.).

Here, SE is introduced – by a psychologist and career coach (Scheidt) – as the 'keyword', as the 'solution' to the problem, i.e., young professionals wanting to do 'something more substantial'. In many ways, this explanation is similar to the symbol of the 'Holy Grail' that is included in A_55 (see above).

These perspectives are interesting, because they imply a critique of work, claiming that the idea of working for a 'conventional' (for-profit) company is lacking purpose or meaning. This may be seen as a systemic critique of the (neoliberal) capitalist economic model, as it seems to fail to provide people – young people in particular – with meaningful jobs. On the other hand, the critique here remains focused on the individual. The proposed 'solution' to the capitalist crisis of meaning is not a systemic reform of the economy. Instead, it is suggested that individuals (young people) should merely look for different jobs. SE then offers an escape, a way out, especially for a certain group of people (degree educated) of a specific generation, so it is argued. SE serves as a promise, a promise to find meaning in work and being able to build a purposeful career – but still *within* the capitalist economy and according to its principles.

The promise of SE providing meaningful work (in particular for young university graduates) is sometimes even presented as some sort of competitive advantage, as a means to attracting young people, who are in the pursuit of meaning. In A_108, for example, it is argued that businesses must take notice of this development, having to meet the expectations of this new meaning-seeking generation in order to recruit talent:

> companies are increasingly competing for the brightest minds. And for them, sustainability orientation is extremely important. This topic will therefore become important for companies, considering the shortage of skilled workers. This includes things such as the vegetarian canteen, meaningful work and social commitment (A_108_Frankfurter Rundschau_24.10.2014).

This 'competitive advantage', again, is sometimes connected to business education and MBA degrees, as demonstrated in the quote above by MBA student Corinna Thomassik (A_48). Even more explicitly, this case is made in A_55, where another MBA student (Grace Sai) is portrayed. According to the article:

> She [Grace Sai] knew exactly where she wanted to do her MBA. "For me, only the *Saïd Business School* came into question," says the Malaysian student. Because the school, which is part of the *University of Oxford*, is considered one of the leading European schools for managers in the field of 'Social Entrepreneurship'. And this is exactly what the 26-year-old wants to expand her knowledge in and to establish a network with like-minded people. (...) The *Skoll Center for Social Entrepreneurship* was founded in Oxford as early as 2003 (A_55_ Die Zeit_30.09.2010).

A_63 also supports this view of SE as 'competitive advantage', for meeting the expectations of the current MBA student generation:

> Maybe so many students are interested in the subject because of the positive image – at *Insead* around a tenth, at the *Saïd Business School* of the *University of Oxford* already more than half of the MBA class. "More and more students are considering social entrepreneurship as a career option and already come to us with an interest in it," says *CASE* Managing Director Nash. (...) "In the past, these students would have gone to a political science school" (A_63_Handelsblatt_11.03.2011).

The framing of SE as a 'career' or 'career option' – as in this quote as well as in some of the other quotes above – is highly interesting. Based on the analysis of the corpus, I argue that this is a new perspective, which is developing in the second period, as I will explore in the following paragraphs.

In the first period (1999–2008), SE was not yet portrayed as a potential 'job' or 'career'. In the second period, it is now possible for job aspirants to point at more examples for 'social entrepreneurship' – or at more people using this term, or labelling themselves as 'social entrepreneur'. Furthermore, as demonstrated in the previous chapter, social entrepreneurs are usually celebrated (internationally and nationally) – almost without exception, the media representation was overwhelmingly positive in the first period. It can be assumed that this creates a strong appeal, making SE an attractive option, in order to follow the footsteps of the celebrated first generation of social entrepreneurs.

Moreover, SE being increasingly understood as 'work' or 'career option' entails various ambiguous aspects. It was found that, in some articles, the focus of the stories seems to shift slightly. In the first period, the main focus always lied on the social activity or 'mission' – i.e., what the social entrepreneur or enterprise *does for others*. The 'job' in the sense of organising and performing the SE activity in itself received little attention. In the second period, instead, there is a stronger focus on the SE activity as such. There is a more explicit and more profound discussion of SE as 'work', and what it means for the people 'working' in this field, including what SE means *for the entrepreneur*.

Some articles discuss that social entrepreneurs also need to make a (decent) living from working in a social enterprise and pursuing a social mission, as in A_84:

> Most social entrepreneurs are not concerned with the highest possible returns, although, of course, they want to be able to make a decent living from their business idea (A_84_Süddeutsche Zeitung_30.08.2012).

In A_74 a social entrepreneur is quoted, also expressing this concern:

> "Of course, I also want to pay myself a salary and maybe build a house later. But the decisive question for me is how I earn this money." (A_74_Welt am Sonntag_04.12.2011).

The most extensive discussion is included in A_65, which interestingly, is the first article in the corpus written by a social entrepreneur himself (Andreas Heinecke).[4] Heinecke addresses the dilemma of keeping a balance between fair pay and social goals – i.e., paying oneself a decent salary while upholding to the

4 As I have laid out in the previous chapter, Andreas Heinecke is one of the most prominent social entrepreneurs in Germany and has staged in many articles in the first period, too. However, this is the first time that an article is actually written by a social entrepreneur. In the first period, the included guest authors were academics or representatives of the wider support ecosystem, such as *Ashoka*.

social mission. What is more, Heinecke discusses fair payment both for the entrepreneur(s) and for their employees:

> Social entrepreneurs dedicate their lives to an idea and take a risk. They give up careers. It often takes decades for an idea to turn into a business. Social entrepreneurs also attract other people who also incur large losses. These alliances of social idealists are often based on self-exploitation. The present is mostly grey, but they hope for better times in order to achieve financial stability next to the social impact. When that point is reached, social entrepreneurs are faced with the question of how to use the profits. Can they accrue to the social entrepreneur, a first proper wage after many years? The answer is: yes and no. Social entrepreneurs certainly have a right to recoup their expenses in building the business. (So, it's good if they keep records on this.) Moreover, profits should be used to pay employees, doing justice to their performance. Civil service pay is a good guide for this. But if a social enterprise turns out to be so successful that it makes high profits over the years, if it is lucratively sold or even publicly traded, then the profits should be used to found new social enterprises or to support other projects committed to the common good (A_65_Die Zeit_28.04.2011).

Heinecke's statement is interesting, because it also includes a critical view, acknowledging that there can also be hardship involved in SE ('self-exploitation') – an aspect that is often disregarded among the cheerful praises of SE and the exceptional, almost 'super-human', features that are attributed to social entrepreneurs. This hardship is shared – from a different perspective – in A_70, in which the journalist begins the article with describing how tired the portrayed social entrepreneurs are:

> Benjamin Itter looks pretty exhausted. He repeatedly has to suppress a yawn and has rings under his eyes. His co-founders are hardly better off (A_70_Die Welt_01.10.2011).

A_83 quotes a social entrepreneur, who has left a well-paid job to open up her social enterprise – finding herself in a less comfortable position than before, in her previous job:

> "I had a well-paid job, life could have been easier for me," she says. Now she has been working up to 20 hours a day without a salary for two years. "But I'm happier than ever." (A_83_Süddeutsche Zeitung_20.07.2012).

This quote is interesting because of its ambiguity: while the quoted social entrepreneur expresses that it is not all shiny and glossy in the SE world, and that there is hard work involved – apparently up to 20 hours a day – she also claims to be 'happier than ever'. To some extent, this claim seems to support the strong desire people have to find 'meaning' in work and that social entrepreneurs have their own reward system or 'currency' – favouring 'happiness' or 'meaning' over a good salary and decent working conditions. However, the question seems to remain as to whether a 20-hour workday can be a good basis for long-term happiness. Certainly, it can be concluded that working conditions around SE are more often addressed and problematised in the second period – the media representation goes beyond an (unrealistic) ideal world of SE, in which everything is positive (and seemingly easy).

Moreover, I argue that there is also a problematic aspect related to the more explicit focus on SE as 'work' or 'career' – as compared to the first period, when the media representation almost exclusively foregrounded the social mission. There seems to be a risk that this shift of the focus might also entail a certain shift in the priorities of SE: the 'career' of the social entrepreneur receiving more attention, possibly at the expense of the social purpose. The representations of SE in various newspaper articles seem to support this concern. In A_70, for example, a group of entrepreneurs (who in the quote above were described as being exhausted) are quoted as following:

> "We always wanted to do business in India," says Jan Holzhauer. Like his colleagues, he knows the country very well, having studied there for a while. "It was clear that we would do something with social entrepreneurship" (A_70_Die Welt_01.10.2011).

The starting point for these entrepreneurs is to 'do business in India' and to 'do something with social entrepreneurship'. The SE activity is initiated not because of a specific pressing social injustice or concern at hand, but because of the wish of the (prospective) social entrepreneurs to engage in SE. Among others, Papi-Thornton (2016) has criticised that this wish to *become* social entrepreneurs (often by young graduates) sometimes may overshadow the real-world problems that SE is supposed to address. While the desire of wanting to be a social entrepreneur is not morally problematic as such, it does raise questions about the priorities. SE and the idea of building a career as a social entrepreneur becomes an end in itself – at the risk that the social concern or mission might lose relevance.

Such a shift in priorities seems reflected in A_64, an article on 'An Austrian in Hyderabad', as the subtitle recalls. The Austrian protagonist is quoted here, explaining that:

> "The city of Hyderabad is the ideal ground for me" (A_64_Die Zeit_24.03.2011).

This focus on Hyderabad as the 'ideal ground' for the entrepreneur ('for me') – i.e., for his personal and professional development – appears problematic. To an extent, the image that is invoked here is even a somewhat neo-colonial one: a European (entrepreneur) exploiting an 'ideal ground' in the Global South, in order to pursue his (career) ambitions.

5.5 Social Entrepreneurship as Business: Ambiguous Developments

The focus shifting towards the economy in the second period, which also comes with an increased understanding of SE as work can also be observed in the explanations of SE. In addition, explanations of SE often address the relationship between profits and social goals, as I will address in this section. In the first period (1999–2009), there were six main approaches of explaining SE: SE as a mix or combination of two worlds, SE as the creation of social value, SE as the solution to social problems, SE as social change, explaining SE through the sector and explaining SE through the person/agent (the social entrepreneur) (see Chapter 4). These six approaches also apply for the media representation in the second period, however, extended by a seventh: explaining SE as business or company. The following table shows how often the seven different approaches appear in the articles for the second period (2009–2014):[5]

5 It should be remembered that frequencies are only indicative in my analysis. In addition, the approaches are not mutually exclusive, and some explanations might combine several approaches.

Table 6: Approaches to Explaining 'Social Entrepreneurship' in the Newspaper Articles (2009–2015)

approach to explaining SE	**example (translation)**	**number of examples**
1. SE as a mix or combination of two worlds	*Social entrepreneurs are people or organizations that provide social services or products, but doing so in an entrepreneurial manner and not depending solely on donations or grants. In short: a cross between Mother Teresa and Bill Gates (A_75_Badische Zeitung_16.12.2011).*	3
2. SE as the creation of social value	*It's called social entrepreneurship. Founding [a company] with social added value, regardless of pure profit orientation (A_63_Handelsblatt_11.03.2011).*	7
3. SE as the solution to social (and sometimes ecological) problems	*Social entrepreneurship means an entrepreneurial activity that is innovative and pragmatic in solving social problems (A_66_Frankfurter Allgemeine Zeitung, 04.05.2011).*	15
4. SE as social change	*A social entrepreneur is someone who achieves social goals through entrepreneurial means. The primary goal is not monetary success, but sustainable, positive social change (A_44_Handelsblatt_12.11.2009).*	1
5. Explaining SE through the sector	*Roughly speaking, social entrepreneurship refers to companies that work in the areas of environmental protection, human rights, the integration of people with disabilities, etc. (A_106_Nürnberger Nachrichten_06.09.2014).*	2
6. Explaining SE through the person/agent (the social entrepreneur)	*The 'social entrepreneurs', a new type of entrepreneur, do not want profit, but social added value (A_91_Die Zeit_27.12.2012).*	14
7. Explaining SE as business/ company	*'social entrepreneurship', as companies and organizations with particularly social goals are called (A_47_Trierischer Volksfreund_16.02.2010).*	14

The overview shows that 'SE as social change' and 'SE as being linked to specific sectors' are rather marginal in this period. Little relevance, too, has the rather vague explanation of 'SE as a mix or combination of two worlds';

as stated in Chapter 4, this approach already became less important over time during the first period. 'SE as the solution to social problems' appears as the preferred approach to explaining SE. The previous chapter has discussed the strong focus on the social entrepreneur in the first period – explanations of SE were often linked to the person, but 'wider' narratives, too, were propagating a quite person-centred version of SE. While this person-centred approach remains important in the second period (with 14 times being one of the most frequently used approaches), at the same time, SE is now often explained foregrounding the organisation: SE as business or company (also employed 14 times).

SE being increasingly explained and understood as business or company is very much in line with the main development for the second period (2009–2014), namely that SE is now more often presented as part of the economy (from a sectoral perspective). Even in the first period, the media representation occasionally emphasises the organisation (instead of the person) and social enterprises were sometimes compared to businesses, as in this article from 2006:

> Initiatives such as *Ashoka* and the *Schwab Foundation* are driving forward a new concept of (social) charity in Germany: social entrepreneurship. The benefactors should run their projects like companies (A_19_Die Welt_17.11.2006, emphasis by the author).

However, SE organisations were not businesses yet. This is different in the second period, as can be observed, for example in A_55:

> Social entrepreneurship is concerned with how a company can solve a social or societal problem with innovative business models and at the same time generate financial profit (A_55_ Die Zeit_30.09.2010, emphasis by the author).

SE is not merely *'like'* companies or businesses anymore – SE *has become* business now. This is similar in A_44, which actually combines the approaches of explaining SE as a company and explaining SE through the entrepreneur (person), moving back and forth between the two:

> This competition is just one example of the boom that the idea of social enterprise is currently experiencing – companies that function according

> to economic principles but that do not pursue monetary goals, and instead want to make the world a better place. (...) Scientists are still arguing about the definition, there is still no consensus among economists about what exactly constitutes a social enterprise. There are over 20 different competing definitions, shows a team led by Shaker A. Zahra from the *Carlson School of Management* at the *University of Minnesota*. However, the researchers agree that social enterprises are primarily companies and not charitable organizations. "Social entrepreneurs are entrepreneurs with a social mission," says Gregory J. Dees of *Stanford University*, summing up the scientists' lowest common denominator. Unlike in traditional companies, "the goal is to fulfil a social task", adds Günter Faltin, professor of entrepreneurship at the *Free University of Berlin*, "and not to generate surpluses" (A_44_Handelsblatt_12.11.2009).

This excerpt from A_44 highlights another important aspect. It shows that SE is a contested phenomenon and that there are different (to some extent competing) definitions for it. What is more, several articles point out different explanations or models for SE that may differ according to their profit orientation. The relationship between (financial) profits and social goals becomes an important criterion – one that serves for identifying and delineating different models of SE. Referring to different social enterprises, A_37 explains that:

> Some of them are profit oriented, others only seek to break even. The thing they have in common is the goal: namely to eliminate social, economic, medical and ecological ills with the help of economic mechanisms (A_37_Süddeutsche Zeitung_24.07.2009).

The diversity of SE and different models for SE is also emphasised in A_63. The article explains that there are different views – and also different representatives in the SE field – with various attitudes towards profit. For some, SE entails 'not only profit' (implying that profit is not merely acceptable, but even a primary goal), while for others, SE must be 'non-profit-oriented':

> The discipline is so young that there is no uniform definition, yet. "In principle, social entrepreneurs can be anyone whose main business goal is not only profit," says Pablo Martin de Holan, professor of entrepreneurship at Spain's *IE Business School* in Madrid. "Innovative solutions to social problems" is how Matthew Nash from the *Center for the Advancement of Social Entrepreneurship* (CASE) at *Duke University* in the United States defines the demands placed

> on social founders. And at the French *Insead*, which launched an initiative in 2006, the aim is primarily to meet social demands. "A social enterprise always prioritizes this over profit," says Christine Driscoll of *Insead*. These approaches have one thing in common: social entrepreneurship does not have to be non-profit per se or non-profit-oriented, as Muhammad Yunus, for example, demands. (A_63_Handelsblatt_11.03.2011).

The relationship between economic and social goals was already relevant in the first period (see Chapter 4) and, therefore, continues to be a main theme in the second period. Overall, the four main types of describing this relationship that were identified in the first period apply to the second period as well. However, adding to this is a fifth view, which highlights the diversity of the different models:

- Profits and social goals are described as being mutually beneficial,
- Profits and social goals are presented as coexistent,
- Profits and social goals are seen as coexistent but with a hierarchy (one domain being more important than the other),
- Profits and social goals are described as in conflict with each other.
- There are different SE models that differ based on their profit-orientation.

In the first period, overall, there was an equal weight between the view that profits and social goals are coexistent and the view that they are in conflict with each other. For the second period (2009–2014), it was found that the representation of financial gain and social goals as coexistent is now (by far) the dominant one: occurring 23 times (compared to 9 accounts of financial and social goals as conflictive). Interestingly, at the same time, the view that profits and social goals may be mutually beneficial (in a 'win-win'-relationship) also loses relevance. The perspective that emphasises different SE models, which differ based on their profit-orientation, occurs 13 times in the second period.

Furthermore, it was found that the coexistence between profits and social goals is described differently in the second period. On the one hand, the discussion focuses less on the fundamental and moral aspects about the relationship between profit (money) and the social cause and goals within SE. A more pragmatic and sometimes a more concrete discussion takes place. The articles then explain why the financial profit is necessary. Sometimes they also explain the rules for how these (financial) profits must be used, as demonstrated in the following excerpt from A_72:

> Social entrepreneurs also want to operate profitably and efficiently in order for their companies to survive on the market. But unlike other companies, they don't siphon off profits, instead reinvesting them straight into solving social problems (A_72_Die Welt_25.10.2011).

A pragmatic argument is provided here: profit is described as necessary, in order for the social enterprise to persist on the market. In addition, it is explained that extracting these profits for private gain would not be allowed and that, instead, they must be reinvested into the company.

A similar perspective on the role of profits can be found in A_84:

> There is no official definition, but I would explain it like this: social entrepreneurs share their profits with their employees and their environment, combining the social with the entrepreneurial. But that doesn't necessarily mean that the profit is donated, for example it also has to be reinvested in the company (A_84_Süddeutsche Zeitung_30.08.2012).

Certain rules are prescribed here for how profits may be used: i.e., sharing them with employees or reinvesting them into the social enterprise (as well as donating to other social projects). Therefore, an interesting connection – that may also be interpreted as a justification for the readers – is established here between profits and the salaries for both the entrepreneurs as well as their employees. As seen in Section 5.4, fair payment and working conditions have become (more) important themes in the second period. What is not included is a more fundamental (moral) debate whether or not the generation of profit is at all compatible with the SE phenomenon and its social goals *per se*. Arguably, this may be interpreted in different ways: on the one hand, the debate is more pragmatic and allows a more realistic account of working (and working conditions) in social enterprises. On the other hand, this could also be seen as a reduction of the discussion, disregarding the (potential) moral aspects (and concerns) entailed in combining economic and social logics.

5.6 More Voices 'Speaking' and Social Entrepreneurs are Not All 'Heroes' Anymore

In the first period, I have identified three main groups of actors in the corpus: the portrayed social entrepreneurs, beneficiaries or target groups of SE and organisations and people of the wider 'ecosystem' (or support system) of SE. These three groups remain relevant in the second period. However, there are also a few differences in the media representation of actors of and around SE, as this section is going to address.

In the first period, it was found that the social entrepreneurs are predominantly portrayed in a very positive light. This is very much the dominant perspective in the second period, too; with a few articles making an exception, e.g., A_42 or A_108, where social entrepreneurs are placed in a somewhat esoteric corner. For the most part, though, social entrepreneurs are presented as skilled, capable, and able to achieve success where many others have failed. However, as I have already addressed in different sections of this chapter, a new aspect is developing in the second period: namely that the story of SE may involve hard work and even hardship. While this does not involve a fundamental critique of the SE phenomenon, it does cast a little shadow on the otherwise very rosy image of SE. Furthermore, this gives room to a more balanced – and also more realistic – view of SE activities and of the working conditions surrounding these.

In addition, it should be noted that in the second period, for the first time, the reader encounters an article (A_65) written by a social entrepreneur – therefore giving (a representative of) this group a low-mediated, more direct voice to 'speak' in the SE discourse.[6] This low-mediated speaker position in the first period was reserved only to the actors of the wider support system or experts (such as academics or leading figures of organisations such as *Ashoka*); however, since this is only one of 76 articles, it clearly remains an exception.

When it comes to the beneficiaries or target groups of SE, it can be said that there are a few more glimpses of the idea of SE as 'empowering' – which is an aspect that is often addressed in academic literature on SE (see Chapter 1) – compared to the first period. Even though it is not a main theme in the second period either, there are a few articles (A_67; A_94; A_106) that emphasise the fact that the beneficiaries or target groups of SE are at eye-level with other stakeholders. They portray the idea that within SE there is an exchange between equals, instead of one group doing something for the other – and, therefore, a hierarchical relationship, as, for example, in traditional charity. In A_67, a beneficiary of *Glovico*, a development project and online language

6 However, even guest contributions are mediated and not a completely 'direct' way for the author of reaching the audience, with journalists and editors curating and editing the text.

school, explains that he prefers working for this company (over other language schools), not only because of the flexible hours and higher pay:

> "That's why I now work mainly with *Glovico*." "With" and not "for" – that is important to him: "I'm treated as an equal, I'm trusted." (A_67_Süddeutsche Zeitung_16.05.2011).

On a more formal note, it is also remarkable that, in this example, the beneficiary is represented in direct speech, allowed to 'speak' in a low-mediated way – giving him a certain degree of agency over the media representation.

As for the third group of actors, the field of support or wider ecosystem of SE, in the first period, it was found that this group – as it is presented to the reader in the articles – primarily consists of wealthy individuals, foundations, corporations, universities and research institutes. Representatives of this group were sometimes authors of guest contributions, therefore, often 'speaking' to the audience in a low-mediated way. This mainly applies to the second period as well, even if there are a few noteworthy developments that I shall address here. Perhaps, the most remarkable finding is that *Ashoka* and the *Schwab Foundation* lose their dominance in the corpus – and, therefore, their interpretive authority over SE ('*Deutungshoheit*') as the main actors, who shape knowledge around SE. *Ashoka* and the *Schwab Foundation* certainly remain important actors, but now, not almost every article is connected to one of these organisations, as it was the case in the first period.

On the other hand, actors (within this third group) that are becoming more important are business schools and universities. One reason for this, certainly, is that SE in the second period is often introduced in the context of business education and MBA programmes. The main story of some articles are particular schools or programmes and the changes that were made, or which are planned, following the financial crisis of 2008 (see also Sections 5.3 and 5.4).

Another important finding is that, slowly, a few political actors and institutions are appearing in the media representation around SE – although, these still remain rather marginal. A German ministry, the *Federal Ministry for Economic Cooperation and Development*, is mentioned for the first time in the corpus in A_71 (in October 2011), as partner and funder of a portrayed social enterprise in the development field. Shortly after, A_72 (also in October 2011) announces the introduction of a programme to support SE – the first of its kind in Germany – by the *Federal Ministry of Family Affairs, Senior Citizens, Women and Youth* in cooperation with the state-owned investment and development bank, *Kred-*

itanstalt für Wiederaufbau (*KfW*).[7] The article (A_72) also mentions that *Ashoka* was involved in the design of the programme – which shows that despite losing its near absolute authority over SE, the organisation is still very influential.

In Chapter 4, I have raised that it is remarkable that the newspaper articles and journalists do not really comment on or problematise the strong links between SE and business elites, who seem to be the (main) supporters of SE in Germany in the first period, according to the media representation. In the second period, on the other hand, one article (A_56) points out this proximity to economic elites – already in the headline:

> *GEW* AGAINST *ASHOKA*: "CONSULTANTS WANT TO INSTRUMENTALISE YOUNG PEOPLE" (A_56_Rhein-Main Zeitung_01.10.2010).

The article then explains:

> The union *Gewerkschaft Erziehung und Wissenschaft* (*GEW*) warns against cooperation with a youth initiative by the organisation *Ashoka*. Last week, representatives of the initiative invited the youth organisations of the political parties and the city school council to take part in a 'Youth Changemaker City' event (...). The project is backed by companies of the consulting industry who "want to exploit young people's social commitment for their own interests in a casting show," stated the *GEW* district association yesterday. (...) The *GEW* points out that *Ashoka* is supported by consulting firms such as *McKinsey*. However, the union rejects a 'problem-solving culture' promoted by the consultants (ibid.).

This is an interesting perspective – and one that stands out. While the article establishes a certain distance to the critical position – given that the critique is placed in (direct) quotes by the union's representative – it gives room to a view that is very critical of SE (at least of the type of SE associated to *Ashoka* and its corporate funders). The article, therefore, shows that there can be different views and opinions on SE and of the actors involved in this field – and that not everybody engages in the cheerful praise of SE. Above all, the article brings attention to actors and interests involved in the SE field – and that these are linked to certain power structures and relations.

---

7 This programme may be seen as the first policy engagement with SE on the federal level in Germany, which, however, did not result in a long-term commitment (see Chapter 2).

A_76 is another article that stands out in this regard. It introduces and compares two books on social business and entrepreneurship with different views on the phenomenon. One book is described as following:

> The authors see social business as an alternative to the classical economy, as a 'grassroots movement' striving for a 'new we culture'. The basic attitude of the authors is characterized by economic scepticism. And so, they also see the approximation to the world of large companies, who are stretching out their hand in the name of corporate social responsibility, as a danger for the young movement, which is still in the experimental stage (A_76_Süddeutsche Zeitung_21.01.2012).

The other book offers a different position:

> Peter Spiegel sees it completely differently. In his book, which is driven by forward-thinking optimism, the head of the Berlin *Genisis Institute*, himself one of the most important players in the scene, drafts an economically compatible model of social business. With profit as the sticking point. More precisely: the question of whether a social business may generate a return for investors. Why not, says Spiegel, pleading for tearing down the barrier that Yunus built into his model (A_76_Süddeutsche Zeitung_21.01.2012).[8]

The descriptions included in A_76 are interesting, because they demonstrate that SE is a contested phenomenon. Different actors have different ideas about the SE movement and who should or should not be involved in it. The first quote makes the relationship between SE and (commercial) companies explicit – and warns against a too close relationship between the two. Instead, the second quote presents a position that considers a close relationship with companies or investors as unproblematic. In addition, it argues against the principle that SE must operate on a non-profit basis (here described as the model promoted by Yunus).

A_56 and A_76, therefore, are some of the few articles that engage in an explicit and overt discussion of actors around SE, with regards to different interests and the social and power relations involved. Overall, however, this is a blind spot in the media representation. Usually, actors (of the wider support

---

8 Paul Spiegel and his *Genisis Institute* were mentioned in Chapter 2 as the organisers of the first *Vision Summits* in Germany (since 2007).

system of SE) are mentioned rather matter-of-factly – without a deeper analysis of these actors, their (potential) interests or position in wider social structures. It is remarkable that these aspects are of such marginal interest in the articles, given that, in fact, it should be the role and function of newspapers to precisely engage in controversial debates – to address, reveal, or even question social and power structures. Arguably, the most significant finding is that articles like A_56 and A_76 appear as such a glaring exception.

5.7 Complex and (More) Ambiguous Logics and Value Statements

Complementing previous sections in this chapter, this section will discuss selected findings on the ('economic' and 'social') logics as well as on the value statements (i.e., what is presented as positive or negative) in the articles for the 2009–2014 period. Section 5.2 has already demonstrated that some articles still draw a critical picture of the state and the social sector – but this is, by far, not as pronounced as in the first period. There is less direct 'state-bashing' or 'bashing' of the established social sector. A greater emphasis lies on the idea of partnership between SE and the established actors and institutions. Nonetheless, SE is sometimes still described as the 'better' form of engagement. However, the differentiation to other forms of engagement or activism now appears more subtle.

SE is still often described as (positively) different. But this argument is made in a more subtle way, for example, via the individuals (the social entrepreneurs), who are given positive attributes – in contrast to other activists and people pursuing social aims. This includes value statements on their attitude, their *habitus*, or on outright superficialities. A_74, for example, positively remarks the appearance of two social entrepreneurs:

> Saskia Ludwig and Frank Dose don't necessarily look like social romantics. In shirts and jackets, the two founders sit in the tasteful (...) lounge (...) and talk about their business idea (A_74_Welt am Sonntag_04.12.2011).

In A_79, a similar observation even makes it into the title of the article, describing social entrepreneurs as:

> 'Do-gooders Without Wool Sweaters' (A_79_Frankfurter Allgemeine Zeitung_12.05.2012).

The sub-title reads:

> THEY WANT TO MAKE THE WORLD A BETTER PLACE WITHOUT CHAINING THEMSELVES TO RAILS (ibid.).

This is definitely a reference to (other) forms of activism[9] – and judging from the wording and the implicit value statements, SE is valued higher than these other forms.

A similar example was found in A_111. Here, the social entrepreneur (Caroline), whose venture seeks to work with new sustainable materials (made of bananas), is pictured as following:

> Caroline calls the banana substance a "meaningful product". But she doesn't want to approach it with a naive do-gooder idea. And she doesn't want to sacrifice herself (A_111_Welt am Sonntag_28.12.2014).

Even if the other – apparently less valuable – form of activism is not explicitly named here, it can be supposed that by 'naive do-gooders' the article refers to activists or people working in social professions. Assuming that these others are 'naive' and 'sacrificing' is clearly a (negative) value statement. Thus, on a different and somewhat more subtle level, traces of the dismissive representation of traditional social fields of the first period (1999–2008) are still there.

The same goes for elements of the 'state failure' logic. State and welfare institutions are still sometimes contrasted to the 'better' or 'more flexible' social enterprises, even though this is usually more nuanced than in the first period. A_72 provides a good example for this perspective. While the article emphasises an idea of partnership and explicitly says that *social entrepreneurs should not replace the social systems, but complement and change them*, it nonetheless comes with a critique of the established institutions:

> The small companies (...) are much more agile and creative than the unwieldy welfare state and the big welfare companies, they bring in new ideas from the most diverse corners. And this is precisely what the state is increasingly dependent on: social entrepreneurs should not replace the social systems, but complement and change them: What can entrepreneurs

9 This is very likely a reference to activism against nuclear power, since blocking railways to prevent the transportation of nuclear waste has been a popular form of protest in Germany for several decades.

> do better, what should the state take over? What can the market solve and what not? (A_72_Die Welt_25.10.2011).

A_46 establishes a contrast between a social enterprise and the UN climate summit (which in 2009 took place in Copenhagen) – presenting the social enterprise as a response to the unsuccessful approach of politics (by the UN and the heads of state):

> While the heads of state of the world were looking for solutions to the impending climate catastrophe in Copenhagen and only found hot air, René Eick is sitting in his gym in Prenzlauer Berg in a black polo shirt and jeans, and is thinking. (...). Because what the summit in Denmark desperately tried to do on a large scale, the mechanical engineer in Berlin has long since tackled on a small scale. According to him, he runs Europe's first green fitness studio (A_46_Berliner Morgenpost_22.12.2009).

SE as the niche and small-scale approach is positively connoted and juxtaposed to (international) politics here: (international) politics as formalised and established, but unable to achieve its goal – and, on the other hand, the imaginative, more casual 'doer', who is operating locally and within the niche.

A similar 'either-or'-logic, contrasting SE to political or activist approaches was found in A_89. A social entrepreneur, whose social enterprise is concerned with bringing financial literacy to young people, explains that:

> "We find ourselves in a large system. Nothing can be changed overnight." With the turbulences currently affecting the financial world, it is more effective in the long term to impart knowledge and to create awareness than to call for bank break-ups (A_89_Die Zeit_25.10.2012).

In this view, instead of emphasising partnership or a complementary relationship, the social enterprise's approach is presented as a 'better' or 'more effective' alternative to politics or activism, i.e., 'calling for bank break-ups', which is clearly a reference to demands by different social groups following the financial crisis of 2008.

Another theme that needs to be addressed are the value statements around (commercial) businesses in the second period (2009–2014). In the first period, the picture was quite clear: the (private) business sector was almost always presented as a positive example or role model, up to a degree of a near glorification of the business world and of its methods and people (managers and entrepreneurs). The transfer of economic logics into social realms was proposed as a popular (and always applicable) 'solution' for public and social institutions to achieve 'better' and 'more professional' results. In the second period, the picture is slightly more complex and ambiguous, as I will explain in the following paragraphs.

On the one hand, the glorification of business can sometimes still be observed (e.g., in A_79, A_85, A_110). Aspects of economization, i.e., transferring economic logics into social fields, continue – for example, in the framing of social fields as 'markets' (e.g., A_57, A_64, A_65, A_72, A_79). An emblematic example is provided in A_72, where a researcher describes the barriers for social enterprises in Germany as following:

> "The practice of awarding contracts in the social sector favours the big ones, smaller and younger social enterprises with unusual concepts hardly seem to have a chance there." *Caritas, Diakonie* and others dominate the market (A_72_Die Welt 25.10.2011).

In the next paragraph, the article then quotes the director of *Ashoka Germany* (Oldenburg):

> *Ashoka*'s boss Oldenburg therefore calls for "real competition" in the social sector as well. It's about more than a few government handouts for do-gooders – it's about the best solutions to social problems being able to prevail on the market (ibid.).

Arguably, this may already represent a next stage of economization – of viewing and understanding social phenomena and the social sector through the eyes and language of business and the economy.

On the other hand, the overall media representation does not show the same degree of glorification of business, its people and methods as in the first period. As explained in Sections 5.2 to 5.4, many articles in the second period also include critical views of the business sector and of the economic model. What is more, some articles engage in a critical discussion on the organisational level, arguing that SE may also challenge economic certainties and business practices. SE then questions the methods of commercial businesses. For example, in A_44 it is argued that:

> social entrepreneurs (...) do not fit into the thought and analysis patterns of traditional business administration. Because social missions are difficult to squeeze into its usual formulas and patterns of analysis (A_44_Handelsblatt_12.11.2009).

A_88, too, provides an interesting account; a social entrepreneur (Porter), whose social enterprise combines a flying school with the delivery of medical supplies in Ghana, is quoted here:

> "I teach a lot of businesspeople to fly. They tell me that I first have to know where I can get the money for such a venture. That's the way business works," says Porter. "But if that means that opportunities go untapped, then business is simply wrong." (A_88_Welt am Sonntag_23.09.2012).

At first glance, this reflects a recurrent narrative of the social entrepreneur 'against all odds'. But at the same time, SE is not just about transferring or applying elements of the business world here, but rather about questioning economic certainties and the logics of business, too (see also A_70, A_83, A_108, A_110).

In A_83, a social entrepreneur (Trinkwalder), explains her 'unconventional' human resource and marketing practices:

> She [Trinkwalder] primarily employs women with "multiple placement obstacles", as it is called in *Jobcenter*-language. On her team is a hearing-impaired alcoholic. "She can come and go as she pleases," says Trinkwalder. "This works out." Trinkwalder completely goes without advertising campaigns. "These are a waste", says the former agency boss. "I save the money and prefer to give it to my ladies and to the suppliers" (A_83_Süddeutsche Zeitung_20.07.2012).

A_70 provides an example on pricing: a social entrepreneur explains how his company's pricing policy differs from the usual practice in the (commercial) fashion industry (which is known for its tough pricing conditions):

> The prices are fixed for a long time. "We don't pass on any pressure, no matter how big customer XY is, or how much power they had to push us to do it." In the organic niche, business is done differently, says Christoph Malkowski. Companies make a larger proportion of advance payments than in conventional sectors (A_70_Die Welt_01.10.2011).

Apart from the glimpse into the 'alternative' pricing practices of this social enterprise, this excerpt is interesting for another aspect: the social entrepreneur here embeds his social enterprise in a wider field of 'organic' production. In fact, social entrepreneurs sometimes try to build on more established traditions and labels, such as 'organic' or 'fair trade' – as can be observed, for example, in A_71, A_74, A_108, or A_110. In A_108, it is explained that these established traditions and labels may help social entrepreneurs to differentiate themselves from commercial companies (which also increasingly claim to act in a socially and environmentally conscious way) and to prevent accusations of 'greenwashing'. However, some of the portrayed social entrepreneurs also decide against these established certifications, arguing that while they welcome the idea behind them, they find them too expensive and that they would prefer to pay more money directly to the producers, instead of spending it on certificates (A_110 and A_111).

5.8 Critiquing but also Stabilising the Capitalist Economy After the Financial Crisis of 2008

Many important aspects of the second period (2009–2014) can be linked to its principal development: SE being increasingly understood and presented as part of the economy, which represents a 'sectoral shift' from the first period, when SE was mainly understood as a (re)form of the welfare infrastructure. This development can be observed not only in the specific examples and fields of SE that are pictured in the articles, but also in wider societal debates, now embedding SE more often in a discussion of business ethics, and less in a discussion of social infrastructure (reform). Different narratives are linked to this, e.g., the representation of SE as a 'meaningful' career (option), especially for students and degree holders.

There is, as always, no single view on SE and its 'wider' meanings. Aspects of the dominant discourse of the first period remain, as I have highlighted throughout the chapter. Yet, important changes were identified. The strong person-centricity of the first period loses relevance – together with *Ashoka* and the *Schwab Foundation*. Although some articles hold on to the image of inefficient or deficient public and social institutions, overall, these are not constantly 'under fire' as this was mostly the case in the first period. Even when institutions of the social infrastructure are criticised, the tone is usually more moderate, and established social institutions are often presented as partners for social enterprises. SE is not necessarily a replacement of the existing institutions and not *per se* 'better', but rather introduced as coexisting and complementing each other. Moreover, the private sector and businesses in general, to some extent, have lost their 'messianic' charm. The promise that everything will turn to the better if organisations (in the public and social realm) would only apply business tools somewhat fades in the second period.

This is hardly surprising when taking into account the wider socio-economic and political context. The second period (2009–2014) falls into the aftermath of the global financial crisis of 2008. On a global scale, the 2008 crisis was the most dramatic financial crisis since the *Great Depression* of the late 1920s and early 1930s. Above all, the crisis came unexpectedly and shook many in their world view. As a result, people increasingly started to question the sustainability of the economic model and capitalism more generally as well as the (mainstream) economics discipline, which had failed to see the crisis coming (Acemoglu 2009; Krugman 2009; Hart et al. 2010; Harvey 2011; Castells et al. 2012; Aigner et al. 2018). According to Hart et al.'s (2010) analysis, "whatever place the financial crisis eventually finds in economic history, one certain victim has been free-market economics" (2010: 4).

Today, this might seem a little overstated. In spite of the severity of the crisis, the neoliberal capitalist system was preserved, without undergoing notable change (Crouch 2011; Adamati & Hellwig 2013) – and the economics discipline still relies widely on neoclassical theory and mathematical models (Aigner et al. 2018). Nonetheless, the established business world – or parts of it, especially banks and the financial sector and big corporations more generally – have lost some of their legitimacy in the public eye. What is more, in the years after the crisis there seemed to be a short intellectual momentum – including more critical views on (neoliberal) capitalism and a newly revived debate about potential alternative economic models (Castells et al. 2012). Arguably, this ideational impact of the crisis is partly reflected in the analysed corpus. It stands out that many articles in the second period (2009–2014) connect SE to the crisis and to the need for different business ethics and principles.

As in the first period thus, the articles manage to establish narratives around SE that neatly fit into the wider socio-economic and political environment – even if it is a different one than in the first period, when large parts of German society shared the view that the labour market and social security needed reform. In the second period, following the financial crisis of 2008, there is an increased public awareness for business ethics and for businesses' social and environmental responsibility. This also includes a more critical perspective towards profit-orientation and towards commercial companies, more generally. Interestingly, A_78 contrasts these developments to the teachings of Milton Friedman:

> The Nobel Prize winner Milton Friedman used to be able to say that the 'social responsibility' of companies lies solely in making profits. No manager would dare to say that today. Almost every larger company has formulated a 'corporate philosophy' and is committed to 'Corporate Social Responsibility' (A_78_Frankfurter Allgemeine Zeitung_13.02.2012).

The media representation of SE then connects these wider developments to SE – or embeds the SE concept and phenomenon within them. Explaining the SE phenomenon and justifying the need for why it exists appears linked to the more general public call for business responsibility and ethics. Against the first period thus, SE in the dominant representation becomes a vehicle to reform the economy (instead of one to reform the welfare infrastructure).

However, I argue that for the most part, the critique of the economy and the calls for more social responsibility remain rather moderate, rarely proposing structural change in the economic model. Structural and radical critique (in the original sense of the word, i.e., targeting the roots of the problem) remains the exception (e.g., in A_50 or A_76). This could be observed, for example, when it comes to the critique of business schools (see 5.3). On the one hand, business schools and their narrow focus on profit and shareholder value are the target of the critique. But at the same time, they are presented as part of the solution to the crisis – not least, in the form of SE. The impression is given that by adding one or a few SE courses, the problem of business education can be fixed. What is more, SE is introduced mainly as an attractive career option for a certain generation of MBA students. SE may even be a 'competitive advantage' for a few business schools on the MBA market. Such a take on SE then remains deeply rooted in the neoliberal idea of competitiveness (Davies 2014a). According to Nicholls (2010), the three most influential academic SE programmes at the time were located in the business schools at *Harvard*, *Duke* and *Oxford*. This not only raises questions of inclusiveness. It also begs the question whether ideas for structural reform of the economic model may come from such high-priced business schools with strong links to the corporate world and business elites. Or whether SE in these contexts is reduced merely to a means to polish the image of an elite circle and its institutions.

Furthermore, through the focus on business education and 'meaningful' work, the critique is primarily centred on individuals. Or put differently: it is diverted from the economic system or model to the individual level. The media representation of SE rarely criticises the structures of the economic system or model as a whole – let alone does it put forward specific proposals for reform or regulation. Instead, the critique in the articles mostly revolves around managers and their behaviour, education, or attitudes. As a result of the 2008 crisis, the 'old' economic figure of the manager has lost its appeal (Heidbrink & Seele 2010). But a new economic figure offers a way out, showing that it is possible to 'do business' and still be morally and socially accepted: the entrepreneur, and in particular the social entrepreneur (Heidbrink & Seele 2010). Paradoxically, perhaps, SE may then open up a way out for economic agents in the capitalist economic system and, in turn, also legitimise it. Through strictly differentiating the concept of 'business administration' from 'entrepreneurship' – as entrepreneurship theory often does (Faltin 2012) – and their respective agents ('managers' versus 'entrepreneurs'), it becomes possible to criticise the economic system, concentrating the critique on one specific agent (the manager) and then to point towards a (different) agent in the system as the solution: the (social) entrepreneur.

This diversion of the focus to the individual level could also be observed in other instances. An interesting example (also quoted above) is provided in A_89, on a social enterprise that provides 'financial literacy'. The social entrepreneur explains:

> "We find ourselves in a large system. Nothing can be changed overnight." With the turbulences currently affecting the financial world, it is more effective in the long term to impart knowledge and to create awareness than to call for bank break-ups (A_89_Die Zeit_25.10.2012).

The capitalist economic model is criticised here. Yet, the 'solution' that is proposed is an individual one. Financial literacy is presented as 'more effective' than political proposals for reform of the financial sector. The proposed solution, therefore, means adapting to the system (on an individual level) – instead of changing it.

As I have outlined in Section 5.5, another important theme in the second period is the relationship between 'economic' and 'social' logics and the role of profits within social enterprises. Overall, the dominant perspective considers that economic and social goals can coexist. Arguably, SE is making a contribution to 'normalising' this relationship, showing that it is possible for organisations to combine the two domains. Against the first period, the discussion becomes less fundamental and more pragmatic, sometimes also more specific. In the first period, the main concern is whether profits and social goals are at all compatible; in the second period, the main questions revolve around the adequate balance and how this relationship may be organised. Aspects such as decent pay and working conditions for entrepreneurs and employees are now included in the debate.

I argue that this 'normalisation' of the relationship between financial and social goals, is ambiguous. On the one hand, it can be viewed as another form of economization: it becomes (or has become) increasingly acceptable that social organisations now apply business methods, or even that they pursue profits – and that commercial companies also may pursue social goals. These processes (on the organisational level) can be seen as part of the blurring of the boundaries between the public, private and third sectors, described, among others, by Ridley-Duff & Bull (2011). On the other hand, I argue that (more strongly) adopting an economic perspective may also introduce new topics and discussions: for example, about the functioning and operations of the enterprises, the salaries of the people working for them, (critical) human resource or marketing practices, or aspects of organisational governance. In addition, the media representation in the second period is more explicit about the diversity of the SE field – when it comes to different social enterprise models, which sometimes have different positions towards profits. Perhaps most importantly, these debates show that the contestation and discussion about SE and the meaning of the 'social' (as well as the practicalities of organising it) is ongoing.

Furthermore, I argue that there are interesting and ambiguous aspects in the debate around SE as work. As said earlier, this debate now often addresses working conditions and salaries. For example, in A_84 it is argued that:

> Good work costs money. This is true for business, but unfortunately not for the social sector. (...) It is a misconception that solving social problems and earning money have to be mutually exclusive. Motivation and recognition are good, but you also want to start a family at some point (A_84_Süddeutsche Zeitung_30.08.2012).

What is remarkable is the fact that the discussion on fair payment and working conditions goes beyond SE here. Via SE, the article – or the social entrepreneur – initiates a wider discussion about payment in social professions. This is, indeed, a theme and argument that entails political potential and one that may resonate with different social and political actors. Yet, 'wider' proposals of this sort still remain an exception in the second period.

In sum, the main development from the first to the second period, the 'sectoral shift' leading to SE being increasingly understood as part of the economy seems rather simple. Yet, this development entails a set of complex and widely ambiguous processes. Some of these seem to discursively challenge and other rather to stabilise neoliberal capitalism. Around 2015, two different and somewhat competing strands of SE become more pronounced, as I will explore in the next chapter.

Chapter 6: Towards an Entrepreneurial Society, or a Transformation of the Economy, or Both? (2015-2021)

6.1 Introduction

This chapter will present the results for the third period identified in the empirical analysis, spanning from 2015 until 2021. 2015 marks the beginning of the third period, in which SE often appears next to other forms of entrepreneurship. Even the very first article in 2015 (A_112) is quite exemplary for this understanding of SE, reporting on a university's programme for students interested in founding a company. SE is now often described as a 'trend' among founders and start-ups. Universities as well as policymakers and local and regional economic development agencies have gotten (more) involved in SE – and new actors have emerged in the SE field, most importantly, the *Social Entrepreneurship Netzwerk Deutschland* (*SEND*), founded in 2017. Some of these actors propagate the second main strand in the third period of SE as 'more' than a form of entrepreneurship, at times linking the concept to the transformation of the economy as a whole. 2021 is the final year covered by the empirical analysis in this book, and, therefore, marks the end of the third period – but should be regarded as an 'open' end to it.

The analysis of the third period (2015–2021) is based on 238 articles. Judging from the media representation (i.e., the number of articles, as demonstrated in Chapter 3), the interest for SE increases in Germany. Arguably, this growing interest in SE also comes with a certain expansion of the SE term and concept, as I will explain throughout the chapter. As in the previous chapter (5), the findings for the third period will sometimes be compared to aspects in the first and second period. In many ways, the third period can be considered as a continuation of the second period (2009–2014), as I will address in Section 6.2. The understanding of SE as part of the economy is further established. However, as 6.3 explains, SE now is not just any part of the economy, but more specifically, presented as part of the start-up world and next to other (commercial) forms of entrepreneurship. Not least due to some actors, who get (more) involved in SE, certain aspects of SE get institutionalised in the third period, as demonstrated in 6.4. Arguably, as more people are familiar with the SE concept, this also comes with a certain normalisation of it – and, more generally, of the idea that social and economic aims can be combined. Section 6.5 will explain that in spite of new powerful actors in the SE field, such as *SEND*, this does not lead to a unified understanding of SE. On the contrary, as interest in SE grows, there rather seems to be an expansion of the term. In 6.6, I will focus on politics and policy around SE and *SEND* in the media representation, to then in 6.7 show how some actors link SE to a specific regional economic model (of Germany or Berlin). Finally, Section 6.8 will close the chapter with concluding remarks.

6.2 Rooted in the Economy and Source of Meaningful Work: More Continuity than Change?

Following the chronological perspective and focusing on the three different periods, it can be argued that the shift from the first to the second period was more pronounced than the shift from the second to the third period. There is no sectoral shift, as the one identified between the first and the second period, when the main focus of SE – judging from the media representations of SE – shifted from the public and social realm to the economy. Instead, many aspects of the third period stand for continuity and some may, in fact, be seen as a continuation or further development or evolution of some of the features of the second period. This section will discuss two of these aspects: SE in the context of meaningful work and SE being understood as part of the economy.

The narratives of 'SE as meaningful work' and 'SE as an attractive career option' that developed during the second period remain important in the third period. 'Meaningful' work is still used as a frequent explanation for the SE phenomenon and for people seeking to become social entrepreneurs. As in the second period, different articles assume that this search for purpose or meaning in work especially concerns a specific ('young' or 'new') generation, or students in particular. Emblematic for this perspective is A_178, titled:

'CAREER WITH A PURPOSE' (A_178_Berliner Morgenpost_14.04.2018)

– where *Ashoka*'s Laura Haverkamp is quoted, voicing the following hypothesis:

> "The younger the generation, the more people there are who seek meaning behind what they are building." (ibid.).

According to Joana Breidenbach, head of the social enterprise *Betterplace*, this search for meaning or purpose also leads people to change careers. In A_135 – titled

> 'Employer for People in Search of Meaning' (A_135_Berliner Morgenpost_17.04.2016)

– Breidenbach explains:

> "Many of our employees have previously worked in traditional commercial companies and, at some point, asked themselves the question of meaning" (ibid.).

Someone who undertook such a career change, a former banker named Strüwer, is portrayed in A_119. The article tells his story as following:

> His career took him to the major Swiss bank *Credit Suisse* in the late 1990s. (...) In 2006, he moved to the head office in Zurich: even better titles, even higher positions, even more money. Holidays in Mauritius, five-star hotels, big cars. And then the day came when Strüwer drove his SUV to work along Lake Zurich (...) and the world became brittle. The financial crisis made headlines, critics of capitalism raged out in the square, and Strüwer thought: "None of this feels real." On the other hand, the upheavals on the financial markets and the birth of his daughter were real: two events that made Strüwer "question the meaning of my work" (A_119_Die Zeit_11.06.2015).

This questioning led Strüwer to support *Ashoka* and the SE sector – and later to become a social entrepreneur himself. Now, he has finally found his purpose – as the end of the story reveals:

> The old standards – titles, position, money – no longer mean anything to Strüwer. He not only works pro bono for *Ashoka*, he also supports the organisation financially. He had to find his way into the new world first. "But now,"

> says Strüwer three years after leaving *Credit Suisse*, "I've come to the right place." (ibid.).

While this story about the 'reformed' banker establishes a link to the financial crisis of 2008, overall, it was found that the crisis of 2008 is much less present in the articles of the third period (compared to the second period). The search for meaning or purpose in work and the rupture with the corporate (or traditional for-profit) world is not anymore necessarily connected to a more general 'post-crisis' discussion of business ethics. A few years later, the distance to the 2008 crisis seems to have widened and, to some extent, the crisis seems to have lost its relevance to still be a popular reference in the media stories. Supporting this view is, for example, the story of a former employee of *Google* and *YouTube* (Christian Sigmund) in A_293, a few years later (February 2021). Sigmund also questions his corporate job and lifestyle, but without alluding to the financial crisis:

> At the age of 25, Christian Sigmund had already arrived where many people want to be. *Google* offered him a marketing job in Dublin, he immediately moved to Ireland, where he had a lot of freedom, a good salary and fun. He later moved to the *Google* subsidiary *YouTube* in London. (...) "I had arrived in the land of milk and honey of employers," says Sigmund. But then, four years later, something appeared that he calls a disturbing feeling. "Why am I doing this?" he wondered. "What's the point?" He didn't care about more people watching a *YouTube* video and *Google* accumulating more profits. He didn't know what else to do, but he felt he was in the wrong place (A_293_Die Zeit_25.02.2021).

According to the article, Sigmund then decides to quit his job and to travel to Peru, where he is confronted with plastic waste pollution. This experience leads him to find his vocation: after coming back to Hamburg, Sigmund looks for like-minded people and together they found *Wildplastic*, a company that uses plastic waste that is collected in Haiti, India and Nigeria to create new products.

Comparing the two stories thus, while both protagonists have a rupture with the corporate world, Sigmund's story apparently does not need the financial crisis of 2008 as a point of reference. His change of mind seems to come from within, from a 'disturbing feeling'. Like in this example from A_293, an explicit link to the financial crisis of 2008 or to wider discussions of business ethics and business education or MBA degrees is widely missing from the newspaper articles. As noted in Chapter 5, the critique of business education and of the MBA in particular was a major theme during the second period. Few exceptions can be found, e.g., in A_182, an article that, indeed, foregrounds business education and business ethics; and in A_126, which portrays a social entrepreneur, who has completed an 'MBA in social entrepreneurship'.[1] On the other hand, an implicit critique lies in this quote from A_293: Sigmund questions working for *Google* or *YouTube* and contributing to their profit accumulation as meaningless.

As mentioned above, another aspect stands for continuity in the media representation between the second and the third period, namely the 'sectoral' understanding of SE as part of the economy. In the previous chapter, I have argued that the main development of the second period is that SE is increasingly understood and represented as part of the economy (and not as part of the public or social sector). This perspective prevails in the third period (2015–2021); it can be argued that, to some extent, this perspective is even consolidated and institutionalised, as I will explain later in the chapter. As always, there are several exceptions to this. For example, A_121 places SE in the context of civil society and voluntary work, or A_168, setting SE into relation to the welfare state. However, on the whole, the dominant sectoral understanding or placement of SE is one of SE as businesses, i.e., as part of the economy.

As explained in Chapter 5, conceiving SE as business may also lead to a more explicit focus on the organisation and to a discussion of SE as work. This sometimes includes addressing decent pay within social enterprises – an issue that remains current in the third period. A_270, one of the few articles written by a social entrepreneur (Zarah Bruhn)[2] – is a remarkable example. The article is titled:

> 'I'M A SOCIAL ENTREPRENEUR – AND THAT'S A STORY OF SELF-EXPLOITATION' (A_270_Frankfurter Rundschau_28.08.2020).

1 However, this is merely biographical information here. The MBA programme itself or business education, more generally, are not discussed.

2 As noted in Chapter 2, Zarah Bruhn (founder of *Social Bee*) is a prominent German social entrepreneur, who in 2022 was appointed Special Envoy for Social Innovation at the *Federal Ministry of Education and Research* (BMBF 2022).

In the article, Bruhn asks the rhetorical question:

> How many successful company bosses with more than 100 employees do you know who share a flat to save money for retirement? (ibid.)

and demands better working conditions for social entrepreneurs and social enterprises, including higher pay. Another article that brings awareness to this issue in the headline is A_257, which describes social entrepreneurs as:

> 'SUSTAINABLE, INNOVATIVE, BUT WITH FINANCIAL WORRIES' (A_257_Berliner Morgenpost_15.02.2020).

However, the aspects that demonstrate continuity between the second and the third period shall not lead to overlook important developments or evolutions. Above all, this concerns the evolution of the understanding of 'SE as business and part of the economy' into a specific kind of business, namely: 'SE as start-up' or 'SE as the *founding* of a company', as I will explore in the following section.

6.3 Social Entrepreneurship and the Start-Up World

In the previous section, I have explained that the understanding and placing of SE as business and as part of the economy remains the dominant perspective in the third period (2015–2021). However, it was found that the understanding of SE as business is not exactly the same as in the second period. In the third period, SE is mainly linked to a specific form or aspect of business – namely: to '*Gründung*', i.e., start-ups, entrepreneurship and founding (a company).[3] In fact, this nuance may arguably be the main development of the third period – as a parallel or competing strand of SE as 'more' than entrepreneurship and linked to the transformation of the economy as a whole (which will be addressed in later sections of this chapter). In the first perspective, social enterprises are increasingly understood as start-ups, and SE as a form or subcategory of entrepreneurship. SE is presented as both an expression but also as a promotor of an entrepreneurial society, as this section is going to explore.

3 While SE as *Gründung* can occasionally be found in the second period, this perspective fully develops in the third period.

First, the understanding of SE as start-up and the particular focus on the founding process of companies (*Gründung*) can be observed, on the one hand, in the definitions and explanations of SE. An example for this perspective on SE is provided in A_112, where a professor of entrepreneurship explains SE as a 'trend' among founders:

> One trend are start-ups in the field of social entrepreneurship. Their main focus is not on financial gain, but on a social purpose (A_112_Mittelbayerische Zeitung_12.02.2015).

A similar description of SE is included in A_268, quoting an employee of a regional business development agency (IGZ) in Bamberg, who claims that:

> So-called social entrepreneurship, i.e., founding a company whose primary goal is not profit, has been more common in the last two to three years, reports Max Dahmer from *IGZ Bamberg* (A_268_Fränkischer Tag_14.08.2020).

A_235 explains SE as:

> sustainable and socially responsible forms of start-up business (A_235_Frankfurter Rundschau_12.10.2019)

These examples, therefore, follow the approach of explaining 'SE as business/company' that was already found in the second period. This is the most frequently used approach to explaining SE in the third period, employed 37 times – e.g., against 19 times of explaining 'SE through the person/agent (the social entrepreneur)'. To some extent, this can be interpreted as a consolidation of the understanding of SE as part of the economy.

However, explaining 'SE as start-up or founding a company' (*Gründung*) should also be differentiated and highlighted as a specific form of 'SE as business'. It places a much stronger emphasis on the activity of *starting* a business and on the initial phase and the processes related to this. In this way, this framing places an emphasis on 'young' companies – and possibly excludes older businesses – given that common definitions of 'start-ups' specify that they are under 10 years old (Kollmann et al. 2021). Furthermore, describing SE as 'start-up' or 'founding' (and not just as 'business') also establishes a link to the modern start-up scene that is associated with a certain type of enterprises – tech companies in particular.

To an extent, this is also reflected in the specific examples for social enterprises or social entrepreneurs that are provided in the media articles. Like in the second period, the examples in the third period (2015–2021) are mainly from fields that would mostly be regarded as belonging to the economy, instead of traditionally 'social' fields. Across all 238 articles of the third period, the most represented fields are 'sustainable production and goods' as well as 'environmental or climate protection' (with examples in 34 articles from each field). From the field of 'education', instead, 16 examples are provided. 'Technology-based approaches', mostly apps, are also well-represented in the third period – with 28 examples coming from this 'field'. It may be questioned, though, whether technology should be viewed as a field, given that (in the context of SE) it is not an end in itself – i.e., technology usually comes together with another field. For example, *Ecosia* – a search engine that uses its revenues to plant trees, which is referenced in A_196, A_210, A_258, A_311, A_349 – combines 'technology' and 'environmental or climate protection'. *Mobile Retter* – an app that seeks to better coordinate rescue workers to reduce time in rescue missions (A_210, A_211, A_258) – combines 'technology' and 'health'. Nonetheless, the emergence of technology-based approaches in the third period is remarkable and further accentuates the proximity of SE to the tech-oriented start-up world.

Furthermore, the perspective of SE as part of the entrepreneurship and start-up world is also reinforced by the spaces and institutional contexts in which SE appears in the newspaper articles in the third period. A few examples for these contexts (often events) in which SE occurs are: the Start-up Initiative of the State of Rheinland-Pfalz (*Gründertreff der Gründungsinitiative Rheinland-Pfalz*) in A_148, or at the *Deutsche Gründer- und Unternehmertage* (*deGUT*) – a yearly fair for starting up and entrepreneurship in Berlin (A_164). A_179 reports on a social enterprise that receives an award as 'Saxony's start-up of the year' (*Sachsens Start-up des Jahres*). A_133 introduces social entrepreneurs, who have obtained an *EXIST Business Start-up Grant*.[4] Several articles (A_130, A_163, A_175, A_240, A_283) reference the German TV show *Die Höhle der Löwen* – similar to the British show *Dragons' Den*, a reality TV format in which entrepreneurs present their business ideas to a panel of five wealthy investors – arguably, the epitome of entrepreneurship references and (pop) culture.

4 The *EXIST* programme is funded by the federal government and has been running since 1998 (BMWK 2022a).

Overall, a considerable share of articles on SE in the third period (2015–2021) addresses this kind of events or awards for (commercial) entrepreneurship and start-ups. A pattern that I could identify is that there are often different categories (and awards) for different 'types' of entrepreneurship – with 'social entrepreneurship' being one of the different categories. For example, in A_190 the *Kreditanstalt für Wiederaufbau (KfW)* awards a 'special prize for social entrepreneurship' (*Sonderpreis für Social Entrepreneurship*) at the *deGUT* fair in Berlin. A_205 addresses a similar 'special prize' (*Sonderpreis 'Social Entrepreneurship'*) at the Start-up Ideas Competition of Thuringia (*Thüringer Gründungsideenwettbewerb*); while A_295 reports on yet another 'special prize' awarded by the *Frankfurt University of Applied Sciences*. Furthermore, a remarkable example is provided in A_143, on *Ernst & Young*, who have been giving out the 'Entrepreneur of the Year' award for 20 years. The award has different categories: a 'special prize' (not further specified), industry, services and IT, consumer goods and trade, start-up and – for the first time, due to the 20th anniversary: a 'special prize for social entrepreneurship' (A_143_Eichsfelder Tageblatt_19.11.2016).

As one of the 'big four' global accounting firms, *Ernst & Young* certainly is a powerful symbol for the established for-profit corporate business world. This award, therefore, establishes a link between SE and the corporate world and business elites. What is more, the 'special prize for social entrepreneurship', on which A_143 reports, is given to Brigitte Mohn. The Mohn family, owners of the *Bertelsmann* media group, is one of the most wealthy and powerful in Germany (Ostermeyer 2015). This raises questions about the understanding – and the function – of SE here. When declaring the charitable engagement of a media mogul as 'social entrepreneurship', SE seems to become an excuse to party for the establishment – a chance to celebrating itself for charitable activities. Overall, however, such prizes are awarded by different actors, including universities, regional economic development agencies and companies. Arguably, these awards and events represent a form of institutionalisation of SE, as I will discuss in the next section (6.4).

Moreover, these events and awards usually position SE next to 'other forms' of entrepreneurship. SE then stands beside commercial forms of entrepreneurship and appears as part of the start-up world. What is more, SE becomes, indeed, a sub-form or type of entrepreneurship – a way of being entrepreneurial in an entrepreneurial society. In turn, SE is presented as both an expression but also as a promotor of this entrepreneurial society.

In different articles, SE is not only represented as a form of entrepreneurship (i.e., as an expression thereof), but also as a facilitator for becoming more entrepreneurial. SE can be the entry into an entrepreneurial life. A_167 illustrates this, portraying two students (Marvin and Brice), who are members of *Enactus*, a student initiative that promotes SE at universities across Germany (also mentioned in Chapter 2). Marvin and Brice explain their interest in SE and in *Enactus* for two reasons: they think that SE is more effective than donation-based approaches and they believe that SE allows them to learn how to become entrepreneurs:

> For the two students, it is important to get involved. "Donating money is too ineffective for us, in the end you never know exactly what it will be used for." says Marvin. "The nice thing about *Enactus* is that we donate our working hours. We develop something that pays for itself. That is meaningful development aid." And Brice says, "It's like watching a child grow." You also learn an incredible amount: how to draft business plans or soft skills such as presentations. Both of them could well imagine becoming entrepreneurs after their studies (A_167_Aachener Nachrichten_04.12.2017).

In this example thus, SE is presented as an approach to development aid – but also as a training programme for students. Students learn entrepreneurial skills via SE – and they can then apply these skills to become entrepreneurs. It is striking, however, that it does not seem to matter *what kind* of entrepreneurs they may later become: whether 'social' or any other type of entrepreneurs.

Another good example for this perspective on SE is offered in A_175, describing a SE workshop of a *School of Entrepreneurship* (linked to regional a university of applied science). A student (Basar) is quoted on the experience:

> "It was interesting to actively design something instead of just listening to others speak," says Basar. "We gained a lot of experience and got to know the basics of entrepreneurship." This is important, not least because three of the students are thinking about the idea of becoming self-employed one day. "Today I know what goes into a market analysis and what it means to work in a team," says the 24-year-old student (A_175_Schwäbische Zeitung_19.03.2018).

One of the organisers of the workshop supports this view of SE as a method to acquire entrepreneurial skills:

> Start-up manager Andreas ter Woort sees the project as an example of the "successful integration and cooperation of different actors in our entrepreneurship ecosystem", as he says. "Events like this strengthen entrepreneurial thinking." Future managers need this not only when founding a company, but also when entering a company (ibid.).

While these programmes and workshops are mostly at universities, some articles also include examples from schools. A_287 describes a competition that is held at schools, again, with different categories for 'entrepreneurship' (in this example including 'real market' and 'social entrepreneurship'). The aim of the event is described as following:

> In the competition, students compete against each other with business ideas, it is about independent action, creativity and entrepreneurial spirit (A_287_Neue Osnabrücker Zeitung_08.12.2020).

In these various examples thus, SE serves as an entry ticket into entrepreneurship – entrepreneurship of any kind. This also comes with a blurring of the lines between SE and other forms of entrepreneurship and supporting and spreading the understanding of SE as a form of entrepreneurship – which, however, can be critically seen as a reduction of the concept (as I have argued in Chapter 1). Critically, this raises the question whether SE is not merely presented as a 'friendly face' next to other – commercial – ventures, ultimately, giving SE the function of a 'social fig leaf'.

This blurring of the boundaries between SE and commercial entrepreneurship (and the for-profit corporate business world, more generally) can be observed in a few other instances. Sometimes, this is also connected to the narrative of people being in the search of 'meaning' or 'meaningful work'. A_196 introduces such a social entrepreneur (Vollmann), whose motivation to start a social enterprise is described as following:

> Vollmann comes from the classic start-up scene and after his third profit-driven start-up, he wanted to do something meaningful (A_196_Berliner Zeitung_14.12.2018).

A_227 portrays a serial entrepreneur, who founded his first start-up right after finishing school. Over the years, he started another business – the third one, now, is a social enterprise in the field of education:

> The heart of its founder beats for company number three. Because here, economic success is only a means to an end. The real goal of the company is to give teachers the tools they need to give the children entrusted to them the best possible support (A_227_Reutlinger General-Anzeiger_13.08.2019).

While the articles draw a clear difference between SE and entrepreneurship, based on the purpose (economic success versus social goals), nonetheless, the nonchalant switching between the two domains is presented as unproblematic: after making money with commercial enterprises, entrepreneurs can be social entrepreneurs.

Furthermore, when SE is presented as a training or education programme this may also come with a shift in the aims and priorities of SE. A similar aspect has been identified in the second period: when SE becomes a 'career (option)', the aim of SE may shift precisely towards the 'career' of the social entrepreneur – at the expense of the social purpose. In the third period, some articles suggest such a shift in priorities, e.g., A_146:

> Frick (43) and von Alvensleben (47) found a niche when they came up with the idea for their company almost a year ago: founding a tailoring shop that produces collections locally and that mainly employs refugees. (...) Von Alvensleben, who has known Frick since 2007, wanted to set up a company in the field of social entrepreneurship. Frick's French friend [or partner] then suggested: "Why don't you do something with refugees?" (A_146_Rhein-Main Zeitung_26.11.2016).[5]

The article presents Frick and von Alvensleben's desire to establish a social enterprise and to become social entrepreneurs as the starting point for their project. The idea to employ refugees only comes in later, almost like an entrepreneurial opportunity that can be seized – and one that is suggested by a third person. Arguably, the priority shifts: in favour of the idea of becoming a social entrepreneur and pursuing SE as a career. SE becomes an end in itself – and the social goals as well as the target groups are only defined later, making them seem somewhat secondary to the main purpose of being a social entrepreneur.

I argue that there is a similar risk when SE becomes an education programme. As a result, the learning outcomes of the participants (mainly univer-

5 'Freund' in German may translate either into 'friend' or 'partner'.

sity students) could be prioritised over the social aims that SE is supposed to address. This seems particularly problematic, when the prefix 'social' becomes optional. As demonstrated in the examples above, SE workshops often have the purpose that their participants gain entrepreneurial skills. Entrepreneurship (regardless of the prefix 'social') then becomes a goal and a value in itself. Several articles suggest that in the third period (2015–2021), it seems to be widely or 'commonly' accepted that entrepreneurship is a (desirable) end in itself. Once more, this frequently appears in the context of (social) entrepreneurship activities at universities. In A_144, for example, Bavaria's State Secretary for Science Bernd Sibler (*CSU*) is quoted at an event at the *University of Passau*:

> "Bavaria needs university graduates who dare to take the plunge into self-employment" (A_144_Straubinger Tagblatt_19.11.2016).

As I have argued throughout, this conceptualisation of SE as entrepreneurship can be seen as a reduction of the SE concept and at the same time, it promotes and legitimises an entrepreneurial society (in which entrepreneurship becomes an end in itself).

On the other hand, it can be argued that SE being represented as entrepreneurship can also have ambiguous aspects to it. Arguably, SE appearing in entrepreneurship events and awards can be seen as an indication for SE finding its entry into spaces of 'mainstream' entrepreneurship. Going further, one might even argue that SE is 'conquering' (these) new spaces. Certainly, it should not be ignored that SE appearing in entrepreneurship contexts can also lead to more resources going into the field – and that it may not (only) be the entrepreneurship context that is shaping (and changing) SE, but also the other way round.

A_190 might support this view. The article reports on a social enterprise (*Ackerdemia e.V.*) winning the 'special prize' for SE by the *Kreditanstalt für Wiederaufbau* (*KfW*) at the *deGUT* fair. *Ackerdemia* builds school gardens and promotes education for healthy food – activities that, arguably, have existed long before the 'social entrepreneurship' term and concept came along. In Chapter 2, I have provided a similar example, of Judy Korn, who started labelling herself 'social entrepreneur' when coming in contact with *Ashoka*, but continuing her previous activities as usual. Social enterprises becoming visible in entrepreneurship events may be an indication that SE projects are now 'taken seriously' in business contexts. Going further, it could be argued that this could be seen as an expansion of 'the social' into economic realms, drawing resources from the economy into traditionally social fields.

A_238 offers another similar example, reporting on a student, who wins a start-up competition at the *University of Erfurt*. The idea of her *Sharing Living Project* is to bring students and older people together in order to provide both generations with affordable housing and for them to help each other in everyday life. Arguably, this intergenerational housing idea has existed for several decades – but it seems unlikely that any business development or start-up money would have gone into it. The initiator of the project would probably have presented their idea to a public or third sector institution – but not to businesspeople and investors. Critically, though, it would need to be questioned whether these events and awards can really lead to significant resources going into these ventures – given that prize money tends to be rather low.

6.4 Institutionalisation and Normalisation of (Some Parts and Aspects of) Social Entrepreneurship

In previous sections, a few developments were mentioned that allude to a certain 'normalisation' of the idea of SE and to an 'institutionalisation' of SE – or of certain aspects of it – in the third period (2015–2021). By 'normalisation', I am referring to aspects that seem to demonstrate that the idea of SE is becoming (or is assumed to have become) more 'common sense'. This includes the (perceived) compatibility of the 'economic' and 'social' domains and logics. By 'institutionalisation', I mean that a SE field is becoming more distinctive and more established in Germany – and that it appears that more resources are going into the SE field. An example for a form of institutionalisation of SE are the different awards for 'social entrepreneurship' that are now handed out by various institutions and in different regions in Germany, as mentioned in the previous section. These awards allocate resources (prize money) to SE and create awareness for SE, arguably, introducing the concept to a broader audience. Furthermore, in Chapter 2, I have explained that the number of yearly newspaper articles is rising (see Graph 1) – which can also be interpreted as an increase in the attention for the SE concept and thus, as a form of institutionalisation. In addition, there are signs for both the normalisation and the institutionalisation of SE, which are related to actors, as I will explain in the following paragraphs.

I argue that the institutionalisation of SE is linked to the emergence and the increased presence and involvement of certain actors in the SE field. Section 6.3 already mentioned that in the third period (2015–2021) there are various awards for SE – often by universities and public institutions, in particular economic development agencies (*Wirtschaftsförderung*). This is a stark contrast to the first period (1999–2008), when this sort of awards only existed around *Ashoka* and the *Schwab Foundation* (see Chapter 4). More generally, it was found that these actors (universities and public institutions) are now more present and more important in the media representation. They participate in shaping SE – what is being understood as SE, and what others get to perceive as SE. Different universities in Germany have now integrated courses on SE. An example for this is provided even in the very first article of the third period, A_112, publicising a 'holiday academy' (*Ferienakademie*) at the *Ostbayerische Technische Hochschule Regensburg* (OTH) for all interested in 'founding a company'. The article announces:

> The 'holiday academy' is aimed at all those interested in founding a company. (...) This year, for the first time, the winter school will be organized by the *OTH Regensburg Start-up Center*. "This is part of our activities relating to the topic of founding a company," says Prof. Dr. Sean Patrick Saßmannshausen, who teaches business administration and entrepreneurship (...). According to Saßmannshausen, interest in start-ups is relatively stable. One trend are start-ups in the field of social entrepreneurship. Their focus is not on financial gain, but on a social purpose (A_112_Mittelbayerische Zeitung_12.02.2015).

Universities are not completely new actors in the SE field. As explained in Chapter 5, business education (at business schools and universities) and its potential reform was a main theme in the second period (2009–2014). Even in the first period (1999–2008), academics or universities appeared in the news articles. However, the big difference is that SE is now (also) promoted by ordinary public German universities and universities of applied science, which make up the bulk of the German university system. For example, the institution portrayed in A_112 (above), the *Ostbayerische Technische Hochschule Regensburg*, is a public university of applied science located in the Bavarian province. In the first and second period, instead, SE mainly occurred in the context of (international) expensive business schools and universities such as Oxford's *Saïd* or the *European Business School* (now: *EBS Universität für Wirtschaft und Recht*). Now, SE is reaching a broader spectrum of universities – a development that can be seen as a spreading out of SE, and therefore, as an institutionalisation of SE. Moreover, the media representation shows that various universities now have integrated SE into their programmes; there are seminars on SE, or educational 'camps' such as the one described in A_112. There are even a few examples of degree programmes (e.g., in A_117; A_147; A_217). These activities imply that resources are going into SE, that knowledge on SE is being produced and distributed, that more and more people are being confronted with the SE concept. In sum: that SE is becoming more established in Germany.

Another important group of actors in the context of the institutionalisation of SE are economic development agencies (*Wirtschaftsförderung*). Very occasionally, single institutions have already appeared in the second period – namely: the national investment and development bank *Kreditanstalt für Wiederaufbau* (*KfW*) (see Chapter 5). But in the third period, this group of actors is much more present – and there is also a spreading out into the surface: it is not only the *KfW* (on the national scale) that promotes and engages with SE, but also regional and local agencies. For Berlin, for example, the subtitle of the article A_219 announces:

> 'IBB [*Investitionsbank Berlin*] is the First German Development Bank to Open Programmes for Social Enterprises' (A_219_Börsen-Zeitung_22.06.2019).

The state (*Bundesland*) of Berlin, is not the only place where economic development agencies get involved in SE (and where this is represented in the analysed media articles). There are many examples in the corpus for the third period (2015–2021), also on the local level and for more remote cities, such as Giessen (in A_269), Göttingen (A_206), or Bamberg (A_268). This indicates that SE is not only happening in – or being described as a phenomenon of – urban centres, but also of smaller cities across different German regions, and sometimes even of rural areas (e.g., A_214; A_228; A_326).

Furthermore, this development, in particular local and regional economic development agencies becoming part of the SE field and shaping it, may also stand for the consolidation of a certain perspective on SE. Arguably, the dominant view that developed in the second period – namely: understanding SE as part of the economy – becomes consolidated in the third period. Economic development agencies contribute to the understanding of SE as part of the economic sector and of social enterprises as business. This understanding might then be institutionalised, for example, through funding programmes for social enterprises. Universities, too, might be contributing to consolidating the perspective on SE as part of the economy. In most of the examples above, SE university programmes are rooted in the fields of business and management, in which SE is often presented as one (sub-) form of entrepreneurship. This is in line with current trends in academic literature (see Chapter 1). Both groups of actors (universities and economic development agencies) thus, not only contribute to an institutionalisation of SE as such, but also to the institutionalisation of the understanding of SE as part of the economy.

In Chapter 2, it was already anticipated that in the late 2010s and early 2020s, policymakers in Germany get more interested in SE. SE was mentioned in different coalition agreements by federal (and state) governments, and SE was debated in the *Bundestag* for the first time in 2018. Two programmes were initiated on *Bundesländer* level: '*Sozialinnovator*' in Hesse and 'Social Economy Berlin'. This, too, represents a form of institutionalisation of SE during the third period. However, politics and policy will be addressed in a separate section (6.6).

Furthermore, in Chapter 5 it has been addressed that there are signs for a certain 'normalisation' of SE, i.e., that the idea of SE is becoming (or is assumed to have become) more 'common sense'. This development seems ongoing in the third period (2015–2021). A first indication for this is that the explanations for SE that the articles provide in the third period are often short and lacking detail. Sometimes, SE is only explained by a translation of the term into German (e.g., as "*Sozialunternehmertum*" in A_170 or "*soziale Unternehmen*" in A_204). In some articles, there is no explanation at all (A_113, A_122, A_127, A_133, A_144, A_164, A_197, A_219, etc.).

Moreover, the rather vague approach to explaining SE as 'a mix or combination of two things' that over the years seemed to have lost relevance (see Chapters 4 and 5) appears to be more present again in the third period. This approach often relies on the formula of 'making money and doing good' – as, for example, in A_114:

> In this model – in German: 'soziales Unternehmertum' – money should be made and good things being done at the same time (A_114_Süddeutsche Zeitung_09.03.2015).

I consider this approach as vague, because it formulates the pursuit of social and financial goals, but does not engage in a deeper discussion of how these goals shall be achieved simultaneously or what this would entail. The pursuit and (co)existence of social and financial aims is mentioned rather matter-of-factly. It becomes a defining – and apparently sufficient – feature of SE. A_276 is another example:

> Doing business? Yes, of course, but in such a way that there is also a profit for society and the environment (A_276_Kieler Nachrichten_17.10.2020).

Apart from the very short explanation, this quote is interesting, because it demonstrates a certain normalisation of SE that extends to the (perceived) compatibility of the 'economic' and 'social' domains and logics, more generally. The formulation 'of course' further accentuates the view that (apparently) there is no conflict between social and financial aims – and makes it seem not only unproblematic, but also easy to marry the two. This 'normalisation' may be seen as a continuation of developments during the second period, in which articles have already less often and less fundamentally questioned this compatibility from a moral standpoint (see Chapter 5).

This 'normalisation' may be seen as the result of wider socio-economic and political developments. The introduction of economic logics into large parts of society, including traditionally social realms (i.e., processes of economisation) is a key aspect of neoliberalism (see Chapter 1). It could be argued that as a result of neoliberalism, the combination and compatibility of financial and social logics and goals has already become more acceptable – leading to an acceptance of SE as well. SE may now be considered less irritating than it used to be – requiring less (detailed) explanation. At the same time, however, SE also facilitates this development, because it provides concrete examples for organisations and activities that join the two logics (economic and social). Arguably, speaking with Fairclough, it seems that there is an interesting dialectical relationship at hand here. SE undergoes a process of normalisation (it becomes more 'common sense') due to wider developments under neoliberalism. But in providing specific (and positive) examples, SE also contributes to a more general normalisation of the relationship between economic and social logics – and to legitimising it.

Another interesting aspect related to the (assumed) normalisation or compatibility of economic and social logics is that some articles link this to a specific generation – similar to the argument that it is a specific generation that seeks purpose in work. This is clearly voiced in A_251:

> Social entrepreneurship is currently one of the big trending topics (...). Because social commitment and entrepreneurship are no longer a contradiction for the younger generations. "There is more and more pragmatism coming in." (A_251_Die Welt_25.01.2020).

A_114 offers a similar account. The article (also in a context of university programmes) establishes a direct link between the normalisation of economic and social logics and the search for meaning. The article quotes both a student with a SE project (Gelhaus) and then the course convenor (Beckmann), who helps explaining the phenomenon:

> Gelhaus says: "For a long time there was voluntary social work on the one hand and business on the other. I can see that now more and more start-ups fit into the middle." Beckmann believes that 10 or 15 years ago, such a course would hardly have been fully booked. The universities have just reacted to the demand. "Today's generation rather asks and looks for values." At parties, you'll often hear the question what meaningful things you've already done. And no longer how much money you earn (A_114_Süddeutsche Zeitung_09.03.2015).

A_193 also puts forward the argument that it is, above all, a 'new' generation that sees economic and social logics as compatible – or at least that they see these as *more* compatible than previous generations. This article, though, focuses on philanthropy and investment, arguing that a 'new' generation of rich donors pursues different investment goals. This attitude is seen as a driving force for the SE field:

> (...) there is the next generation of wealth owners who have inherited in recent years. They often pursue a new approach to investing, in which they no longer necessarily differentiate between classic philanthropy and investments that are only intended to generate returns. Their thought pattern goes more in the direction of investing their money sustainably altogether and wanting to do something good with it (A_193_Frankfurter Allgemeine Zeitung_21.11.2018).

Arguably, this is an ambiguous interpretation of the SE phenomenon. Instead of a mere economisation, it is suggested here that the merging of social (including environmental) and economic logics may also be seen as a (more) holistic approach to economic activity. This strongly reminds of the idea of sustainability or sustainable development.

This perspective is voiced in A_249, too, again with the claim that it is particularly a 'young generation' that is driving this development:

> The young generation in Germany is loudly demanding ecological and sustainable action (A_249_Berliner Morgenpost_16.12.2019).

Similar to this, A_311 claims that:

> The digital natives and the following *Fridays-for-Future*-generation insist even more radically on corporate responsibility than their predecessors (A_311_Frankfurter Allgemeine Zeitung_28.06.2021).

6.5 More Actors and the Expansion of the 'Social Entrepreneurship' Term and Concept

The previous chapter demonstrated that in the third period, SE is explained less often and with less detail. This can be seen as the result of a certain 'normalisation' of the relationship between economic and social logics. This normalisation may be interpreted in different ways. On the one hand, it can be seen as part of more general economisation trends. On the other hand, it can also be understood as a more holistic approach towards economic activity. Furthermore, I have provided examples that demonstrate that explanations of SE in the third period often remain vague. Overall, the media representation of SE in the third period thus, provides various explanations and wider interpretations of the SE term, concept and phenomenon. In spite of the rise of new important actors, no uniform understanding of SE has developed in Germany. On the contrary, there seems to be an expansion or diffusion of the SE term and concept in the third period (2015–2021), as I will explore in this section.

Not all explanations of SE in the third period follow one of the seven different approaches to explaining SE that were identified in the first two periods (see Chapters 4 and 5).[6] While the first six approaches were able to cover nearly all explanations for SE in the first period, and expanded by the seventh approach (explaining 'SE as business/company'), almost all explanations in the second period, this is not the case for the third period. A considerable number of explanations (about 35%) do not fit into this framework.[7] At the same time, a new distinct approach to explaining SE could not be identified. In addition, Section 6.4 already showed several examples for rather vague explanations of SE in the third period (2015–2021). Overall, the media representation suggests that a 'common' understanding of SE has not yet developed in Germany – in spite of the growing popularity of the SE term (see Chapter 2).

Quite the contrary, some findings suggest a certain expansion of the SE term and that, on occasion, the SE term is used in a rather arbitrary way. In numerous articles, the delineation between SE and other phenomena does not seem very clear – for example, differentiating SE from commercial businesses. At times, SE is merely explained as businesses that act responsibly or that take responsibility, e.g., in A_175 where SE means that

> [i]n addition to maximising profit, social responsibility should be a value (A_175_Schwäbische Zeitung_19.03.2018).

Not only is 'maximising profit' mentioned first. The formulation that social responsibility 'should' be taken into account 'in addition', too, is quite weak and makes 'social responsibility' seem somewhat optional. In any case, social responsibility is placed secondary to profit. This explanation, therefore, does not make a substantial difference between SE and commercial businesses or start-ups. A similar example is provided in A_220. Once more, this is an article that makes use of the argument that SE is particularly attractive for a specific generation – and that describes social entrepreneurs in the following way:

> Young entrepreneurs increasingly want to take on social responsibility. They do not just foreground pure profit maximisation (A_220_Südkurier_22.06.2019).

6 The seven approaches are: SE as a mix or combination of two worlds, SE as the creation of social value, SE as the solution to social problems, SE as social change, explaining SE through the sector, explaining SE through the person (the social entrepreneur) and explaining SE as business/company.

7 Still, about 65% (82 out of 126) of the explanations identified in the articles for the third period use one or more of the seven approaches.

According to this representation, SE is not 'pure' profit maximisation – 'profit *maximisation*' is nonetheless accepted. This perspective allows making profits within SE that go beyond those required out of long-term economic necessity – for example, for making investments for the future of the enterprise or to be able to provide decent salaries for the entrepreneurs and their employees. While these representations that explicitly allow profit maximisation are few, they stand in contrast to the second period, in which the delineation against profit *maximisation* was consistent across all articles. Allowing profit *maximisation*, however, bares the risk that the SE concept becomes unprecise. It foregrounds the economic over the social goals – which is a contradiction to most definitions of SE (see Chapter 1). In addition, these representations make a differentiation between SE and corporate social responsibility (CSR) – which subsumes the social goals under a 'business case' (Lohmeyer & Jackson 2018) – difficult, if not impossible. As a result, the SE term and concept becomes arbitrary and, ultimately, useless.

Such an arbitrary use of the SE term and concept was found in different instances. In A_178, for example, the reader is offered an 'either-or'-explanation with different options for what SE may be:

> The term ['social entrepreneur'] describes a type of entrepreneurs who use their economic energy to contribute to the solution of a social problem, or who follow principles such as sustainability and social responsibility in their work (A_178_Berliner Morgenpost_14.04.2018).

A_218, reporting on an event on SE, opens a discussion, using questionable examples in the subtitle of the article:

> 'Is *Netflix* a Social Enterprise? Or the Private Taxi Service *Uber*?' (A_218_Landshuter Zeitung_19.06.2019).

The first sentence of the article then focuses on *Uber*:

> Companies like *Uber* want to change something in society (...) (A_218_Landshuter Zeitung_19.06.2019).

The lack of delineation or even the establishing of a link between SE and for-profit platform corporations like *Uber* or *Netflix* certainly is a very arbitrary media representation of SE. The article fails to explain in which way SE is different from these companies. This missing delineation certainly opens the door for greenwashing or 'social-washing' – a critique that was voiced against the early SE movement (as described in Chapter 2).

However, it must be noted that this is only one perspective. Other articles explicitly try to distinguish SE from traditional (for-profit) businesses and their CSR activities. A counterexample can be found, for example, in A_187, where it is explained that:

> While the core business of other companies that claim to do good often has little to do with charity and commitment, social value is firmly anchored in the DNA of social enterprises. Their business plans are based on striving for an environmentally friendly production chain, fair conditions for farmers or suppliers and a humane employee culture. Social start-ups want to solve social and humanitarian problems – and earn money by doing so (A_187_Focus_08.09.2018).

The formula 'earn money by doing good' is employed here, too – suggesting that the coexistence of the two domains (social and economic) is unproblematic. However, SE is clearly differentiated from traditionally commercial businesses.

An arbitrary use and lack of delineation of the SE term that I have addressed above was also found related to social or ecological projects – not only to for-profit businesses. In 6.3 and in Chapter 2, I have addressed the fact that social or ecological projects that have already existed before, now sometimes receive the label 'social entrepreneurship'. For example, a few decades ago, there probably were similar social enterprises to *Ackerdemia* (A_190), a social enterprise that was mentioned earlier, with the aim of building school gardens and promoting healthy food, but these would not have been referred to as 'social entrepreneurship' back then. Article A_271, for example, reports on a waste collection campaign, in which volunteers collect garbage from the coasts in the North of Germany, labelling the activity as 'social entrepreneurship'. However, this sort of activity seems indistinguishable from other social or environmental campaigns and raises the question about the 'economic' or 'entrepreneurial' dimension. These examples thus, indicate an expansion of (the use of) the SE term and concept into a different direction as well.

The findings of the analysis show that explanations in the third period (2015–2021) are often vague and sometimes rather arbitrary. Overall, in spite of the growing popularity of the SE term and concept in Germany, there is not yet a 'common' understanding of SE that is shared by large parts of society. At least, this does not extend to the media and to its representation of SE. On the contrary, there are signs for a certain expansion of the SE term – which does not only mean that the term is used more often (quantitatively), but also that it seems to be (increasingly) used to refer to different things (qualitatively).

It could be argued that this expansion is related to the fact that more actors are becoming interested and involved in SE in Germany during the third period. In Section 6.4, I have already mentioned that universities and economic development agencies as well as policymakers start to appear in the media representation of SE. Chapter 2 has provided an overview of the SE field in Germany, demonstrating that, over the years, important new actors have emerged (e.g., *Social Impact* or *Impact Hub Germany*) and established actors are starting to take notice of SE (e.g., the development bank *KfW*). More people are by now 'speaking' about SE. Arguably, the founding of the *Social Entrepreneurship Netzwerk Deutschland* (*SEND*) in 2017 marks a turning point. *SEND* quickly becomes a central player in the German SE scene, which is also reflected in the newspaper articles.

SEND is mentioned for the first time in December of 2018 (in A_196) and quickly manages to gain media attention. Next to universities, which I have addressed previously in this chapter, *SEND* has an exceptionally prominent position in the media representation in the third period. On the other hand, other actors – *Ashoka* and mainly the *Schwab Foundation* – lose relevance, as Table 7 shows.

Table 7: Overview of Articles Including Selected Actors: 1999–2021

	first period (1999–2008)	**second period (2009–2014)**	**third period (2015–2021)**
total number of articles	35	76	238
articles mentioning:			
Schwab Foundation	13	6	1
Ashoka	14	13	10
universities	10	34	86
SEND	0	0	41

Ashoka and the *Schwab Foundation*'s dominance had already faded in the second period (see Chapter 5). They continue to lose presence in the third period. In fact, the *Schwab Foundation* almost entirely disappears from the newspapers (appearing for the last time in A_131).[8] Both the disappearance of the *Schwab Foundation* and the rise of *SEND* become even clearer when looking at the years 2015–2018 and 2019–2021 separately, as in Table 8:[9]

Table 8: Overview of Articles Including Selected Actors: 2015–2018 and 2019–2021

	2015–2018	**2019–2021**
number of articles	87	151
articles mentioning:		
Schwab Foundation	1	0
Ashoka	6	4
universities	40	46
SEND	1	40

As explained in Chapter 2, *SEND* quickly manages to become a prominent voice and to shape the SE field in different ways, which is also reflected in the news articles. For instance, *SEND* plays an important role in explaining or defining SE, as, for example in A_270, where *SEND* is referenced:

> According to the definition of the *Social Entrepreneurship Netzwerk Deutschland*, social enterprises are a mixture of classic start-ups and non-profit organizations (A_270_Frankfurter Rundschau_28.08.2020).[10]

In this example, *SEND* is referenced to explain SE – and, therefore, given a certain authority over the SE field. In addition, as mentioned in Chapter 2, *SEND*

8 2012 is the last year that the *Schwab Foundation* awards the 'Social Entrepreneur of the Year' in Germany.

9 *SEND* in the corpus is mentioned for the first time only in December 2018 (in A_196). Therefore, Table 7 separates the years before and after 2019 (i.e., before and after *SEND* has been mentioned by the newspapers).

10 It should be noted that this quote does not actually reflect the definition that *SEND* provides, which is much more detailed (see Chapter 1).

has since 2018 been publishing a yearly report (*Deutscher Social Entrepreneurship Monitor*), which aims at providing data about the German SE ecosystem for decision-makers in politics, business and civil society (SEND 2022a). This *Monitor*, too, is mentioned in several articles (e.g., in A_196, A_218, A_256, A_257, A_267, A_303, A_307) and further establishes *SEND*'s role as an authority in the field, who provides and shapes knowledge on SE in Germany. In this way, *SEND* contributes to what is 'commonly' understood as SE. Furthermore, some articles are either an interview (A_249) with leading *SEND* figures, or a guest contribution by them (A_327; A_347).

Apart from its role as explainer of SE, *SEND* appears in a few other ways in the newspapers. One way is linked to classic lobbying activities: in these instances, *SEND* appears putting forward demands to support the interests of social enterprises and trying to create awareness for SE (e.g., A_210, A_249, A_265, A_293). *SEND* criticises the lack of political support for SE in Germany and reminds governments of their commitment to SE that had been promised in different coalition agreements (see Chapter 2). In 2020, the *COVID-19* pandemic is an important topic – as *SEND* attempts to advocate for financial support for social enterprises affected by the crisis.[11] A_260 quotes a survey conducted by *SEND*, stating that 85 per cent of social enterprises are facing existential threats. In A_265, *SEND*'s Katrin Elsemann explains that existing support programmes are not suitable for social enterprises:

> "So far, the *KfW* loans were not able to reach our target group," says Katrin Elsemann, Managing Director of the *Social Entrepreneurship Network Germany* (*SEND*). Either because they haven't been on the market for long enough or because they do not make large profits due to their social orientation. (...) Given that [social enterprises] usually only barely break even, loans that have to be repaid are often not an option (A_265_Süddeutsche Zeitung_08.07.2020).

Various articles demonstrate that *SEND* was quickly able to gain political attention. Even the first article mentioning *SEND* (A_196) reports on *SEND*'s *Monitor* that is being presented to the public in the *Bundestag*. Being able to present SE in this context (i.e., at the national parliament) seems like a

11 Apart from *SEND*, social entrepreneur Andreas Heinecke, head of *Dialog im Dunkeln*, who also appeared in previous years (see Chapters 4 and 5), is quoted in several articles. Heinecke, too, tries to raise awareness for social enterprises affected by the consequences of the pandemic.

remarkable lobbying success. A_218 substantiates this view, attributing the appearance of the term 'social entrepreneurship' in the coalition agreement of 2018 (see also Chapter 2) to the work of the organisation (A_218_Landshuter Zeitung_19.06.2019). *SEND* also collaborates in two official government programmes on *Bundesländer* level: the '*Sozialinnovator*' in Hesse and 'Social Economy Berlin' (also see Chapter 2). This demonstrates that today, policymakers and public administrations widely seem to recognise *SEND* as the representative (and 'voice') of the SE field.

Overall, the media representation shows that *SEND* has a quite dominant role in the (later) third period. However, this does seem to lead to the fact that *SEND*'s understanding of SE is becoming dominant as well – different than *Ashoka* and its take on SE in the first period (see Chapter 4). As this section has demonstrated, so far, no uniform understanding of SE has developed in Germany. At times, the SE term and concept appears quite vague and arbitrary – sometimes even more so than in previous years.

6.6 Politics of and beyond Social Entrepreneurship

In Chapter 2 and throughout this chapter, I have already argued that in the third period, SE is gaining more attention in the realm of politics. Furthermore, the previous section has explained the emergence of *SEND* as a new and important actor. At times, *SEND* also engages in topics and debates that, arguably, go beyond SE, as will be addressed in this section.

From 2019, *SEND* appears in several articles linked to a debate on so-called 'dormant' bank accounts – i.e., accounts of deceased people that have not been claimed for years. Following international examples, including the UK's *Big Society Capital*, among others, *SEND* proposes to use the money of these dormant bank accounts to establish a 'social investment' fund for social enterprises. *SEND* has managed to position itself as a political actor at the centre of this debate and appears next to other actors, e.g., as a counterpart to the *Association of German Banks* and as an ally of the *Association for Heir Finders*, as described in A_237:

> [*SEND*] is aiming for a new legal regulation and calls for the funds from the 'ownerless' accounts to be invested in social funds in the future and used for charitable purposes. The idea is not new: In Great Britain, banks have been transferring the money from such accounts to funds for over ten years

> if no one has claimed it after 15 years. Katrin Elsemann, Managing Director of *SEND*: "Germany is the only country among the G7 where there is no legal regulation for dealing with dormant assets." The *SEND* network is committed to promoting social and societal innovations and sees such funds as an opportunity to further promote social entrepreneurship. (...) However, the *Association of German Banks* is critical of this (...). The *Association for Heir Finders*, on the other hand, supports the network's demand (A_237_Kölner Express_17.10.2019).

This is an example of *SEND* actively trying to shape politics and policy and bringing awareness to a certain topic, i.e., engaging in political agenda setting. What is more, I argue that this engagement, strictly speaking, goes beyond the narrow field of SE.

Of course, *SEND* is suggesting that these 'dormant' funds should be invested in the SE sector, seeking to increase the amount of capital going into it. However, proposing an idea for where the government shall raise money seems unusual – and, arguably, goes beyond lobbying for the SE field as such. What is more, the idea of accessing these dormant bank accounts may be decoupled from the use of the funds that *SEND* envisions. This can be observed in A_263, where this topic appears in a more general context of increasing the state's revenues following the pandemic, which has put public households under stress:

> Combating the economic consequences of the coronavirus pandemic is becoming expensive: Federal Finance Minister Olaf Scholz has budgeted 1,200 billion euros for direct aid, loans and guarantees. For this purpose, Germany is taking on new debts for the time being – if the Federal Republic wants to repay them, it will need a lot of money. The taxpayers would then have to pay for it, and with it the many average-earning private households, the wealthy and the companies. Those who obey the law. But why not look elsewhere, among criminals and tax dodgers? Six suggestions for where the finance minister could raise a lot of money (...) (A_263_Süddeutsche Zeitung 16. /17.05.2020).

The dormant bank accounts are then proposed as one of these six policy solutions (among others, e.g., combating tax evasion or taxing forex trading). Therefore, in this example, the idea to access dormant bank accounts is introduced as a means to raise money for the state in general, but not necessarily with *SEND*'s purpose in mind, i.e., spending these funds to support SE.

There are other instances, in which *SEND* representatives make political claims that go beyond topics directly related to lobbying for social enterprises. Most notably, this was found in A_249, in an interview with Markus Sauerhammer, chairman of the board of directors of *SEND*, who calls for a more active role of the state in ensuring that businesses would take ecological and social aspects into account. Sauerhammer explains:

> The state has an enormous influence because it provides the framework. Currently, the market externalises ecological and social costs, i.e., they are not included. If we don't create a framework that includes these social and ecological issues, then many companies will continue to pretend that they are doing something about social problems (A_249_Berliner Morgenpost_16.12.2019).

The interviewer then asks what this framework should look like – to what Sauerhammer responds:

> The CO_2 tax is a building block. It is right to give climate-damaging substances a price and also to make it clear that this will become more expensive. (...) A framework on social conditions, such as the minimum wage, is just as important. However, it is important not only to look outside our own front door, but to think in terms of global value chains (ibid.).

This perspective is interesting. A CO_2 tax, the minimum wage (which is still a rather new instrument in Germany, having been introduced only in 2015) as well as the regulation of global value chains are all policy proposals that certainly go beyond a narrow understanding of lobbying for SE. In demanding a regulatory framework that is favourable for social enterprises, Sauerhammer ultimately proposes instruments that aim at a transformation of the economy or society as a whole. On the one hand, this regulation is aimed at establishing conditions that allow social enterprises to flourish. It should help to level the playing field for social enterprises (against) traditional commercial businesses. However, these regulations would also force traditional for-profit businesses to comply to certain social and environmental standards. In this perspective thus, SE is presented as an example that should be guiding the development for *all* businesses – what Sauerhammer calls 'transformation aid':

> (...) the pioneering work starts on a small scale. In my view, social entrepreneurship also has a lot to do with transformation aid. These compa-

> nies prove that something works and the established players are looking closely (ibid.).

Furthermore, the arguments put forward in these quotes entail a critique of commercial businesses and of the economic model. 'Externalities', i.e., the ecological and social costs that are caused by business activity and externalised by the market, are presented as a problem – one that SE shall help to overcome.

What is more, the *SEND* representative in the interview demands regulation and a more active role of the state. This demand by actors of the SE field is interesting – and, arguably, stands in a stark contrast to the media representation in the first period, when the state was pictured as widely incapable of effectively addressing social challenges. This should better be left to private actors, so the widespread view (see Chapter 4). Instead, the perspective shared here sees the state as a powerful and important actor – and one that is a (potential) partner of the SE movement.

In A_327, two other *SEND* representatives address topics that go beyond a narrow understanding of lobbying for SE. In a joint guest contribution, Katrin Elsemann (managing director of *SEND*) and Laura Haverkamp (active both at *Ashoka* and *SEND*) put forward a few proposals (however, remaining a little more abstract than Sauerhammer above). They criticise the fact that large parts of society seem to assume that technology is supposed to be able to solve social problems. Instead, they propose a stronger focus on 'social innovation':

> We will not succeed in changing nutrition if we do not change our attitude towards food. Innovation also lies in bringing children closer to nature, in creating value chains for non-standardised food, or in reviving the public commons. We will not succeed in changing mobility if we do not rethink the relationship between work and life. (...) We will not succeed in protecting the climate if we do not show routes of alternative consumption, get people excited about climate protection and protect them with new agricultural concepts (A_327_taz_14.09.2021).

Furthermore, they criticise that:

> As long as we only measure growth in monetary terms, we lose sight of what is being destroyed – the social and ecological costs that are passed on to the general public. And we don't recognize the value we create for the common good (A_327_taz_14.09.2021).

Similar to the example from A_249 thus, the authors part from a critical perspective, addressing the social and environmental costs caused by business activity (externalities). SE, on the other hand, is presented as a concept that offers a more holistic view on progress and development. In addition, Elsemann and Haverkamp, too, see the role of SE as a pioneer that should serve as an example for the economy and society as a whole:

> Imagine if we lived in a society where progress would be measured by the planet and people's well-being (including as many people as possible). A society that would promote added value and prevent damaging practices. In a society in which we would start and manage companies and organisations around the idea of contributing to an egalitarian, sustainable and inclusive world (A_327_taz_14.09.2021).

To some extent, Elsemann and Haverkamp are promoting the idea of SE here – engaging in classic lobbying work. However, they also offer a more general vision for the economy and society. Their focus is not limited to the SE niche. Instead, they make recommendations for change in the economic system as a whole and for the logics and principles, according to which businesses should be organised.

There are other specific examples in which either *SEND* (representatives) or social entrepreneurs engage in certain political issues (which go beyond SE as such). Article A_233 reports on the *Fridays for Future* strikes in September 2019 – and briefly quotes a *SEND* representative, who is participating in the protests. A_283 mentions the political activism of the founders of *Einhorn*, arguably, some of the best-known social entrepreneurs in Germany, who have been involved in different public campaigns and causes. One of their political engagements was participating in a campaign with the aim to lower taxes for menstruation products (A_283_Sächsische Zeitung_17.11.2020), calling out the gender discrimination related to this taxation practice.[12]

An interesting perspective is offered in A_242. The article claims that entrepreneurs in general – not only social entrepreneurs – are increasingly concerned with social and environmental causes and that they would even support

12 Before 2020, menstruation products in Germany were taxed with the regular consumption tax rate of 19% instead of the reduced rate of 7% that applies for products of basic need, such as food, etc. (Tagesschau 2019).

more regulation in these areas. The article is based on the findings of a study (the *German Start-up Monitor*), which found the following:

> It was also shown (...) that 'green' and social topics are becoming increasingly important for founders: 36 percent see themselves as part of the Green Economy or of social entrepreneurship ('soziales Unternehmertum'). And when it comes to the expectations of politics, after the classics of reducing bureaucracy and support in raising capital, the third place on the wish list is a better promotion of the commitment to environmental protection and social sustainability. This point was even more important to the respondents than the expansion of broadband and 5G networks (A_242_Potsdamer Neueste Nachrichten_05.11.2019).

In addition, the article tries to substantiate the claim that entrepreneurs are increasingly concerned with social and environmental issues with the voting preferences of the entrepreneurs. Among the surveyed, most entrepreneurs favour the *Green Party* (*Bündnis 90/Die Grünen*) with 43.6%, followed by the liberal *FDP* with 27,7% and the conservative *CDU* with 11,7% (A_242_Potsdamer Neueste Nachrichten_05.11.2019).This (new) link between the German *Green Party* and entrepreneurship is an interesting hypothesis, but exploring it would certainly go beyond the scope of my research. However, when it comes to SE, the media representation in the third period, indeed, seems to suggest that the *Green Party* is the main supporter of SE (among the main political parties in Germany).

As I have mentioned throughout the chapter, policymakers start showing interest for SE in the third period – and they begin to appear in the analysed newspaper articles. In some instances, policymakers simply express their support for SE. This includes policymakers of different parties, e.g., Berlin's State Secretary for Economic Affairs (*Staatssekretär*), Christian Rickerts (who is not a party member, but was appointed by the *Green Party*) in A_230, the Commissioner for the Digital Economy and Start-ups at the Federal Ministry of Economic Affairs, Thomas Jarzombek (*CDU*) in A_234, or two members of the *Bundestag*, Andreas Lenz (of the *CSU*, which is the conservative *CDU*'s sister party in Bavaria) and Sabine Poschmann (of the social democratic *SPD*) in A_258. Several politicians show support for financial aids for social enterprises during the *COVID-19* pandemic, including *Bundestag* member Dieter Janecek of the *Green Party* in A_260, the parliamentary group of the *Green Party* in A_261 and Rolf Mützenich of the *SPD* (in both A_261 and A_265).

Furthermore, policymakers appear in the newspaper articles around specific policies – most importantly around the two programmes introduced on *Bundesländer* level in 2020: '*Sozialinnovator*' in Hesse and 'Social Economy Berlin' (see also Chapter 2). In A_269, the '*Sozialinnovator*' programme in Hesse is described as the initiative of Kaya Kinkel, a *Green* member of the state parliament (*Landtag*):

> The state of Hesse has also recognised the potential of social enterprises (...). Following an initiative by state parliament member Kaya Kinkel (*Bündnis 90/ Die Grünen*), the state of Hesse was the first federal state to develop a support programme tailored to social entrepreneurs. "With this funding programme, we have the opportunity to identify and promote social innovation here in Hesse," says Kaya Kinkel (A_269_Giessener Anzeiger_22.08.2020).

In A_281, Ramona Pop, Senator of Economic Affairs of Berlin (for the *Green Party*) is quoted, announcing the 'Social Economy Berlin' programme (A_281_Potsdamer Neueste Nachrichten_06.11.2020). Pop has also appeared earlier (in A_257), proclaiming that some of the funding programmes of the *Investitionsbank Berlin* (*IBB*), the business development bank of the state of Berlin, would be opened for social entrepreneurs.

Furthermore, several politicians appear in the corpus related to some of the proposals by *SEND* – above all, in the debate on dormant bank accounts that was addressed earlier in this section.[13] Once more, the earliest and most direct support seems to come from the *Green Party*. The first article (in the corpus) that addresses this topic, A_237, reports:

> The handling of dormant accounts is (...) also being discussed in politics. The Greens recently made a small enquiry [*kleine Anfrage*] on the subject. In it, the parliamentary group asked to what extent the concept of a population register, which already exists in Great Britain, could be transferred to Germany (A_237_Kölner Express_17.10.2019).

---

13 Two articles (A_241 and A_244) also briefly address part of the policy history of the dormant bank accounts. Regardless of the intentions for how to spend the funds, there had been attempts by German politicians to access these. An attempt had been made in the state parliament of North Rhine-Westphalia in 2016 by the *SPD* and the *Green Party*, as A_241 explains. According to A_244, it was the *SPD*'s Norbert Walter-Borjans who had a leading role in the matter – at the time, however, without success (A_244_Solinger Morgenpost_09.11.2019).

A_239 claims that *SEND*'s Markus Sauerhammer is supported by Lisa Paus of the *Green Party*. Sauerhammer is quoted, reminding the federal government of its commitment to better support SE:

> "In the coalition agreement, the governing parties have agreed to give more support to social entrepreneurs and social innovations" (A_239_Der Tagesspiegel_20.10.2019).

The article then brings in Paus's statement:[14]

> The *Green* politician Paus sees it similarly. "Societally relevant projects in the areas of education, climate protection or integration often lack the appropriate funding," she says. "Here you could create a useful addition and without burdening the federal budget." (ibid.).

Over time, politicians of other parties join in, too. By 2020, the *FDP* also supports funding social enterprises through dormant bank accounts, as reported in A_265 and A_279. A_279 mentions Lower Saxony's Finance Minister Reinhold Hilbers's (*CDU*), who supports a register for these accounts (which is a necessary first step for this policy). But the earliest and clearest support had been coming from (members of) the *Green Party*. In A_313, *SEND* and the *Green Party* are even mentioned in the same breath, making it almost seem as if the social investment fund would be somewhat of a joint policy proposal of the two actors:

> Since there is so much forgotten money in the banks in Germany, social entrepreneurs from the *Social Entrepreneurship Network Germany* (*SEND*) and the *Green Party*, among others, as early as in the end of 2019 called for taking the British as an example. If no one accesses an account there within 15 years, the assets are attributed to a non-profit development bank and used for social purposes (313_Nürnberger Nachrichten_15.07.2021).

---

14 Arguably, Paus in the quote does not necessarily commit to spending the funds for the support of SE – her phrasing of the situation is more general, for example, also leaving the door open for using these funds for different (public) purposes. Nonetheless, the article is constructed in a way that signals that *SEND*'s proposal is fully supported by Paus's quote.

In the wake of the state parliament elections in Baden-Württemberg, A_292 reports on the different election manifestos of the major political parties (*CDU, SPD, FDP, Green Party, Die Linke*), focusing on economic policy. Once more, the *Green Party* is highlighted. According to the article, the *Green Party*'s manifesto most explicitly addresses starting-up and entrepreneurship – and it is the only party that mentions a particular focus on SE (as reported in A_292).

A_308 establishes a link between the *Green Party* and SE at the municipal level. Andreas Eichenseher, a *Green* City Council of Bamberg, is quoted here, declaring that

> A 'green' vision for Bamberg's economy is the promotion of 'Social Entrepreneurship' (A_308_Fränkischer Tag_14.06.2021).

These examples suggest that SE seems to fit well into the economic policy agenda of the German *Green Party*. However, these examples are still few – and often tied to individuals, not necessarily to a systematic, large-scale policy strategy. Therefore, it would be too early to make assumptions about potential political 'alliances' at this point – and this would certainly go beyond the analysis on which this book is based.

A different example was found in A_334: here it is a leading politician of the *FDP*, who embraces SE. In a guest contribution, Thomas Sattelberger (*FDP*), Parliamentary State Secretary (*Parlamentarischer Staatssekretär*) in the *Federal Ministry of Education and Research* proposes 10 points for Germany's future as an 'innovative nation' ("*Innovationsnation*") (A_334_Handelsblatt_19.10.2021).[15] Sattelberger, whose ministry later also appointed social entrepreneur Zarah Bruhn as Special Envoy for Social Innovation calls for giving the German 'Social Market Economy' an update ("*Update der Sozialen Marktwirtschaft*"). He puts forward 10 policy proposals. One of the 10 points consists in more support for SE and in using funds from dormant bank accounts for this purpose. Most probably, due to the support by leading politicians of the *Green Party* and of the *FDP*, the idea of accessing dormant bank accounts also made it into the coalition agreement between *SPD, Green Party* and *FDP* a few months later, in December 2021 (Scheper 2021).

15 A few months later, after the *Bundestag* election of 2021, Sattelberger became Parliamentary State Secretary (*Parlamentarischer Staatssekretär*) in the FDP-led *Federal Ministry of Education and Research*. Sattelberger was also quoted in Chapter 5, appearing as an 'MBA critic' and manager (before he became a politician).

This section has included a few examples of policymakers linking SE to a specific geography (Germany as a whole, or a certain region or city) as well as to a certain vision about the economy – e.g., the 'Social Market Economy' by Thomas Sattelberger (*FDP*), or a 'green vision for Bamberg's economy' by Andreas Eichenseher (*Green Party*). These narratives that seek to embed SE as part of or as a driver of a specific regional (economic) model will be explored in the next section.

6.7 Social Entrepreneurship as Part of a Regional (Economic) Model?

Throughout this chapter, several aspects have been pointed out that indicate a stronger connection in the third period between SE and 'place', i.e., Germany as a country, or certain regions or cities. This includes the involvement of regional economic development agencies (or banks) that increasingly seek to promote SE. Different actors on the city-level, e.g., in Giessen (in A_269), Göttingen (A_206), or Bamberg (A_268), now appear involved in SE. Two states (*Bundesländer*) have launched programmes to support SE: the '*Sozialinnovator*' in Hesse and 'Social Economy Berlin'. SE can now (also) be found at public German universities in different regions (see Section 6.4). All these are factors not only of the institutionalisation of SE, but also of a certain geographical spreading out of SE in Germany. However, I argue that this development entails much more than just place or geography. In the third period, SE is sometimes embedded in a specific local or regional (economic) development narrative and linked to the economic model of this particular place, as this section is going to explore.

In the third period (2015–2021), different actors, who seem to have noticed SE as an attractive concept for local and regional (economic) development and planning, link SE to their specific locality or region. Apparently, SE offers different actors (such as state governments) the opportunity to cast a positive light on their local and regional economy, showing that their region is relevant for SE and that they are promoting the SE idea. This was found in the analysis, most explicitly, for Berlin. For example, Senator Ramona Pop (*Green Party*) tries to create a narrative of Berlin as a SE pioneer, when announcing that certain (funding) programmes of the *Investitionsbank Berlin* (*IBB*) have been opened for social entrepreneurs:[16]

> "Berlin is a pioneer here too: among the German federal states, Berlin is the number one for companies in the social economy. I am pleased that we can now also support social entrepreneurs with their innovative ideas as part of economic development," explained Economics Senator Ramona Pop (*Green Party*) (A_257_Berliner Morgenpost_15.02.2020).

The narrative of Berlin as a particularly relevant and promising place for SE is also promoted by the chairman of the management board of the *Investitionsbank Berlin* (*IBB*), Jürgen Allerkamp, in a guest contribution (A_219):

> (...) the number of companies that are not primarily profit-oriented is growing. The topic is very trendy. (...) Berlin is at the forefront. In times when the socialisation of real estate is being debated – which we as *IBB* consider wrong –, young people demonstrate every Friday for a climate-friendly future and Berlin is trying to manage the transport transition, the capital presents itself as the spearhead of a social movement (A_219_Börsen-Zeitung_22.06.2019).

It is remarkable that Allerkamp connects (the funding for) SE to Berlin specifically – and he also alludes to other current topics of public interest and activism. Clearly, he presents an understanding of SE as 'more' than entrepreneurship and as 'more' than economic development. However, Allerkamp also delimits SE from other types of activism or causes, namely, from the 'socialisation of real estate'.[17] It could be argued that SE is presented as a 'proper' or acceptable form of activism here – against more radical forms of activism, such as the 'socialisation of real estate'.

A_230, too, links SE to Berlin and mentions the state government's plans to make Berlin a 'capital for social entrepreneurs'.[18] The State Secretary

16 The opening of some of the *IBB*'s programmes for social enterprises was already addressed in 6.4.

17 With the 'socialization of real estate', Allerkamp refers to a current debate around a campaign in Berlin that seeks to force large private housing companies (*Deutsche Wohnen* and others) to sell property to the state of Berlin. Still, it is interesting that Allerkamp uses the term 'socialisation' and not 'expropriation'. In this debate, the former is usually used by the supporters of the campaign and the latter by its opponents.

18 Prior to *Social Economy Berlin*, there was also a short pilot programme initiated by the Berlin Senate called *Social Innovation Capital* (SenWEB 2020).

(*Staatssekretär*) of the State Department for Economic Affairs, Christian Rickerts, presents his vision for SE in Berlin. Rickerts explains that the state government plans to make Berlin a 'capital' for social entrepreneurship and social innovation – and that the city can build on a long tradition to achieve this:

> According to Rickerts, social entrepreneurship offers the perspective of directing entrepreneurial activity to the big questions of the time. "The purpose of the company should therefore help to prevent social injustice or global environmental destruction. In most cases, profit maximization takes second place," explained the politician (...). Berlin already has a long tradition of social enterprises. For example, since 1992, the *Weiberwirtschaft* on Anklamer Strasse in the Mitte district has been helping women to gain a foothold as entrepreneurs in a business world that is still often dominated by men. The non-profit company *Pfefferwerk Stadtkultur* has also been one of the city's social enterprises since 1991 and operates 17 day-care centres, among other things. "Berlin has long been a place for trying to improve the world," Rickerts summarized (A_230_Berliner Morgenpost_01.09.2019).

Apart from linking SE to Berlin as a specific place, this testament is interesting because Rickerts not only alludes to 'social injustice' and 'global environmental destruction', but also embeds SE into a more general social economy or social enterprise tradition. He refers to *Pfefferwerk Stadtkultur* and to the *Weiberwirtschaft*, which according to Birkhölzer's (2015: 4–24) typology may be classified as a 'socio-cultural centre' (*Sozio-kulturelle Zentren*) and a 'self-managed enterprise resulted of alternative and women's movements' (*Selbstverwaltete Alternativ- und Frauenbetriebe*) respectively, which have developed in a different historical and political context than the current SE term and movement (also see Chapter 2). However, in the article the commonalities and not the differences between the various social economy or social enterprise movements are stressed. SE is thus, presented as the continuation of an alternative economy scene and movement in Berlin. In fact, the 'Social Economy Berlin' programme that was introduced by the Berlin Senate one year after this article (A_230) seems to follow this approach. It carries the 'social economy' term in its name and it brings actors from different (historical) social economy movements together (which I will briefly discuss in Chapter 7, as this goes beyond the analysis of the newspaper articles).

This narrative of Berlin as an important and promising place for SE, is also promoted by actors other than government, including *SEND*. The interview with Markus Sauerhammer (A_249) discussed above even states this in the headline:

> "BERLIN IS A HOTSPOT FOR SOCIAL ENTREPRENEURSHIP" (A_249_Berliner Morgenpost_16.12.2019).

Sauerhammer boldly claims that:

> Berlin is already the global hotspot for social entrepreneurship, although Germany as a whole fell far behind the other economically strongest nations in the world in the most recently published study 'The Best Country to Be a Social Entrepreneur'. In Berlin, however, we suddenly have good ground. This is also due to the history of this city. Communism and capitalism met here, people from East and West live together here today and bring different perspectives to the discussion. Here, the world is not black or white. Berlin is also a digital centre, which means that there are also many people who come to this city specifically because of this transformation process. This creates a mixture for future- and solution-oriented thinking that other places do not have (ibid.).

In another article (A_257), *SEND* repeats this claim of Berlin as the centre for SE in Germany, making use of the same 'hotspot' phrase again and substantiating it with findings from its yearly study: the (second) *Deutscher Social Entrepreneurship Monitor*. In addition, Sauerhammer is quoted in the article, welcoming the efforts of the state government to support SE in Berlin (A_257_Berliner Morgenpost_15.02.2020).

In the analysed articles, other regions and cities appear linked to SE as well. This includes e.g., Bamberg in A_308, Stuttgart in A_185, or Lower Bavaria (*Niederbayern*) in A_228 and A_326. A_228 also mentions that the Lower Bavaria region has received a title as 'European Social Economy Region' by the *European Commission* and highlights the importance of SE for regional development – in rural areas in particular. The importance of SE for rural areas is also stressed in A_214, announcing an event discussing SE in Saxony-Anhalt.

I argue that these narratives that link SE to specific places in Germany (or to Germany itself) are remarkable and that they can be seen as more than just location or regional marketing (which is certainly also an aspect of it). To an extent, they also represent a 'geographical shift' as compared to other periods –

one that goes beyond portraying a few examples for SE, in order to show that SE exists in Germany (too), which was a theme that developed from the middle of the first period (see Chapter 4). Instead, in the third period, SE is now being presented as a phenomenon that has 'genuinely' emerged from Berlin or Germany – and that it is rooted in a particular socio-economic and political tradition. These narratives, therefore, entail more than the geographical spreading out and the institutionalisation of SE in Germany, because they also establish a link between SE and the local or regional (context-specific) economic model.

Furthermore, the value statements that are made on different economic and social models have changed over the years. In the first period (1999–2008), SE mainly appears linked to the economic and social model of the US. The German model was described as backwards and in need of reform, in order to become more like the US model (see Chapter 4). This is very different in the third period (2015–2021): the German model (or the local economy of certain places such as Berlin) is now often presented as the 'better' version (and vision) for economic development. The US model, on the other hand, seems to have widely lost its appeal in the media representation. The newspapers no longer present the US as a positive role model for economic and social development. Quite the contrary, the US model – and Silicon Valley in particular – is now often referred to in a negative way, as a 'bad' example and counterpart to the model offered by Berlin or Germany.

This change in perspective can be clearly observed in the corpus in the references to Silicon Valley, which differ considerably across the different periods. During the first period, Silicon Valley was mainly presented as a positive example – as, for example, in A_1, where Silicon Valley also serves as a point of reference to explain SE:[19]

> "It [SE] combines the passion for a social goal with the discipline, innovative spirit and willpower that we know from young entrepreneurs in Silicon Valley." (A_1_Die Zeit_ 08.04.1999).

On the other hand, the image and the judgement of Silicon Valley that is portrayed in the newspaper articles is quite different in the third period. In A_207, a social entrepreneur is paraphrased who clearly differentiates between SE – which he considers to be a 'Berlin' phenomenon – and commercial entrepreneurship, which he associates with Silicon Valley:

19 Here, the article quotes the business scholar Gregory Dees.

> He [the social entrepreneur] thinks that pure capitalism is stupid. Berlin is not like Silicon Valley, but a place of the "hippie tech scene": a community of young people who play in the big game, but with social awareness and the will to change things (A_207_taz.die tageszeitung_13.04.2019).

As explained above, a link is therefore established between SE, the place and the local or regional (context-specific) economic model. A_185 offers a similar view. The article makes a contrast between two different models: Stuttgart (which according to the article relies on SE) and, on the other hand, Silicon Valley:

> (...) that is the specific start-up location in Stuttgart. Social entrepreneurship with reference to the Swabian tradition – as a clear antithesis to Silicon Valley (A_185_Süddeutsche Zeitung_31.07.2018).

A_186 focuses on Dublin, which is said to have become the 'European Silicon Valley'. The article addresses the striking inequalities in the city, where some have high-paying jobs in the tech world and are living comfortable and cosmopolitan lives, while others struggle – a situation that has been reinforced by the financial crisis of 2008, as the article reports. A social entrepreneur, co-founder of the social enterprise *Fumbally Exchange*, is then introduced to the story, who seeks to combat the high level of inequality in Dublin:

> So, she got active. With others (...) she founded the co-working space *Fumbally Exchange*. The goal: to earn money, but at the same time to support society. It is a counter-model to turbo capitalism. She calls the approach 'social entrepreneurship' (...). Their idea: companies not only work for their own balance sheet, but also to give something back to the community. Profits should be reinvested to promote social projects (...) (A_186_Süddeutsche Zeitung_21.08.2018).

In this example thus, SE is directly and explicitly presented as an alternative (model) to the model of 'turbo capitalism' – which the article associates with Silicon Valley.

As I have previously mentioned, several newspaper articles establish a connection between SE and Germany's economic and social model, more generally – i.e., beyond the level of the local or regional economy, as it was often the case in the examples above. This includes references to the German 'Social Market Economy' (*Soziale Marktwirtschaft*). The concept of the 'Social Market Economy' (SME) is complex and contested – and discussing it in detail would go beyond the scope of the discussion here. However, it should be noted here that in public, political and media debates in Germany the 'Social Market Economy' does not necessarily refer to the ordoliberal economic policies or the economic theory promoted by (the early) SME thinkers – which Bonefeld (2012), among others, has summarised concisely. Instead, as Nonhoff (2006) explains, the SME mainly serves as a (vague) idea of an economy that responds to people's needs. The 'social' is then understood in non-capitalised letters – similar to its meaning in the context of social entrepreneurship, which I have discussed in Section 1.2. This notion of the 'social', of course, may then be interpreted in many different ways (by different actors).

This being said, several articles try to establish a connection between SE and the idea of a SME. Section 6.6 has mentioned that Thomas Sattelberger in A_334 proposes SE as an opportunity to give the Social Market Economy an 'update'. Another example is A_219, which was already quoted above. Allerkamp of the economic development bank *IBB* makes use of the SME *motif* here, writing:

> In the anniversary year of the *Grundgesetz* [the German constitution], which formed the framework for the success story of the Social Market Economy, social entrepreneurship is a strong symbol. If we remind ourselves that property shall result in a particular obligation [to society], the Social Market Economy will continue to contribute to the well-being and prosperity of our country (A_219_Börsen-Zeitung_22.06.2019).

SEND's Sauerhammer in A_249, also invokes this idea, embedding SE in the German SME tradition:

> In the early days of the Social Market Economy, Germany was basically a social innovator. At that time, cooperatives came into being, as did welfare organizations and trade unions. Health insurance, accident insurance and old-age provision also date from that time (A_249_Berliner Morgenpost_16.12.2019).

Thus, Sauerhammer not only establishes a link to older social economy movements (cooperatives and welfare associations) and to trade unions. He also links SE to social security provision and, therefore, to a specific welfare system.[20] Furthermore, the features of the German welfare system are positively

20 This quote is also an example for what I have mentioned a few paragraphs earlier, namely that popular references to the 'Social Market Economy' in Germany often re-

connoted in this statement – which, once more, marks a stark contrast to the common tenor of the first period (1999–2008), when Germany's economy and social security system both were mostly portrayed as inefficient or even deficient.

A_256, too, establishes a link between the German SME and SE. The article calls for a better regulation of markets by the state. SE is introduced as an opportunity to 'revive' the SME tradition and as an example and source of inspiration for policy proposals. Next to SE, the article mentions the *European Green Deal*, the *Fridays for Future* strikes and the government's plans to phase-out of coal power (A_256_Die Zeit_13.02.2020). In this perspective, SE is presented as some sort of role model, on which the state may base on regulation and policy. This view is quite similar to the idea of SE as 'transformation aid' that was discussed in Section 6.6.

6.8 Overlaps with Other Concepts: More 'Confusion' and Ambiguity than Ever?

The previous section demonstrated that SE is sometimes related to other concepts. So far, I have addressed the 'social economy' (e.g., around the 'Social Economy Berlin' programme) and the idea of the 'Social Market Economy'. In addition, in the third period, SE often stands next to 'entrepreneurship' – and, sometimes, SE even appears integrated or subsumed under an idea of 'entrepreneurship' (as I have explained throughout this chapter). Strictly speaking, the relationship between SE and other ideas, concepts or *leitmotifs* goes somewhat beyond the scope of my research. Based on Birkhölzer (2015), my empirical analysis has deliberately remained close to the 'social entrepreneurship' term. Nonetheless, this section should briefly mention the fact that, in the analysed articles, SE frequently appears next to other terms and concepts, which seem to have overlaps and (potential) intersections with SE. Apart from 'entrepreneurship', the 'social economy' and the 'SME' (which were already addressed), this includes 'sustainability' and 'social innovation', among others.

'Sustainability' is another important term and concept , which appears to intersect with SE on multiple occasions. Sustainability and sustainable devel-

main vague, roughly referring to an idea of an economy that is somehow 'more social' than pure capitalism (also see Nonhoff 2006).

opment are, in fact, mentioned in the articles in all three periods. In the first period, already 7 of 35 articles name 'sustainability' or derivatives of the term. This slightly increases over time: 28 of 76 articles in the second period and 106 articles of 238 in the third period connect SE and sustainability. Perhaps, this seems little surprising, given that the language of sustainability has been integrated into policy discourse and even into everyday language since the late 1980s (Redclift 2005). Arguably, the term and concept of sustainability and sustainable development have gained popularity and relevance ever since (Brand & Wissen 2017). Right at the beginning of the third period (in 2015), the *United Nations* agreed on and introduced the historic 17 *Sustainable Development Goals* (*SDGs*) – a significant step in the global sustainable development discourse and agenda. In the analysed articles, the *SDGs*, too, appear as a point of reference and in relationship with SE (e.g., in A_176, A_232, A_289, A_293, A_314).

Another important term and concept that is linked to or that intersects with SE is 'social innovation' (also briefly mentioned in 6.6 and 6.7). What is more (yet, this goes beyond the analysed articles), it appears that 'social innovation' is being picked up by policymakers. The term and the idea of 'social innovation' clearly plays a role in both programmes that promote SE in Germany on the *Bundesländer* level. A short pilot programme and predecessor to 'Social Economy Berlin' was titled 'Social Innovation Capital', and the state programme in Hesse goes by the name '*Sozialinnovator*'. As seen in Section 6.6, leading figures of the SE scene also establish a connection between SE and social innovation. For example, Katrin Elsemann (*SEND*) and Laura Haverkamp (*SEND* and *Ashoka*) argue in A_327 that addressing social challenges requires more than technology, and they propose a stronger focus on 'social innovation'.

Many other terms, ideas, concepts or *leitmotifs* have been found in the corpus. Sometimes, social enterprises have also been labelled as 'green' (e.g., in A_171, A_242) or as 'impact' enterprises (e.g., n A_207, A_293, A_296). The *European Green New Deal* was mentioned as a point of reference in Section 6.7. In both the second and third periods, there are references to *Fair Trade* (e.g., A_70, A_71, A_84, A_137, A_293, A_345). One article (A_274) establishes a link to the *Plural Economics* (*Plurale Ökonomik*) debate and movement, which seeks to challenge mainstream economics education. In a few articles, there are overlaps between SE and the *Gemeinwohl-Ökonomie* (e.g., in A_202). In Birkhölzer's (2015) understanding, the *Gemeinwohl-Ökonomie*, which originated in Austria and is organised in the *International Federation for the Economy for the Common Good e.V.*, could also be considered a recent social economy or social enterprise movement with a distinct identity, shared values and organisational structures.

The list of terms and concepts that overlap or intersect with SE could be continued, but would exceed the scope of the discussion here. My main point was simply to unveil a few of these links and overlaps, which I consider relevant for two reasons. First, they show that SE is (still) contested and malleable – various meanings can be given to SE and this can (also) be achieved by linking SE to other concepts or ideas (such as 'entrepreneurship', 'sustainability' or the 'SME'). Second, it is possible that SE may merge or even be embedded in a different (more powerful) discourse in the future. While this certainly goes beyond my analysis, I believe that it is possible that aspects of SE and other discourses could merge, or that SE could even be absorbed by another – more powerful – concept or discourse (and will explore this further in Chapter 7).

My analysis has demonstrated that despite its growing popularity, SE remains weakly institutionalised in the third period. More actors are emerging in the SE field. Universities, policymakers and regional economic development agencies have gotten (more) involved in SE. First policies to promote SE are being implemented. With the *Social Entrepreneurship Netzwerk Deutschland (SEND)*, social entrepreneurs have established a network and lobby organisation. However, this does not seem to have led to a unified or 'common' understanding of SE in Germany shared by large parts of society. At least, this does not extend to the media and to its representation of SE, which, on the contrary, shows a certain expansion of the SE term. Two main strands of SE were identified in the third period. SE is often understood and presented as (a form of) entrepreneurship, as a 'trend' among founders and as part of the start-up world. On the other hand, SE is understood as a movement that aims at transforming the economy (and society) as a whole. The processes around constructing the meaning(s) of SE are many and ambiguous, and they are ongoing. The 'conceptual confusion' around SE persists – perhaps, it is greater in the third period than ever before.

Chapter 7: On the Rise and on the Move – but where to? Discussion, Reflection and Outlook

7.1 Introduction

The aim of this book is to contribute to a better sociological understanding of the contested concept of social entrepreneurship (SE) in the specific context of Germany between 1999 and 2021. Four main research themes were investigated: ***Diversity and dominance***: exploring different understandings as well as identifying dominant representations of the SE concept. ***Representation and Relevance***: analysing what a broader audience gets to learn about the SE phenomenon, i.e., parts or aspects of SE that are getting noticed by wider society, beyond the niche spaces of the SE scene. ***Development over time***: tracing the evolution of the SE concept in Germany from the late 1990s (when the 'social entrepreneurship' term first started to appear) until the early 2020s (when interest for SE in the German public and politics is starting to increase). ***Notions of 'change' and politics:*** examining the 'change' that SE seeks to achieve and the idea of economy and society that SE envisions and exploring the (potential) societal or political role that is ascribed to SE in Germany, including its relationship to neoliberalism.

For these purposes, relevant literature on SE was reviewed (in Chapters 1 and 2) and the theoretical framework of discourse analysis was explained and operationalised (in Chapter 3), in order to conduct an empirical study of newspaper articles. This research design and choice of data leads to certain limitations of the findings of my research that need to be taken into account. Strictly speaking, the empirical findings are on certain *representations* of SE in newspapers. Therefore, my empirical results mainly refer to a mediated and an 'outside' view on SE. Yet, I argue that these mediatic representations are a valid choice for my research themes and questions. As explained in the Introduction and in Chapter 3, my study is concerned with analysing different understandings of SE but also with identifying dominant versions of SE, in particular, aspects of the SE concept and wider narratives linked to it that receive attention from a broad(er) societal audience. It is, therefore, precisely this 'outside' view on SE that I was principally interested in capturing: i.e., what a broader (or 'mainstream') audience gets to perceive of the SE concept, which ideas of and around SE 'make the news' and reach into wider society.

The central contribution lies in the periodisation: three periods were identified in the analysis: from 1999 to 2008, 2009 to 2014 and 2015 to 2021. Accordingly, the research findings were organised and presented in three results chapters. In this final chapter, I will now summarise the key insights and findings and discuss in which way they contribute to previous academic research. The insights and findings in different ways add to, substantiate, differentiate, exemplify or demonstrate findings of previous scholarship. Some of them challenge or expand previous literature and some are original contributions. In addition, due to certain limitations of my approach, several aspects and themes on which my analysis has touched upon require further or complementary research approaches, as I will outline throughout the chapter.

7.2 The Three Periods in the Social Entrepreneurship (Media) Discourse

Inspired by previous research, mainly from the UK, this book has provided an empirical study on representations of the SE concept and their development in Germany. A key and novel finding of the empirical analysis is the identification of three periods within the investigated two decades: From 1999 until 2008, in which SE was conceptualised mainly as a reform of the welfare infrastructure. From 2009 until 2014, when SE was increasingly seen as part of the economy. In the third period (from 2015), there are two important currents: one views SE simply as 'entrepreneurship' and the other one as transformative for the economy as a whole, as being part of a wider social economy movement, or as part of a certain (regional) economic model. This periodisation and showing how each period comes with different explanations of SE, which are intertwined with wider narratives and different visions for society, is the central contribution of my research. It integrates and synthesises the four research themes outlined above, as summarised in the following table:

Table 9: Periodisation According to the Media Representation of Social Entrepreneurship

Time period and given title	**1999–2008:** SE Coming to the Aid of the 'Sick Man'	**2009–2014:** SE Becoming Part of the Economy	**2015–2021:** SE – Towards an Entrepreneurial Society, or a Transformation of the Economy or Both?
Dominant description(s) of SE	SE as part of welfare production and (reform of) the social infrastructure.	SE as business and part of the economy.	a) SE as a part of the start-up world, a particular form of business (entrepreneurship) and b) SE as a vehicle for deeper societal transformation.
Main sector and fields for SE	Traditional social and public sector (work integration, education).	The economy gains importance (poverty reduction and development, sustainable production and goods, education).	The economy (sustainable production and goods, environmental or climate protection, technology, work integration).
Main target of reform addressed by SE	The traditional social sector and the state and their institutions and ways of functioning	Both the traditional social sector and the state as well as businesses and business logics in the private sector	Both the traditional social sector and the state as well as the private sector
Important narratives	Business methods are presented as overwhelmingly positive and contrasted against a very inefficient or even deficient image of the state and social sector. Heroic individuals with managerial skills are presented as good and necessary examples.	Business methods and techniques are often still presented as valuable. But, at the same time, the perspective that business and business education also require reform (business ethics) gains importance. SE offers an opportunity to provide 'meaningful work'.	Entrepreneurship becomes an end in itself – SE offers an opportunity to develop entrepreneurial skills, and boundaries to commercial entrepreneurship fade. On the other hand, SE is more often linked to a specific model of economic development and to the transformation of the economy as a whole. The state is often presented as a partner for this transformation.

Time period	**1999–2008:**	**2009–2014:**	**2015–2021:**
Link to the wider political and socio-economic environment	Fuelled by high unemployment, public acceptance for neoliberal reform of the labour market and social security is high in Germany during this time period, leading, among other things to the largest reform programme in recent history: the *Agenda 2010*. SE often appears embedded in this particular reform spirit and language at the time.	This period is congruent with the aftermath of the financial crisis of 2008. During this time, the sustainability of the neoliberal economic model is increasingly questioned by different societal actors. Practices in the private sector become a target of critique, albeit this critique mainly remains on an individual and less on a structural or systemic level (e.g., focusing on the behaviour of managers instead of political action).	One the one hand, there is a hype around entrepreneurship and start-ups (including tech companies), all things entrepreneurial are presented as socially desirable. On the other hand, the 'Silicon Valley' model of development is questioned. Critique is more often structural, and linked to debates around sustainability (e.g., the UN's *Sustainable Development Goals*), and SE appears as part of a different model of (economic) development.
Exemplary and illustrative quotes	*When it comes to child care, there are a lot of problems. "There have to be private offers because the state system can no longer or doesn't want to shoulder everything. What the state has to offer is not enough and it is getting worse and worse"* (A_18_Süddeutsche Zeitung_17.11.2006).	*The economic crisis is causing that social entrepreneurship is gaining relevance. More and more MBA students question the previous economic models of profit maximization. "Many want to build careers in a more socially responsible way"* (A_36_ Handelsblatt_06.03.2009).	for a) *One trend [in the start-up scene] are start-ups in the field of social entrepreneurship. Their focus is not on financial gain, but on a social purpose* (A_112_Mittelbayerische Zeitung_12.02.2015). for b) *(...) the pioneering work starts on a small scale (...) social entrepreneurship also has a lot to do with transformation aid. These companies prove that something works and the established players are looking closely* (A_249_Berliner Morgenpost_16.12.2019).

In this way, my research makes an academic contribution mainly in four regards: strengthening sociological research on SE, helping to understand SE in the specific German context based on empirical research, tracing the development of the SE concept over time and (more generally) contributing to the interdisciplinary study of (socio)economic phenomena (in applying discourse analysis to this object of study). The findings of the analysis help for the sociological 'making sense' of SE and contribute to the study of SE as a social and political phenomenon and movement, in this way connecting SE with perspectives and debates in sociology, political economy and socioeconomics. In addition, it reiterates the importance of understanding SE in interplay with its specific political and socio-economic context, and that SE – as well as the research focusing on it – cannot simply be transferred from one place to another.

Yet, despite having highlighted the importance of a context-specific understanding of SE, it should also be noted that there are similarities between SE in Germany and SE in other contexts. For example, my analysis has demonstrated that, similar to the global euphoria about SE, a generally positive view of SE is reproduced in the German media – even though, over time, the reporting on SE becomes more down to earth and realistic. Often, SE is presented as the bearer of positive change – and this is mostly taken for granted instead of evidenced, almost as if it would not require any explanation. This overly positive portrayal of SE and the 'social change' SE is supposed to bring about (regardless of the context) is sometimes mirrored in academic literature, too (as explained in Chapter 1). Similarly, my analysis also supports the claim that SE is receiving more and more attention, which is voiced in SE literature ever since the first publications – at least for Germany in the time frame 1999–2021, in providing (indicative) empirical evidence, namely, in the rising number of newspaper articles (see Graph 1).

For the first period (1999–2008), my analysis has demonstrated that a certain version of SE is predominant in the media in Germany. This includes a portrayal of SE that is, among other things, individualistic and person-centred, focused on the individual social entrepreneur. SE is mainly described as 'new', 'innovative' and 'changemaking'. Social entrepreneurs in the articles are represented as skilled ('exceptional') individuals and appear linked to competitions and awards as well as to members of the business elite, such as Klaus Schwab. In addition, SE is characterised by favouring private and market-based solutions and is often embedded in narratives of welfare reform and state failure (see Chapter 4). Thus, my analysis is also a contribution to substantiate the existing literature (in part theoretical and/or focusing on other contexts) with empirical findings and exemplifies observations of, among others, Dart (2004), Nicholls (2010), Dey & Steyaert (2010), Teasdale (2012), Papi-Thornton (2016) – but for the specific context of Germany, approximately between 1999–2008.

Having identified dominant accounts and narratives of SE for each period should, however, not lead to disregard that SE in Germany (as in other contexts) is and remains a phenomenon or movement that is contested, appearing ambiguous and, at times, incoherent. Explanations of SE and the wider narratives that these are connected to entail normative contradictions (Ranville & Barros 2021). These contradictions may be found within single explanations as well as within the overall SE discourse, as demonstrated in my empirical analysis (see Chapters 4–6). I argue that 'resolving' this conceptual confusion *once and for all* (in the sense of answering what sort of phenomenon SE *really is*) seems impossible and does not seem desirable either. Moreover, my empirical findings are merely based on representations of SE in German newspapers. Other arenas, in which meanings and knowledge around SE is produced will need to be taken into account by future research to grasp an even broader picture of the diversity of meanings and goals associated with SE.

In sum, despite having identified dominant versions of SE in different periods, a central claim of my book is that the meaning(s) of and around SE are dynamic, that they evolve over time and that the contestations of these meanings are ongoing. The three periods shall by no means be viewed as static and clear-cut. In addition, the year numbers should be regarded as indicative – in particular the wider narratives that appear intertwined with the SE concept and that relate to long-term political and socio-economic developments that do not change abruptly from one year to another. There is also a great deal of complexity and ambiguity within the shifts leading from first to second and from second to third period (as the following section is going to discuss).

7.3 Ambiguous Social Entrepreneurship: Criticising *and* Legitimising the Capitalist Economy

SE remains sociologically complex and ambiguous. Despite the dominant SE discourses that were identified during the analysis, which allowed to distinguish the three different periods between 1999 and 2021, it must be noted that across all periods, there are different, to some extent competing, understandings of SE. This also applies for the developments or shifts between and during the periods (or leading from one period to another), as I will reiterate in this section.

In Chapter 5, I have explained the 'sectoral shift', leading from the first to the second period: SE is now increasingly presented as a phenomenon that occurs in the economy, and this perspective is then consolidated in the third period (see Chapter 6). In addition, organisations that compose the SE field (social enterprises) are increasingly conceptualised as businesses (and not merely *like* business) – what may be seen as part of or as an organisational expression of this (sectoral) shift of SE towards the economy. As explained in Chapter 5, this shift entails, on the one hand, aspects of economization, implying a transfer of business logics into social fields and organisations, and, arguably, contributes to the acceptance or 'normalisation' of combining social and economic goals, and that organisations may be able to pursue both at the same time. To some extent, there is a blurring of the boundaries between 'the economic' and 'the social' (e.g., Ridley-Duff & Bull 2011). Institutions in the public or 'social' realm are now more often described with the language and concepts of business, for example, as 'markets'. My analysis thus, shows similarities to the turn to 'social business' described in Nicholls (2010) and in Teasdale (2012). Nicholls (2010) and Teasdale (2012) have identified a shift in the SE discourse in the early 2000s, with SE being increasingly understood as 'business solutions to social problems' (away from SE being rooted in and part of the third sector).[1]

However, my findings also show that 'SE becoming business' is more complex and ambiguous than only injecting business logics into the social realm. This development also introduces new narratives, e.g., foregrounding certain organisational aspects of SE and initiating a more explicit discussion about work, about (decent) pay for social entrepreneurs as well as for their staff and about organisational governance within the SE field, as can be observed in the second and third period. Beyond my empirical analysis, it is also interesting to note here that – taking *SEND* as a reference – organisational governance has found a place in the German SE scene. *SEND*'s definition for SE includes a governance dimension (next to the social and the economic/entrepreneurial dimension), similar to the definition by *EMES* (see Chapter 1). To some extent, this institutionalises the (normative) notion that social enterprises should take aspects of (democratic) organisational governance into account.

1 Mind, however that the context that these authors describe is a different one: SE in England ca. 2001–2005.

Occasionally, the discussion around work and (decent) pay within SE has also been linked to the wider topic of decent pay in 'social' fields, more generally (see Chapter 5). This is a perspective that would be worth exploring in further research. Arguably, there could be an interesting nexus to feminist research around care work and pay in 'social' professions, which is historically and socially constructed as 'female' and remains underpaid (e.g., Gather et al. 2007; Maier 2013). This perspective seems relevant, in particular, as SE is sometimes celebrated as 'female', since there is a higher proportion of women entrepreneurs and leading staff in social enterprises as compared to tech start-ups (e.g., SEND 2022a: 66). In my empirical analysis, this was not yet a major theme, even though a few articles have made an attempt to establish a link between SE and women (entrepreneurship), even in the first period (see Chapter 4). Research that explores these issues, however, should be critical and mind the risk of reproducing gendered stereotypes and power relations in constructing SE as a 'female' version of entrepreneurship.

Alongside discussions of SE as work, SE is sometimes portrayed in a more realistic and balanced way in the newspaper representation. In contrast to articles that only stress the remarkable (almost super-human) skills of social entrepreneurs, these articles mention that social entrepreneurs sometimes experience hardship and that achieving both social and financial success is often difficult (see Section 5.6). These articles also increasingly address that there are different models for SE, e.g., differing in their approach towards profits. Some SE models exclude and others allow profits, and again others prescribe the purposes for which profits may be spent. In addition, the SE discourse then revolves less around the 'exceptional' or even 'heroic' individual social entrepreneur and becomes less person-centred. In line with these developments, *Ashoka* and the *Schwab Foundation* lose their extraordinarily dominant position after the first period, as more actors start to engage with SE.

Moreover, it is now increasingly 'the economy' that is presented as the 'problem' and in need of reform or 'change' – instead of the institutions of the social and public realms, which were the main target of critique and reform in the first period (in line with the *zeitgeist* revolving the *Agenda 2010*). In centring the debate more around business and the economy, a discussion and critique of business and the economy and their practices can be initiated as well. Sometimes, economic principles and practices are challenged, and different (alternative) business methods and practices are proposed. While the glorification of business, its people and methods can still be observed after the first period, it is by far not as evident as it used to be in the first period. The shift towards the economy thus, does not only imply an economisation (organisations becoming more like businesses, adopting the principles of management, etc.), it is also a development that allows a critique of businesses and the economy, as demonstrated in Chapters 5 and 6.

However, it also needs to be noted that the critique of the (neoliberal) economic model often remains somewhat superficial, foregrounding business education and the personal values of a 'new' generation (of students), who now are found to seek 'meaningful' work and to make different career choices, pursuing 'purpose' instead of high salaries. The critique hardly extends to the economic system as such and to what should change about it – let alone are political proposals put forward, in order to achieve structural change in the economy. Paradoxically, the figure of the social entrepreneur then sometimes seems to have a legitimising and stabilising function for (neoliberal) capitalism, even when the articles criticise the capitalist economy. This is possible, because the entrepreneur – and in particular, the social entrepreneur – is presented as a new (ideal) economic figure. As Heidbrink & Seele (2010) have explained, the figure of the manager (especially of banks and other big corporations), which used to be appealing for many, remains widely discredited after the financial crisis of 2008 – which, to some extent, is also mirrored in the news articles (see Chapters 5 and 6). The (social) entrepreneur, on the other hand, personifies the promise that apparently it is still possible to participate in the economy, to 'do business' after the crisis, in a morally acceptable way. Somehow, SE is introduced as a response to problems in the economic model, offering what appears to be a 'quick fix': in becoming (social) entrepreneurs, it seems possible to 'repair' the system. This, however, entails logical fallacies and diverts the discussion away from the systems level onto the individual level. A problem is recognised within the economic system – but the offered solution is not to change the system, but, instead, to become a (social) entrepreneur. Through differentiating 'business administration' from 'entrepreneurship' (e.g., in Faltin 2012) and differentiating their respective protagonists (managers versus entrepreneurs), it becomes possible to criticise the (economic) system, but concentrating the critique on one specific actor (the manager) and then pointing towards a (different) actor in the system – the entrepreneur – as the 'solution'. The critique is then individualised and, ultimately, may have a legitimising and stabilising function for (neoliberal) capitalism.

Legitimacy is an interesting theme within SE – on which, among others, Dart (2004) has made crucial contributions. Dart (2004) has demonstrated that the SE movement has derived legitimacy from appearing similar to business (and acting like business), which according to the neoliberal *zeitgeist* was regarded as a superior form of organisation (e.g., as compared to public institutions). While I have been warning against simply transferring insights from one context to another (in this case: from Dart's observation as a scholar based in Canada to Germany), my empirical analysis was able to show that Dart's (2004) observation widely applies to the German context as well – in the corresponding time period. During the first period (1999–2008), legitimacy *for* SE is established on the ground of SE sharing the (assumed) virtues of private businesses. More importantly, perhaps, as explained above, my research has been able to point out another aspect when it comes to legitimacy: namely, that it is a two-way street and that SE may also, in turn, legitimise the (capitalist) economic model.

7.4 The Importance of the Diversity and the Sector(s) of Social Entrepreneurship

An important finding of my research is the 'sectoral shift' in the German SE discourse between the first and the second period, when the dominant perspective on SE – as portrayed in newspapers – shifted from 'SE as a reform of the social (welfare) infrastructure' to 'SE as part of the economy'. I argue that this shift has revealed the importance of what I call the 'sectoral perspective' or the 'sectoral focus', and that this has, so far, received too little notice in academic literature. Perhaps, this plea for giving more attention to the sectoral perspective (i.e., to 'where' SE is taking place, in which fields or area of society) might apply for contexts other than Germany as well.

What is more, the sectoral perspective – and this specific shift towards the economy – challenges the view of 'SE as welfare reform' that, arguably, is still the main sociological interpretation of SE in academic literature. Based on my empirical findings, I argue that it becomes harder to accept the interpretation of SE as a (neoliberal) reform of the welfare infrastructure when more and more social enterprises emerge (at least judging from those that appear in the media representation), which trade, for example, in textiles and clothing (as e.g., in A_70, A_83), food and drink (A_72), agricultural products (A_75) or sustainable energy (A_84), among other things, as it is the case from the second period. Overall, based on the literature review and on the empirical analysis, I argue that (so far) it seems that the parts of SE that are taking place in 'the economy' are less represented in interpretations of SE as a political phenomenon.

Related to this, arguably, the impetus that SE may give for *reforming* the economy and businesses – may, to some extent, be disregarded, too. On the other hand, there might be an overemphasis of SE as reform of the social and public sectors (welfare) – at least contrasted against the findings of my empirical analysis for Germany and for the years after 2008. Based on these findings, I argue that looking at SE through a welfare lens only (*a priori*) highlights only aspects or parts of the SE field and discourse and implies a reduction of the SE concept.

While I can only make informed guesses about the reasons behind this (potential) over- or underrepresentation of certain aspects of SE, throughout my literature review and empirical research a few thoughts have developed on the role of the 'sector' – and its possible effect on the interpretation of SE as a political phenomenon. First, one reason might be the disciplinary belonging of researchers. It might be that the parts of SE that occur within the economy are underrepresented in this discussion, because these are mainly researched by business scholars, who are unlikely to investigate the sociological questions around the political meaning(s) of SE. Second, scholars rooted in sociology, social policy or third sector studies, who tend to ask these questions, have mostly focused on SE in areas of the social or public domain, such as health, education, and so forth. Interpretations of SE as a political phenomenon or movement then also mainly rely on insights from these fields. Given that these are areas, which, generally speaking, have undergone processes of privatisation and seen an increase in competitiveness and economic calculation as governing principles in the past few decades, SE appears as related to these developments. SE may then be explained *a priori* as an expression of neoliberal reform in the public or the third sector. To some extent, this view might also be entailed in Nicholls & Teasdale's (2017) 'nested paradigms' – in which SE finds itself in a 'mixed economy of welfare' meso-paradigm. Similarly, some authors place SE as 'entrepreneurship in the social realm' simply by definition, as, for example, management scholar Dees (2001 [1998]), who inscribes this sectoral positioning in defining that "[s]ocial entrepreneurs play the role of change agents in the social sector" (Dees 2001 [1998]: 4). While understanding SE as part of the welfare infrastructure matches my empirical analysis for the first period (1999–2008), it disagrees with the findings for later periods. Another possible explanation, therefore, is simply the historical context and that most studies investigating and interpreting the political meaning(s) of SE (until now) are based on SE in a different point in time. Finally, a self-critical explanation may be that the part of SE that occurs within the economy is *over*represented in the analysed newspaper articles and, therefore, in my empirical findings. These and other (possible) limitations of my research will be discussed more in detail in Section 7.7.

Put differently, in bringing attention to (possible) 'sectoral' aspects when it comes to making sense of SE as a political and sociological phenomenon, this book is a reminder to acknowledge the diversity of SE. Under the SE umbrella one may find ventures as different as microcredit institutions, work integration social enterprises, fair-trade chocolate producers, kindergartens, or tech companies, etc. SE occurs in many different fields or 'sectors'. There is also a methodological argument to make here for future research projects. Having identified the weight of the sectoral focus, this can serve as a warning against assessing SE as a political phenomenon on the basis of very few cases (or case studies). This entails the risk that the SE phenomenon is then interpreted only according to the specific sector that one or a few cases (social enterprises) are situated in. This is something to take into account for future research, especially when it comes to the research design and sampling decisions.

7.5 The Complex Interrelations between Social Entrepreneurship, Capitalism and the State

SE often appears related to 'big' concepts, such as 'capitalism', or 'the state'. The analysed material representing the SE discourse, therefore, does not only contribute to the construction of meanings of SE itself – but also to notions of these concepts, as I will address in this section. First, I am going to address SE in relation to (neoliberal) capitalism, its organisations (businesses) and its subjects (entrepreneurs and managers). The empirical analysis has demonstrated that, in the first period, the articles draw a very positive picture of capitalism, mainly through the favourable and allegedly superior characteristics of markets, businesses, managers and entrepreneurs. This image somewhat changes in the second period. Arguably, due to the financial crisis of 2008, the established business world – or parts of it: especially banks and the financial sector and big corporations, more generally – have widely lost their ability to serve as possible role models and to provide legitimacy for the economic system as a whole. On the organisational ('meso') level, business, is no longer a 'good example' *per se*. This might, in part, explain the need for a deeper contextualisation of profits (which I have addressed in 5.5). On a 'micro' level, the figure of the manager has lost its appeal, which is a development that Heidbrink & Seele (2010) directly link to the crisis of 2008 and to the role managers (mainly in banks but also in other institutions) had here.[2]

Furthermore, it was found that, in the third period, some aspects of the critique of the economic model are a bit more substantial. The two most notable findings are that, first, the US model of capitalism (including Silicon Valley) seems somewhat out of fashion. Second, a different (more positive and active) role of the state is portrayed in the third period. Overall, these narratives and proposals may be interpreted as a call for a different model of capitalism, as I will explain in the following paragraphs.

Across the three periods, there are interesting accounts of the relations between SE and different models of capitalism – namely the US versus the German model of capitalism – as well as of Silicon Valley as a symbol for a certain form of the capitalist economy. Arguably, having identified references to different models of capitalism in the analysed newspapers (see Chapter 6) also marks a novel contribution. An interesting contrast could be observed across the different periods in the references to the economic and social model of the US. In the first period, the US is mainly represented as a role model for Germany, which, at the time, is suffering from high unemployment. Similar to this, Silicon Valley in the first period serves as symbol of inspiration and as an example for Germany to follow. By contrast, in the third period, the US model seems to mostly have lost its charm – for which, again, probably the financial crisis of 2008 is one of the reasons. The references to Silicon Valley, too, have undergone a significant change. Once pictured almost like a utopia – now, Silicon Valley appears as a bad example, one to which SE is contrasted to, as (part of) a counter-movement or as an alternative model.

Furthermore, the picture of the state and politics – and the relations between these and SE – evolves in between the different periods. The German economy and welfare state, which were presented as deficient or at best as ineffective in the first period, in later years, above all, in the third period, are sometimes positively connoted. This includes a favourable view of social security, *Wohlfahrtsverbände*, cooperatives, trade unions, among others. While SE is sometimes still positioned against politics – i.e., as being more effective or better suited than solutions provided by politics and the state – this is much

2 Even though this entails ambiguous aspects, given that the figure of the (social) entrepreneur offers an apparent 'alternative' to the manager, in turn legitimising the capitalist system (as I have explained in 7.4).

more explicit in the first than in the second and third period. Broadly speaking, the articles' image of the state changes over the years: at first, the state and its institutions are pictured as deficient. They should, in part, be replaced by private actors. The perspective shifts towards a representation of the state as rather coexisting or in partnership with SE. The state more often appears as a partner for SE – and not as a completely incompetent entity that shall make space for smaller, agile and private units.

In the third period, politics also appears as a viable instrument for SE actors, as an arena, in which SE actors, too, are participating. *SEND*, for example, engages in politics and in policy proposals – some of which go beyond topics that target the SE field. Put differently: *SEND* engages in politics that go beyond the classic lobbying work, such as increasing funds directed to social enterprises. At times, SE organisations (such as *SEND*) and their representatives call for state action and for (additional) regulation, in order to establish a framework that acknowledges the social and environmental impact of economic activity. This includes instruments aimed at internalising costs that are produced by businesses and absorbed by the public as 'externalities', e.g., via a tax on CO_2 (see Chapter 6).

On the one hand, members of the SE scene present these proposals as a call for establishing a framework that is favourable for social enterprises, because such measures would help to level the playing field for organisations and businesses with social and environmental ambitions against purely profit-oriented actors. But they can be interpreted as more than that. As some SE representatives have described, SE may be seen as 'transformation aid' for the economy as a whole. In effect, if the state would issue legislation that is inspired by social enterprises, the rules would then apply for all businesses in the economy – regardless of the motivation behind it. Indeed, this could represent an option for SE to unfold political potential. For the time period until 2021, however, it cannot seriously be answered whether or not there have already been influences on general (economic) policy derived from the SE field or its actors, or whether this is likely to happen in the future (at least for Germany). While this intersection between policy – and potential agenda-setting by SE – goes beyond the scope of the discussion here, it certainly seems to offer a very interesting route for further research.

Nonetheless, I argue that the fact that SE actors engage in policy (proposals), 'doing' politics and proposing legal solutions, already seems relevant. First, because in calling for legislation, SE acknowledge the importance of politics. When (some) SE actors propose market regulation, they are demanding a stronger and (more) active role of the state – which most definitely establishes a remarkable contrast to the *laissez-faire* spirit that was dominant during the first period. Politics is presented as helpful and as necessary – for SE but also for the economy and society as a whole. Second, the call for state action or legislation also impacts the relationship between the state and SE directly. As noted earlier, in the second and third period, the view prevails that SE shall not replace the state and politics. Instead, most articles maintain that there is a role for (private) SE actors in the economy and society, but that other tasks need to be resolved by the state and in a political process. This perspective also entails acknowledging that SE and the potential solutions provided by SE have limitations. SE may provide transformation *aid* – but large-scale transformation requires political action and policies implemented by the state.

To some extent, this portrayal of SE and the state as partners may also be interpreted as a challenge to the often assumed (false) dichotomy between state and market. It helps to acknowledge that in all capitalist systems, states have made and continue to make the rules for the economic system – including the organisation of economic activity via markets (Polanyi (2015 [1944]). (State) power has been and remains necessary to establish and maintain markets, which are no 'natural state' of humanity or of human civilisation, as some liberal and neoliberal thinkers tend to propagate.

On the other hand, it may be critically questioned how substantial such impulses emerging from the SE field can be for transforming the economy as a whole. It seems uncertain whether or not these would be able to provide more than a few economic incentives, with the aim of incrementally guiding production and consumption in a more sustainable direction – which, certainly, would be nothing groundbreakingly new or exclusive to SE. For a long time, different direct taxes have existed all around the world, with the aim of steering consumptive behaviour towards a healthier lifestyle – for example, taxes on tobacco or alcohol. On the side of production, companies in many countries can rely on tax benefits and aids, for example, to invest in energy efficiency measures. Thus, whether establishing a framework that is beneficial for SE would merely offer some tweaking of the tax incentives here and there, or whether this could also lead to more transformative or 'radical' policies, remains to be seen.

When regarding these findings through a critical angle, e.g., based on Davies's (2014a) understanding of neoliberalism – with competitiveness and economic calculation as its core principles (see Chapter 1) – one could even argue that establishing such a framework may be yet another facet of neoliberalism. Sticking with the example of a CO_2 tax, such a tax may be seen as an instrument that actually *replaces* politics – i.e., trying to find a *political* solution for the ecological harms caused by CO_2 emissions – by economic calculation: in giving CO_2 a monetary value. Similarly, it should be noted that the idea of 'levelling the playing field' for social enterprises does not break with the spirit and organisational principle of competitiveness. Improving the capability of social enterprises to *compete* on the market would not change the fact that the world would still be divided into winning and losing businesses. Even though the parameters, by which 'winners' and 'losers' are determined, would then no longer be financial profits alone. Following this thought, the propagated 'transformation aid' that SE potentially propels could merely be a form of (neoliberal) capitalism absorbing its critics (Boltanski & Chiapello 2007). Again, a concluding evaluation of these developments would be premature here and should be investigated further in upcoming research projects.

On a more practical note, this book has also been able to shed light on SE within day-to-day politics in Germany. In the Introduction, it could be demonstrated that representatives of the different political parties are easily able to embed SE into their different political agendas. Everyone can interpret SE so that it fits their ideological background. The empirical analysis then found that – according to the media representation – out of the main political parties in Germany, the *Green Party* seems to have the most prominent role in the SE discourse (so far), and that it appears as the most explicit ally of the current SE actors (see Chapter 6). However, considering how niche and little institutionalised the SE field currently still is, this link does not seem very established or persistent, yet. It seems likely that any political party that would decide to put SE on their flag, making SE a major policy issue would be able to do so – under their respective premises and understanding of SE, shaping the SE field accordingly. This certainly represents a certain risk for the SE sector and movement, as I will address in the next section.

7.6 Social Entrepreneurship and Other Concepts: Overlaps and (Lack of) Boundaries

Strictly speaking, the relationship between SE and other ideas, concepts or *leitmotifs* exceeds the scope of my research. Nonetheless, this section will further discuss the proximity and (potential) intersections between SE and other ideas and concepts that was briefly addressed in Chapter 6. I argue that (potential) overlaps and boundaries (or lack thereof), as well as the interaction with other ideas and concepts and the (political) actors related to these are of crucial importance for SE and its possible development in the future. My empirical findings do not really provide answers here, yet, it is possible to point towards avenues for further research. It has been demonstrated that SE often appears as embedded in or next to other concepts, such as 'entrepreneurship', the 'Social Market Economy', 'social innovation', 'sustainability', or the 'social economy', among others. Questions arise here concerning the relationships between SE and these other ideas and concepts, and how these relationships will develop in the future. If, perhaps, aspects of SE and other discourses will merge, or, whether SE could even be absorbed by another – more 'powerful' – concept or discourse.[3] These considerations also feed into the discussion whether it makes sense, at all, to speak about a distinctive SE discourse (which I will explore in 7.7).

In Chapter 1, I have raised the issue that academic literature (mainly in business studies), often subsumes SE under 'entrepreneurship'. Chapter 6 has demonstrated that, currently, this understanding of SE as part of or as a form of entrepreneurship is a dominant perspective in Germany. Embedding SE within 'entrepreneurship', however, can be seen as a reduction of the concept – and arguably disregards that SE may have political potential. When standing next to other forms of entrepreneurship, there is a risk that SE is being presented as a 'friendly face' or as a 'social fig leaf' next to other – commercial – ventures. When the prefix 'social' becomes optional in these situations, SE merely has the role of promoting and legitimising an entrepreneurial society, in which entrepreneurship is an end in itself.

Another prominent neighbouring concept and discourse that appears in the analysed articles, even from the first period, is 'sustainability'. 'Sustainability' and 'sustainable development' are popular conceptual frameworks. Since the adoption of the UN's *Sustainable Development Goals* (*SDGs*) in 2015, the idea of 'sustainability' is increasingly able to offer a political and practical programme and guideline – and on a global scale. Important SE actors already make reference to the *SDG* framework. *Impact Hub Berlin*, for example, declares its commitment to the *SDGs* on its website (Impact Hub Berlin 2022).

3 In theory, it would also be possible for SE to absorb other concepts or discourses. Given the still marginal and weakly institutionalised status of SE, however, this seems more unlikely at the moment.

In a workshop hosted by the *Social Entrepreneurship Akademie* in April 2020, in which I participated, the *SDGs* served as the basis, on which the participants should develop an idea for a SE venture. Participants should pick an *SDG* and then design a project around it.[4] As funding bodies, including foundations and public institutions alike, are also increasingly ascribing to the *SDGs* – expecting the same from their recipients or partners – the SE scene might follow. In the long run, being integrated into the *SDG* concept, its policies and logics, indeed, seems like a possible development for SE.

Another concept that appears related to SE is the 'Social Market Economy' (SME). SE is sometimes presented as a (potential) building block for a new or renewed version of the German SME model – or of a 'Social and Ecological Market Economy', as it is sometimes complemented or reframed in recent years (BMWK 2022b). To some extent, the SME can also be related to the debate about SE and a specific local or 'German' economic model and to regional economic development (see Chapter 6). This discursive link between SE and the SME seems promising for further research. While the SME itself is a highly contested term and concept, the popular use of the term in Germany often refers to a vague idea of an economic model that is somehow more 'social' than 'pure' capitalism (Nonhoff 2006). In this regard, SE and the SME have much in common. Yet, it remains to be seen whether the intersection between SE and SME will expand further in the following years. Most definitely, it seems too soon to tell whether SE would then be able to make any substantial contribution to a new SME model – and whether this new SME model would be more than just a rhetoric figure.

Another interesting concept that appears interrelated with SE is the 'social economy'. As explained in Chapter 1, some academic literature *a priori* seeks to place SE within the 'social economy' (Pearce 2003; Kay et al. 2016). This can also be seen as a way of prescribing that SE should represent some sort of alternative to (neoliberal) capitalism and function according to different principles. What is more, the 'Social Economy Berlin' programme (mentioned in Chapters 2 and 6), which is funded by the state government, to some extent, seems to connect to this tradition. The 'Social Economy Berlin' programme integrates actors and organisations of different social economy traditions: mainly *SEND*

4 In the past few years, I have encountered several workshops of this kind by different organisations related to the SE scene.

and *Technologie-Netzwerk Berlin*.[5] This approach could thus, be interpreted as an attempt (by state policymakers and administrators) to integrate SE more strongly into a wider social economy tradition and community. Whether or not this will turn out to be successful, still remains to be seen.

Apart from the 'social economy' umbrella, several (other) social enterprise movements and their actors seem relevant for the future of SE. For example, both *Fair Trade* and the more recent *Gemeinwohl-Ökonomie* were mentioned in the analysed articles. Beyond the empirical analysis, a few jointly-organised events came to my attention, for example, between *SEND* and the *Gemeinwohl-Ökonomie* or between *SEND* and the *Federal Association of Green Business* (*Bundesverband nachhaltige Wirtschaft e.V.*), a network and lobby organisation of mainly medium-sized businesses. Before the 2022 state parliament election in North Rhine-Westphalia, the regional groups of *SEND* and *Gemeinwohl-Ökonomie* even issued a joint paper, in which they commented on the economic policy proposals of the main political parties (SEND 2022b). These emerging collaborations and networks should most definitely be explored in further research, to investigate in which way these might shape the SE movement and whether SE could become part of a broader social economy movement.

Another relevant term and concept is 'social innovation'. Different SE actors, including *SEND* and their representatives repeatedly ascribe to the 'social innovation' label and promote the 'social innovation' narrative. For example, in the article A_327, Elsemann (*SEND*) and Haverkamp (*SEND* and *Ashoka*) argue that addressing social challenges requires more than technology, and they propose a stronger focus on 'social innovation' (see Chapter 6). Several of the most important actors in the SE scene (including *SEND*, *Phineo*, *FASE* and *Ashoka*) have launched an agency called *Kompetenzzentrum Soziale Innovationen* (Social Impact 2022b), which is part of the *European Social Innovation Alliance*, which pursues the aim of "working towards a pan-European social innovation infrastructure on all levels – locally, regionally, nationally, and transnationally" (Social Impact 2022c). A reason for increasingly focussing on 'social innovation' might be strategic, given that the EU and the federal government are increasingly seeking to support and promote 'social innovation' across different ministries (BMBF 2021). Perhaps, 'innovation' might also be a term that

5 *Technologie-Netzwerk Berlin* ascribes to the 'social economy' concept and tradition. Karl Birkhölzer, who has also made important contributions to social economy and third sector scholarship and who is referenced repeatedly in Chapter 2, was one of the founders of the organisation.

scares fewer actors than 'entrepreneurship', which comes with the 'ideological baggage' of the Schumpeterian figure of the heroic, creative entrepreneur (see Chapter 1) – and is alien to most third sector actors. A hint for this could be that one of the partners of the *Kompetenzzentrum Soziale Innovationen* is the *Diakonie* (one of the five large German welfare associations). Certainly, more research would be required here.

Furthermore, as explained in Chapter 6, in the third period, there is a remarkable closeness between SE and the start-up world. SE is now mainly described as a founding or start-up – not just as any type of business, which also establishes a closer link to the commercial founding and tech scene. To some extent, this perspective on SE is also being institutionalised, e.g., by certain networks and resources going into the SE field (such as awards for entrepreneurs and founders that include a 'social entrepreneurship' category). Beyond my empirical analysis, it should also be noted that *SEND* has emerged out of the *German Startups Association* (*Bundesverband Deutsche Startups e.V.*), the main lobby organisation for commercial start-ups (see Chapter 2). *SEND*'s history and (part of) its network, therefore, can also be interpreted as an institutionalised link between SE and the start-up world.

On the one hand, a closeness to technology and to commercial entrepreneurship may bring (new) resources into the SE field, which can then be used for the social aims pursued by social enterprises. Following this reasoning, the strategy of keeping tech and commercial entrepreneurship close may be seen as a form of 'tactical mimicry' as described by Dey & Teasdale (2016), i.e., applying a certain language for tactical reasons and attracting resources to the field. On the other hand, herein lies a risk that the SE concept is reduced to a form of entrepreneurship. SE may be absorbed by the (commercial) start-up world and its political potential contained. Moreover, Chapter 6 has also demonstrated that this proximity between commercial and 'social' entrepreneurship is sometimes found on the individual level. Or put differently: this proximity is personified in certain entrepreneurs, who become social entrepreneurs – and vice versa. Several articles report on social entrepreneurs, who have become social entrepreneurs only after having achieved financial success (as well-paid employees or as entrepreneurs in the business world). In addition, various articles describe courses on SE, in which young people (mostly university students) gain entrepreneurial skills – which they might then apply to become (commercial) entrepreneurs. This raises serious concerns about the purpose, function and priorities of such educational programmes, as they sometimes seem to reduce SE to a facilitating function, as an entry ticket into entrepreneurship (of any kind).

There are also questions of inclusivity and participation related to this. Such questions have previously been raised (Voß 2015) and could only be addressed marginally. Certainly, there are interesting routes for further research around inclusivity and participation in the German SE movement that are worth exploring. When SE is only presented as an option for financially secure or even wealthy individuals, this would make SE indistinguishable from charity. SE would then resemble the charitable activities of benevolent industrialists, who want to 'give back' to their workers or to the local community – as many industrial families have done over centuries, e.g., by setting up foundations. Most certainly, such a take on SE would strip it from its political potential. I argue that this charity-like approach to SE (engaging in SE only after accumulating financial wealth) remains rooted in a dichotomy of the economy versus the social and charitable world. Arguably, this undermines the basic idea of SE of a somewhat more holistic understanding of economic activity that in itself should address social aims or achieve 'positive social impact'. There is also a moral dilemma entailed here: in order to become social entrepreneurs, individuals would first need to inherit or to accumulate wealth. However, this is problematic when assuming that in the current economic system (much) economic activity is harmful – as explanations or definitions of SE often do, at least implicitly (see Chapter 1). This creates a paradox: in order to 'do good' (through SE), one would first have to engage in harmful economic activity to achieve financial security. In addition, when SE only becomes an activity for the wealthy, this would mean a decoupling of SE and wage labour. This would then counteract the debates about decent pay and working conditions in social enterprises, which I have discussed as a route for SE to unfold political potential in Section 7.4.

Looking beyond the empirical analysis of the news articles, it seems that the lack of boundaries to the commercial and tech world (and its charitable activities) has recently reached a new stage. In June 2022, *SEND* has started a new project: *emp:our now*, which is funded by *Google*'s charitable arm: *Google.org* (SEND 2021e). Again, one side of the coin of engaging with *Google* might be clever 'tactical mimicry' – in order to draw resources to 'genuinely social' fields. On the other hand, this opens a door for 'social washing' for companies such as *Google*. There is a risk for SE actors of being instrumentalised so that large companies can polish their image by showcasing their 'social responsibility', regardless of the impact of their main economic activities. In this way, SE actors may become the 'fig leaf' of commercial entrepreneurship and, ultimately, of neoliberal capitalism.

Overall, it can be argued that the links, overlaps and boundaries (or the blurring of boundaries) and the interaction between the SE concept and its actors and other actors and movements will be crucial for the developments in the coming years. As the interest in SE has started growing in the early 2020s, it seems likely that different actors (in the economy, politics and civil society alike) will play an important role in steering the German SE movement in one or another direction. This being said, it seems that all the different overlaps and interactions come with both opportunities and risks. Collaborating with actors around another concept opens up the opportunity of bringing more attention, people, and resources to the SE movement. Aligned with other concepts and actors, SE may reach greater scale or leverage. However, there is also the risk that these other actors or discourses will appropriate or even instrumentalise SE for different purposes.

7.7 Social Entrepreneurship Discourse(s) and Newspapers: Reflections on the Methodological Approach

As mentioned in Chapter 3, it is relevant to note that the findings of the empirical analysis are based on newspaper articles, and that this might entail certain limitations. The choice of data has an impact on the findings, and certainly, only a part of the SE discourse is represented in the newspapers – and, therefore, in my findings. More specifically, my analysis has grasped:

- the part of SE discourse(s) that makes it into the news,
- the part of SE discourse(s) that journalists and editors find interesting – i.e., aspects of SE that make marketable news stories and/or that relate well to trending topics and current affairs,
- the part of SE discourse(s) that the media is able and willing to represent, possibly excluding more radical versions or aspects of SE.

In this section thus, I shall further reflect on the implications that this has for the reach of my findings and how additional research may help to fill the research gaps that remain unresolved.

Focusing on an 'outside' perspective was an intentional choice – as an attempt to look beyond the SE niche or 'bubble', and to investigate, what aspects of SE reach a broader audience. I wanted to find out what larger parts of society get to perceive of SE. Of course, newspapers do not reach all members of society – yet a very considerable part of them. On the other hand, it must be clear that my findings cannot be seen as an all-encompassing and balanced depiction of the SE field. In particular, my analysis offers limited insights on the 'inside' view, on how the SE scene and the actors who constitute it, such as social entrepreneurs and their support and lobby organisations, may try to construct a 'common agreement' or identity. My findings thus, do not necessarily represent the dominant perspective on SE *within* the SE field, its practitioners and support organisations. These might agree, but also disagree, with the media representation of SE. In addition, the media representation of SE does not have to be congruent with understandings of SE in other important arenas in public and social life, e.g., in the arena of education (such as universities), politics (such as parliament or policymaking), the economy (businesses or business forums) or civil society, etc.

For this reason, a study focusing on the 'inside' of the SE scene, its network(s) of practitioners, support organisations, etc. would be a fruitful complement to my research – e.g., by conducting interviews, applying ethnographic methods and/or analysing websites or the social media activities of the relevant SE actors. Such further research would be necessary to better understand the internal workings of the SE movement. In addition, it would then be possible to compare the 'inside' construction and the 'outside' depiction of the SE phenomenon and movement, and to identify similarities as well as differences between them. This comparison would be very interesting, in order to assess, whether there is an overlap between such 'inside' and 'outside' understandings of the SE concept and whether or not SE actors would feel the media representation an adequate one. An inside view would also allow to better capture different 'voices' within the SE discourse. As I have explained in Chapters 4–6, social entrepreneurs and other members of the SE scene and wider support ecosystem are allowed to 'speak' in the newspaper articles. Ultimately, however, the protagonists of the stories have little agency over their representation in the final product, given that newspaper articles are mediated texts, which are researched, written, edited and published. The explanations of SE as well as the wider narratives around SE, which are captured in my analysis, are significantly shaped by journalists. Likewise, research that focuses on understandings of SE in other important arenas in public and social life would be offer quite fruitful complementary perspectives, e.g., through analysing representations of SE in universities, business forums, policy documents, or the like. Keeping in mind, however, that SE in Germany is still in its infancy, and that in the areas of politics and policymaking, for example, it would be hard to find relevant and substantial material that dates back a similar time span (as I have explained in Chapters 2 and 3).

This being said, it must also be noted that newspapers are embedded in certain social and power relations that determine, which articles are produced, and how these are produced, as I have already mentioned in Chapter 3. It may be possible that the newspapers have only represented the parts of SE that *could* be represented within the constraints of the social and power relations within neoliberal capitalism, in which the media are embedded (Fairclough 1995). Following this thought, it could be possible that parts of SE that present a challenge or an alternative to neoliberal capitalism – namely, more 'radical' versions of SE – are widely excluded from the media discourse, because they are beyond the limits of what can be said (within the constraints of the neoliberal power structures). If it is beyond the newspapers' horizon to imagine an alternative to the neoliberal model of capitalism, then such takes on SE, understanding SE as (part of) an alternative model, will be excluded in the first place, therefore, containing the radical political potential of SE. Newspapers, especially the more conservative outlets, might represent only a reformist version of SE, one that is more conforming to the current economic and social system. Likewise, there is good reason to assume that other power relations, too, have shaped the media representation from which I gathered my empirical results, including inequalities that derive e.g., from gender or race relations. Various critical perspectives on power relations – such as feminism, post-colonial theory, critical disability studies, or intersectionality – may challenge the media representation when it comes to the subjects of SE, asking why certain social entrepreneurs are represented, and how inclusive or exclusive these representations of social entrepreneurs are (McRobbie 2020). Hence, further research could help to explore the (potential) effects that the media's power structures might have on the representation of SE.

Another important point seems to revolve around the flexibility and malleability of the SE concept, against the background of the media's function in informing the general public about current affairs. The central contribution of my book is that it was able to trace a development of representations of the SE concept in Germany over time. Related to this, I have made a strong case for understanding SE in dialogue with the more general political and socio-economic environment. I have demonstrated that, in the first period, SE appears linked to public debates over the reform of the labour market and the social security system, and later, SE appears linked to the financial crisis of 2008. While I stand by the assertion that the broader political and socio-economic environment is important for understanding SE in a particular context, there also lies a possible critique with regards to the analysed material. Given that journalists report on current affairs, there might be a bias in the media representation that results from journalists constructing their stories in a way to fit SE in, connecting SE to what is trending at the moment. Following this view, it is possible that the relationship between SE and themes that are currently relevant in the wider political environment – at least those receiving news coverage – may be too pronounced in my findings.

Viewed from a different perspective, this, once again, points to the fact that it is possible to embed SE in various wider narratives, e.g., that it seems possible to link SE to whatever is going on in the world right now. This feeds into an important aspect that I want to discuss regarding the theoretical framework and the methodology applied to my empirical research, namely: whether it makes sense to speak of one SE discourse – or whether it would be better suited to think of several SE discourses (in plural).

At times, I was questioning the manifestation of a distinct SE discourse, and that, instead, it would be better to think of SE as appearing within different discourses – such as a 'reform of welfare' discourse, a 'reform of the economy' discourse, an 'entrepreneurship' discourse, a 'sustainability' discourse, a 'what makes good organisations' discourse, an 'empowerment' discourse, and so forth. There seem to be valid arguments for regarding SE as a 'scattered' phenomenon or movement that appears in many different discourses. However, I come to the conclusion that despite the flexibility and malleability of the SE term and concept, which makes it appear somewhat 'scattered', there is also a strong common thread in the complete analysed time frame: from 1999 to 2021. I propose to understand the 'different' SE discourses in terms of dominant and less dominant versions or currents of the SE discourse, but not as completely different discourses. Generally speaking, the different versions or currents have existed from the beginning, but they may be more pronounced in one period than in another – and they may evolve over time. For example, the idea of SE as 'entrepreneurship', which is very pronounced (even dominant) in the third period, does not appear all of a sudden. As demonstrated in Chapter 1, this perspective can already be found in early academic literature on SE (e.g., in Dees (2001 [1998]). In addition, the understanding of SE as 'entrepreneurship' can also be seen as a continuation of or building on the idea of 'SE as part of the economy', which (in the media representation) only becomes dominant in the second period.

Different versions, narratives and currents of the SE discourse exist simultaneously – and they are not mutually exclusive and might, at times, appear intertwined. Yet, there is enough coherence and consistence to speak of a distinct SE discourse. In itself, my analysis is also a testament to this coherence, given that I have been able to trace specific developments across the entire period of investigation (1999–2021). Supporting this view is also that I was able to rely on the 'social entrepreneurship' term during the empirical research process (see Chapter 3). While still weakly institutionalised, the 'social entrepreneurship' term proved to be a successful signifier to refer to the social practice that I intended to study (in the German context). Furthermore, in recent years, the 'social entrepreneurship' term is becoming more established – in particular, as certain actors ascribe to it, most importantly *SEND*, founded in late 2017. As explained in Chapter 6, different institutionalisation processes are occurring in the third period, which include SE courses at universities, the promotion of SE by local economic development agencies, etc. Arguably, these deepening institutionalisation processes further sustain speaking of a distinct SE discourse in the German context – and that it will remain relevant in the coming years. Overall, the SE discourse is composed of "utterances which seem to be regulated in some way and which seem to have a coherence and a force to them in common" (Mills 1997: 7). This makes it possible to speak about a discourse of social entrepreneurship (in Germany). This being said, nonetheless, I consider that it is possible that the SE term and concept could merge with – or *be integrated* into – another concept, such as 'sustainability', 'social innovation', or 'entrepreneurship', in the future (as explained in Section 7.6). Any forecast on this development would be premature – and the future of the SE discourse will most likely depend on the activities of resourceful actors and the way, in which these will shape it. Further research should definitely pay attention to these potential prospects.

7.8 The Political Potential of Social Entrepreneurship

What to make then of the 'social entrepreneurship' phenomenon and movement from a sociological perspective, and what can I say to my former self, who, prior to embarking on this research had his own hopes for SE, as a way of experimenting with alternative economies that are more just and sustainable than current business models, and therefore, as a means to reform the economy (as mentioned in the Introduction)? What 'political potential' of this sort could be observed throughout the research for this book?

There seems to be a quantitative and a qualitative dimension here – with the flexibility and ambiguity of the SE concept being an opportunity as well as a risk. On the one hand, SE seems to appeal to many actors, it is able to enter different spaces, and to attract resources from different sources, e.g., through 'tactical mimicry'. It should also be considered that, perhaps, flexible concepts can have great longevity, because of their ability to adapt to different (external) circumstances. Capitalism itself would be a good example for this, which has time and again been able to adapt to and to integrate criticism, as we know from Boltanski & Chiapello (2007). On the other hand, its flexibility and ambiguity seem to make the SE concept fragile, and prone to appropriation or instrumentalisation by other concepts or actors. Previous studies (mainly for the UK) have already pointed out how policymakers have managed to use and appropriate SE for various policy goals (Teasdale 2012; Dey & Teasdale 2016; Mason & Moran 2019). The remarkable influence of business elites on SE (see especially Chapter 4) should also be remembered here – and while they are not as dominant in the German SE field as in the early phase, they are still showing interest for SE. The new closeness between SE and the start-up (and tech) world may also present a risk for SE of being reduced to a form of entrepreneurship, and ultimately, being stripped from its political potential when it comes to establishing alternative economies. Similar to commercial entrepreneurship, to which Davies (2014a) – *in theory* – attests political potential, too, the political potential of SE could then be contained by capitalism as a system and by business elites, who manage to hold close links to entrepreneurs.

In order for SE to more fully develop its political potential thus, SE actors would need to clarify their political agenda and to forge and cultivate effective alliances. In order to be part of a transformation towards an alternative model, SE actors would need to be (more) critical with their alliances and beware of reproducing (implicit) economisation processes, such as uncritically transferring mainstream business logics into social realms, or engaging in cheerful praises of business virtues. To use the idea of 'transformation aid' that has been voiced by SE representatives, this would require formulating political proposals that go beyond incremental change – proposals that ultimately challenge neoliberalism's organising principles of competitiveness and economic calculation. In order to provide substantial 'transformation aid' that is worthy of the name, it would be necessary to draw a clearer vision of a framework for an economic model, as well as to design strategies to implement it. Alliances between SE actors and other actors, or movements – in particular with other social economy movements – could offer a promising avenue. In shedding light on the background and development of the SE phenomenon and movement, my study may, to some extent, help to facilitate the communication and possible cooperation between SE and actors in politics and between different 'generations' of social economy movements. That is, if the term 'entrepreneurship' is not too off-putting for the respective political and civil society actors to get involved, appearing as compromised, as Davies (2014a) has raised – as it comes with (too) much neoliberal 'ideological baggage'. Moreover, the (potential) interplay of policy and SE, too, is a crucial aspect – both for political and practical relevance and as a topic for further research. Yet, the idea that SE could inspire policy ideas and action, i.e., put forward proposals, which are then put into regulation for all, remains rather hypothetical at the moment.

Given that policymakers of all stripes and various actors in the economy and in civil society may try to use SE for different (policy) goals and agendas, the involvement of these actors may swing the SE movement in different ways. There are different forces at play, and the future of SE seems uncertain. Different paths seem possible for the future development of the SE movement, most probably, depending on which resource-rich actors will be shaping it. At the moment, SE hardly seems able to propose a substantial 'alternative' to capitalism, certainly not in a 'radical' sense, i.e., addressing the roots and fundamental structures of the system. Instead – and assuming that the perspectives that consider SE to be 'more' than entrepreneurship are dominant (which is debatable) – SE could be seen as a (small) building block for moderate or gradual reform of the economy, for it to be more responsive to ecological and social justice concerns. Perhaps, SE can help to contribute to a discussion on the varieties of capitalism or to reinvigorate social-democratic or socially responsible versions of capitalism in the 21st century. But it would have to be closely monitored that this would actually result in action and reform and not merely in rhetoric.

The idea of SE, therefore, might not seem ambitious enough for those seeking fundamental systemic change. Against the background of a future without any 'alternatives' whatsoever, though, SE may offer hope for moderate reform. Considering the dire state of the economic model, economic though and economic policies, SE should not yet be easily dismissed. SE may not be able to provide all the answers, but, perhaps, be able to ask the right questions – and to contribute to a debate about the future of our economic and social model, to debates about the future of capitalism, and to help pinpointing where it is doing harm. SE may also contribute to discussions around more holistic understandings of progress and development – and to some, these might seem like sufficient reasons to continue researching and engaging with this phenomenon.

Reference List

Acemoglu, C. (2009). The Crisis of 2008: Lessons for and from Economics. *Critical Review*, 21 (2–3), pp. 185–194, doi:10.1080/08913810902933788.

Achleitner, A.-K., Heister, P. & Spiess-Knafl, W. (2010). Venture Philanthropy und Sozialunternehmertum. In: Hoelscher, P., Ebermann, T., Schlüter, A. (eds.) *Venture Philanthropy in Theorie und Praxis*. Stuttgart, Lucius & Lucius, pp. 81 89.

Achleitner, A.-K., Heister, P. & Stahl, E. (2007). Social Entrepreneurship. Ein Überblick. In: A.K. Achleitner, Pöllath, R. & Stahl, E. (eds.) *Finanzierung von Sozialunternehmern. Konzepte zur finanziellen Unterstützung von Social Entrepreneurs*. Stuttgart: Schäffer Poeschel, pp. 3–25.

Admati, A. & Hellwig, M. (2013). The Bankers' New Clothes: What's Wrong with Banking and What to Do about It. Oxford: Princeton University Press.

Aigner, E., Aistleitner, M., Glötzl, F. & Kapeller, J. (2018). The focus of academic economics: before and after the crisis. Johannes Kepler University, Institute for Comprehensive Analysis of the Economy. *ICAE Working Paper Series*, 75.

Ashoka (2013). Ashoka Jahresbericht 2012. Ashoka: München.

Ashoka (2020). Ashoka – Heimat der Changemaker. [online] Available at: https://www.ashoka.org/de-de (Accessed 29 August 2020).

Austin, J., Stevenson, H. & Wei-Skillern, J. (2006). Social and Commercial Entrepreneurship: Same, Different, or Both? *Entrepreneurship Theory and Practice*, 30 (1), pp. 1–22.

Bacq, S. & Janssen, F. (2011). The multiple faces of social entrepreneurship: A review of definitional issues based on geographical and thematic criteria. *Entrepreneurship & Regional Development*, 23, (5–6), pp. 373–403.

Baker, P., Gabrielatos, C., Khosravinik, M., Krzyżanowski, M., McEnery, T. & Wodak, R. (2008). A useful methodological synergy? Combining critical discourse analysis and corpus linguistics to examine discourses of refugees and asylum seekers in the UK press. *Discourse & Society*, 19 (3), pp. 273–306.

Balgar, K. (2011). Zur ‚Verortung' von Social Entrepreneurship. In: Jähnke, P., Christmann, G. & Balgar, K. (eds.) *Social Entrepreneurship: Perspektiven für die Raumentwicklung*. Wiesbaden: Springer VS, pp. 87–102.

Bandinelli, C. (2017). Social Entrepreneurship: Sociality, Ethics and Politics. Doctoral thesis, Goldsmiths, University of London.

Bandinelli, C. & Arvidsson, A. (2013). Brand Yourself a Changemaker! *Journal of Macromarketing*, 33 (1), pp. 67–71.

Beckmann, M. (2011). Social Entrepreneurship – Altes Phänomen, neues Paradigma moderner Gesellschaften oder Vorbote eines Kapitalismus 2.0? In: Hackenberg, H. & Empter, S. (eds.) *Social Entrepreneurship – Social Business: Für die Gesellschaft unternehmen*. Wiesbaden: Springer VS, pp. 67–85.

Betzelt, S. (2001): The Third Sector as a Job Machine? Conditions, Potentials, and Policies for Job Creation in German Nonprofit Organizations. Frankfurt: Peter Lang Verlag.

Betzelt, S. (2019). Autoritäre Tendenzen in der Sozialpolitik? Wie Grundrechte im 'Hartz-IV' System ausgehöhlt werden – und was dies mit Rechtspopulismus zu tun hat. In: Heinrich-Böll-Stiftung Sachsen (ed.) *Politik im autoritären Sog*. Dresden: Heinrich-Böll-Stiftung Sachsen, pp. 53–67.

Birkhölzer, K. (2015). Social Enterprise in Germany: A Typology of Models. *ICSEM Working Papers*, 15, Liege: EMES European Research Network.

Birkhölzer, K. (2018). Historische Entwicklung und Wirkungsanalyse sozialer Unternehmen in Deutschland. Berlin: Technologie-Netzwerk Berlin.

Birkhölzer, K., Göler von Ravensburg, N., Glänzel, G., Lautermann, C. & Mildenberger, G. (2015). Social Enterprise in Germany: Understanding Concepts and Context. *ICSEM Working Papers*, 14, Liege: EMES European Research Network.

Bode, I. & Turba, H. (2022). Deformation qua Externalisierung? In: Betzelt, S. & Fehmel, T. (eds.). *Deformation oder Transformation? Analysen zum wohlfahrtsstaatlichen Wandel im 21. Jahrhundert*. Wiesbaden: Springer Fachmedien, pp. 117–148.

Bode, I. & Vogd, W. (eds.) (2016). *Mutationen des Krankenhauses. Soziologische Diagnosen in organisations- und gesellschaftstheoretischer Perspektive*. Wiesbaden: Springer VS.

Boltanski, L. & Chiapello, E. (2007). The New Spirit of Capitalism. London: Verso.

Bonefeld, W. (2012). Freedom and the Strong State: On German Ordoliberalism. *New Political Economy*, 17 (5), pp. 633–656.

Borzaga, C. & Defourny, J. (2001). Conclusions: Social Enterprises in Europe, a Diversity of Initiatives and Prospects. In: Borzaga, C. & Defourny, J. (eds.) *The Emergence of Social Enterprise*. London: Routledge, pp. 350–370.

Borzaga, C., Galera, G., Franchini, B., Chiomento, S., Nogales, R. & Carini, C. (2020). Social enterprises and their ecosystems in Europe. Comparative synthesis report. Executive summary. Luxembourg: Publications Office of the European Union.

Bosma, N., Schott, T., Terjesen, S. & Kew, P. (2016). Global Entrepreneurship Monitor 2015 to 2016: Special Report on Social Entrepreneurship. London: Global Entrepreneurship Research Association.

Braham, P. (2013). Key Concepts in Sociology. London: SAGE.

Brand, U. & Wissen, M. (2017). Social-ecological transformation. In: Richardson, D. et al. (eds.). *The International Encyclopedia of Geography*, doi:10.1002/9781118786352.wbieg0690

Bröckling, U. (2007). Das unternehmerische Selbst: Soziologie einer Subjektivierungsform. Frankfurt: Suhrkamp.

Bruder, I. (2021). A Social Mission is Not Enough: Reflecting the Normative Foundations of Social Entrepreneurship. *Journal of Business Ethics*, 174, pp. 487–505, doi: 10.1007/s10551-020-04602-5.

Bundesinitiative Impact Investing (2020). Gründungsgeschichte. [online] Available at: https://bundesinitiative-impact-investing.de/about/ (Accessed 6 September 2022).

Bundesministerium für Bildung und Forschung (BMBF) (2021). Ressortkonzept zu Sozialen Innovationen. Berlin: Bundesministerium für Bildung und Forschung.

Bundesministerium für Bildung und Forschung (BMBF) (2022). Zarah Bruhn zur Beauftragten für Soziale Innovationen ernannt, Pressemitteilung 26/2022. [online] Available at: https://www.bmbf.de/bmbf/shareddocs/pressemitteilungen/de/2022/03/300322-Bruhn-Beauftragte.html (Accessed 6 September 2022).

Bundesministerium für Familie, Senioren, Frauen und Jugend (BMFSFJ) (2011). Bundesfamilienministerium und KfW stellen neues Instrument zur Wachstumsfinanzierung von Sozialunternehmen vor. [online] Available at: https://www.bmfsfj.de/bmfsfj/aktuelles/alle-meldungen/bundesfamilienministerium-und-kfw-stellen-neues-instrument-zur-wachstums finanzierung-von-sozialunternehmen-vor-97002 (Accessed 6 September 2021).

Bundesministerium für Wirtschaft und Klimaschutz (BMWK) (2021). Sven Giegold: Staatssekretär im Bundesministerium für Wirtschaft und Klimaschutz. [online] Available at: https://www.bmwk.de/Redaktion/DE/Dossier/Visitenkarten/visitenkarte-giegold.html (Accessed 6 September 2022).

Bundesministerium für Wirtschaft und Klimaschutz (BMWK) (2022a). Existenzgründungen aus der Wissenschaft (EXIST). [online] Available at: https://www.bmwk.de/Redaktion/DE/Artikel/Mittelstand/gruendungsfinanzierung-exist.html (Accessed 17 September 2022).

Bundesministerium für Wirtschaft und Klimaschutz (BMWK) (2022b). Sozial-Ökologische Marktwirtschaft heute: Leitbild der deutschen Wirtschaftspolitik [online] Available at: https://www.bmwk.de/Redaktion/DE/Dossier/soziale-marktwirtschaft.html (Accessed 28 September 2022).

Butterwegge, C. (2007). Rechtfertigung, Maßnahmen und Folgen einer neoliberalen (Sozial-) Politik. In: Butterwegge, C., Lösch, B. & Ptak, R. (eds.) *Kritik des Neoliberalismus*. Wiesbaden: Springer VS, pp. 135–220.

Butterwegge, C. (2015). Harz IV und die Folgen. Eine Kritische Bilanz Nach Zehn Jahren. *Gesundheits- und Sozialpolitik*, 1 (1), pp. 38–53.

Cagarman, K., Kratzer, J. & Osbelt, K. (2020). Social Entrepreneurship: Dissection of a Phenomenon through a German Lens. *Sustainability*, 12, 7764, doi:10.3390/su12187764.

Caritas (2020). Wir über uns: Caritas-Statistik: Millionenfache Hilfe – Die Caritas in Zahlen. [online] Available at: https://www.caritas.de/diecaritas/wir-ueber-uns/die-caritas-in-zahlen/statistik (Accessed 30 August 2020).

Castells, M., Caraça, J. & Cardoso, G. (2012). The Cultures of the Economic Crisis: An Introduction. In: Castells, M., Caraça, J. & Cardoso, G. (eds.) *Aftermath: The Cultures of the Economic Crisis*. Oxford: Oxford University Press, pp. 1–16.

Cho, A.H. (2006). Politics, Values and Social Entrepreneurship: A Critical Appraisal. In: Mair, J., Robinson, J. & Hockerts, K. (eds.) *Social Entrepreneurship*. Basingstoke: Palgrave Macmillan, pp. 34–56.

Chouliaraki, L. & Fairclough, N. (1999). Discourse in Late Modernity: Rethinking Critical Discourse Analysis. Edinburgh: Edinburgh University Press.

Christlich Demokratische Union Deutschlands (CDU), Christlich-Soziale Union in Bayern (CSU) & Sozialdemokratische Partei Deutschlands (SPD) (2018). Ein neuer Aufbruch für Europa Eine neue Dynamik für Deutschland Ein neuer Zusammenhalt für unser Land. Koalitionsvertrag zwischen CDU, CSU und SPD, 19. Legislaturperiode. [online] Available at: https://www.bundesregierung.de/breg-de/themen/koalitionsvertrag-zwischen-cdu-csu-und-spd-195906 (Accessed 6 September 2022).

Christlich-Soziale Union in Bayern (CSU) & Freie Wähler (2018). Für ein bürgernahes Bayern: menschlich – nachhaltig – modern. Koalitionsvertrag für die Legislaturperiode 2018–2023 [online] Available at: https://www.bayern.de/staatsregierung/koalitionsvertrag-2018-2023/ (Accessed 6 September 2022).

Christmann, G., Richter, R., Sept, A., Troendle, V., Jahnke, T. & Spiri, N. (2021). Marktorientierte Sozialunternehmen in Brandenburg: Darstellung der existierenden Unternehmenslandschaft und Feststellung vorhandener und fehlender Gründungsvoraussetzungen. Potsdam: Ministerium für Wirtschaft, Arbeit und Energie des Landes Brandenburg.

Coffey, A. & Atkinson, P. (1996). Making Sense of Qualitative Data. London: Routledge.

Cook, B., Dodds, C. & Mitchell, W. (2003). Social entrepreneurship – false premises and dangerous forebodings. *Australian Journal of Social Issues*, 38 (1), pp. 57–73.

Crouch, C. (2011). The Strange Non-Death of Neoliberalism. Cambridge: Polity Press.

Dacin, P., Dacin, T. & Matear, M. (2010). Social Entrepreneurship: Why We Don't Need a New Theory and How We Move Forward From Here. *Academy of Management Perspectives*, 24 (3), pp. 37–57.

Danko, A. & Brunner, C. (2010). Social Entrepreneurship – Zum State-of-the-Art der aktuellen Forschung. *Zeitschrift für KMU und Entrepreneurship*, 58 (2), pp. 157–174.

Dart, R. (2004). The Legitimacy of Social Enterprise. *Nonprofit Management & Leadership*, 14 (4), pp. 411–424.

Dart, R. (2019). Bursting the bubble: the mythologies of many social enterprises and enterpri$ing nonprofits. In: Dey, P. & Steyaert, C. (eds.) *Social Entrepreneurship: An Affirmative Critique*. Cheltenham: Edward Elgar, pp. 65–74.

Davies, W. (2014a). The Limits of Neoliberalism. Authority, Sovereignty and the Logic of Competition. London: SAGE.

Davies, W. (2014b). Neoliberalism: A Bibliographic Review. [online] Available at: https://www.theoryculturesociety.org/blog/william-davies-a-bibliographic-review-of-neoliberalism (Accessed 22 September 2022).

Davies, W. (2017). The Limits of Neoliberalism. Authority, Sovereignty and the Logic of Competition, revised ed. London: SAGE.

Dees, G. (2001 [1998]). The Meaning of 'Social Entrepreneurship'. [online] Available at: https://centers.fuqua.duke.edu/case/wp-content/uploads/sites/7/2015/03/Article_Dees_MeaningofSocialEntrepreneurship_2001.pdf (Accessed 20 September 2022).

Defourny, J. & Nyssens, M. (2010). Conceptions of Social Enterprise and Social Entrepreneurship in Europe and the United States: Convergences and Divergences. *Journal of Social Entrepreneurship*, 1 (1), pp. 32–53.

Defourny, J. & Nyssens, M. (2012). The EMES Approach of Social Enterprise in a Comparative Perspective. *Working Papers Series*, 12/03, Liege: EMES European Research Network.

Defourny, J., Nyssens, M. & Adam, S. (2021). Introduction: Documenting, Theorising, Mapping and Testing the Plurality of SE Models in Western Europe. In: Defourny, J. & Nyssens, M. (eds.) *Social Enterprise in Western Europe*. London: Routledge, pp. 1–18.

Der Spiegel (2004). Sozialhilfe: Kein Geld mehr für 'Florida Rolf'. *Spiegel* [online] Available at: http://www.spiegel.de/politik/deutschland/sozialhilfe-kein-geld-mehr-fuer-florida-rolf-a-289809.html (Accessed 23 September 2022).

Deutscher Bundestag (2019). "Social Entrepreneurs als Akteure der ökologischen und sozialen Modernisierung der Wirtschaft stärken" – Antwort der Bundesregierung auf die Kleine Anfrage der Abgeordneten Dieter Janecek, Markus Kurth, Dr. Danyal Bayaz, weiterer Abgeordneter und der Fraktion BÜNDNIS 90/DIE GRÜNEN, Drucksache 19/6844. [online] Available at: https://dserver.bundestag.de/btd/19/072/1907293.pdf (Accessed 6 September 2022).

Dey, P. (2010). The symbolic violence of 'social entrepreneurship': language, power and the question of the social (subject)', paper presented at the Third Research Colloquium on Social Entrepreneurship, Saîd Business School, University of Oxford, 22nd-25th June, 2010.

Dey, P. & Steyaert, C. (2010). The politics of narrating social entrepreneurship. *Journal of Enterprising Communities: People and Places in the Global Economy*, 4 (1), pp. 85–108.

Dey, P. & Teasdale, S. (2016). The tactical mimicry of social enterprise strategies: Acting 'as if' in the everyday life of third sector organizations. *Organization*, 23 (4), pp. 485–504.

Diaz-Bone, R. (2006). Zur Methodologisierung der Foucaultschen Diskursanalyse. *Forum Qualitative Sozialforschung / Forum: Qualitative Social Research*, 7(1), Art. 6, doi: 10.17169/fqs-7.1.71.

Diaz-Bone, R. & Krell, G. (eds.) (2015). *Diskurs und Ökonomie: Diskursanalytische Perspektiven auf Märkte und Organisationen*, 2nd ed. Wiesbaden: Springer VS.

Diaz-Bone, R., Bührmann, A., Gutiérrez Rodríguez, E., Schneider, W., Kendall G. & Tirado, F.: (2007). The Field of Foucaultian Discourse Analysis: Structures, Developments and Perspectives. *Forum Qualitative Sozialforschung / Forum: Qualitative Social Research* 8 (2), Art. 30, doi: 10.17169/fqs-8.2.234.

Doherty, B., Haugh, H. & Lyon, F. (2014). Social enterprises as hybrid organizations – A review and research agenda. *International Journal of Management Reviews*, 16 (4), pp. 417- 436.

Dörre, K. (2011). Hartz-Kapitalismus. Vom erfolgreichen Scheitern der jüngsten Arbeitsmarktreformen. In: Heitmeyer, W. (ed.) *Deutsche Zustände. Folge 9*. Frankfurt: Suhrkamp, pp. 294–305.

Dustmann, C., Fitzenberger, B., Schönberg, U. & Spitz-Oener, A. (2014). From Sick Man of Europe to Economic Superstar: Germany's Resurgent Economy. *Journal of Economic Perspectives*, 28 (1), pp. 167–88.

Ehnts, D. & Zeddies, L. (2016). Die Krise der VWL und die Vision einer Pluralen Ökonomik. *Wirtschaftsdienst*, 96 (10), pp. 769–775.

Eikenberry, A. & Kluver, J. (2004). The marketization of the nonprofit sector: civil society at risk? *Public Administration Review*, 64 (2), pp. 132–140.

EMES International Research Network (2020). Who we are. [online] Available at: https://emes.net/who-we-are/ (Accessed 28 August 2020).

Esping-Andersen, G. (1990). The three worlds of welfare capitalism. Cambridge: Cambridge University Press.

European Commission (2014). Ein Überblick über Sozialunternehmen und ihre Ökosysteme in Europa – Zusammenfassung. Brussels: Publications Office of the European Union.

European Commission (2021). EU action plan for social economy. [online] Available at: https://ec.europa.eu/info/law/better-regulation/have-your-say/initiatives/12743-EU-action-plan-for-social-economy_en (Accessed 6 September 2021).

Evers, A. & Laville, J.-L. (eds.) (2004). *The Third Sector in Europe*. Cheltenham: Edward Elgar.

Fairclough, N. (1992). Discourse and Social Change. Cambridge: Polity Press.

Fairclough, N. (1993). Critical discourse analysis and the marketization of public discourse: the universities. *Discourse & Society*, 4 (2), pp. 133–168.

Fairclough, N. (1995). Media Discourse. London: Edward Arnold.

Fairclough, N. (2000). New Labour, New Language? London: Routledge.

Fairclough, N. (2010). Critical Discourse Analysis: The Critical Study of Language, 2nd ed. London: Routledge.

Fairclough, N. & Wodak, R. (1997). Critical Discourse Analysis. In: van Dijk, T. (ed.) *Discourse as Social Interaction (Discourse Studies: A Multidisciplinary Introduction. Vol. 2)*. London: SAGE, pp. 258–284.

Faltin, G. (2008). Social Entrepreneurship. Definition, Inhalte, Perspektiven. In: Braun, G. & French, M. (eds.) *Social Entrepreneurship – Unternehmerische Ideen für eine bessere Gesellschaft. Dokumentation der 4. HIERO Ringvorlesung zu Unternehmertum und Regionalentwicklung an der Universität Rostock im Wintersemester 2007/2008*. Rostock: Hanseatic Institute for Entrepreneurship, Selbstverlag. pp. 25–46.

Faltin, G. (2012). Kopf schlägt Kapital: Die ganz andere Art, ein Unternehmen zu gründen. München: Deutscher Taschenbuch Verlag.

Fehmel, T. & Betzelt, S. (2022). Einleitung. In: Betzelt, S. & Fehmel, T. (eds.). *Deformation oder Transformation? Analysen zum wohlfahrtsstaatlichen Wandel im 21. Jahrhundert*. Wiesbaden: Springer Fachmedien, pp. 1–21.

Flick, U. (2012). Qualitative Sozialforschung: Eine Einführung, 5th ed. Reinbek/Hamburg: Rowohlt.

Foucault, M. (1961). Madness and Civilization: A History of Insanity in the Age of Reason. New York: Random House.

Foucault, M. (1966). The Order of Things: An Archaeology of Human Sciences. New York: Random House.

Foucault, M. (1969). The Archaeology of Knowledge: And the Discourse on Language. New York: Pantheon Books.

Foucault, M. (1975). Discipline and Punish: The Birth of the Prison. New York: Random House.

Foucault, M. (1978/1979 [2004]). Geschichte der Gouvernementalität (I, II). Frankfurt: Suhrkamp.

Fowler, R., Hodge, B., Kress, G., & Trew, T. (1979). Language and Control. London: Routledge & Kegan Paul.

Friedman, M. (1970). The Social Responsibility of Business is to Increase its Profits. *The New York Times Magazine*, 13 September 1970. [online] Available at: http://umich.edu/~thecore/doc/Friedman.pdf (Accessed 25 January 2020).

Garrow, E. & Hasenfeld, Y. (2014). Social enterprises as an embodiment of a neoliberal welfare logic. *American Behavioral Scientist*, 58 (11), pp. 1475–1493.

Gather, C., Maier, F. & Veil, M. (2007). Thematische Einführung (Schwerpunktheft “Geschlechterverhältnisse in der Ökonomie”). *Feministische Studien*, 25 (2), pp. 183–188.

Gebauer, J. & Ziegler, R. (2013). Corporate Social Responsibility und Social Entrepreneruship. Entwicklungen, Debatten und Perspektiven für Forschung und Praxis. In: Gebauer, J. & Schirmer, H. (eds.) *Unternehmerisch und verantwortlich wirken? Forschung an der Schnittstelle von Corporate Social Responsibility und Social Entrepreneurship*. Berlin: Institut für ökologische Wirtschaftsforschung.

Göler von Ravensburg, N., Krlev, G. & Mildenberger, G. (2018). Social Enterprises and Their Ecosystems in Europe – Country Report Germany. Luxembourg: Publications Office of the European Union.

Göler von Ravensburg, N., Mildenberger, G. & Krlev, G. (2021). Social Enterprise in Germany: Between Institutional Inertia, Innovation and Cooperation. In: Defourny, J. & Nyssens, M. (eds.) *Social Enterprise in Western Europe*. London: Routledge, pp. 85–101.

Graupe, S. (2013). Ökonomische Bildung: Die geistige Monokultur der Wirtschaftswissenschaft und ihre Alternativen. *Coincidentia: Zeitschrift für europäische Geistesgeschichte*, 2, pp. 139–165.

Gredel, E. (2018). Digitale Methoden und Werkzeuge für Diskursanalysen am Beispiel der Wikipedia. In: Huber M. & Krämer, S. (eds.) *Wie Digitalität die Geisteswissenschaften verändert: Neue Forschungsgegenstände und Methoden, Special edition of Zeitschrift für digitale Geisteswissenschaften*, 3, doi:10.17175/sb003_005.

Grenier, P. (2009). Social entrepreneurship in the UK: from rhetoric to reality? In: Ziegler, R. (ed.) *An Introduction to Social Entrepreneurship*. Cheltenham: Edward Elgar, pp. 174–205.

Grohs, S., Schneiders, K. & Heinze, R. (2016). Outsiders and Intrapreneurs: The Institutional Embeddedness of Social Entrepreneurship in Germany. *Voluntas*, doi:10.1007/s11266-016-9777-1.

Hackenberg, H. & Empter, S. (eds.) (2011). *Social Entrepreneurship – Social Business: Für die Gesellschaft unternehmen*. Wiesbaden: Springer VS.

Halberstadt, J. & Hölzner, H. (2018). Social Entrepreneurship. In: Grunwald, K. & Langer, A. (eds.) *Sozialwirtschaft*. Baden-Baden: Nomos, pp. 592–605.

Hall, S. (1997). Introduction. In: Hall, S. (ed.) *Representation: Cultural Representations and Signifying Practices*. London: SAGE, pp. 1–12.

Hall, S., Massey, D. & Rustin, M. (2015). After Neoliberalism: Analysing the Present. In: Hall, S., Massey, D. & Rustin, M. (eds.) *After Neoliberalism: The Kilburn Manifesto*. London: Lawrence and Wishart, pp. 9–23.

Hart, K., Laville, J.-L. & Cattani, A. (2010). Building the Human Economy Together. In: Hart, K., Laville, J.-L. & Cattani, A. (eds.) *The Human Economy*. Cambridge: Polity, pp. 1–20.

Hartz, P. et al. (2002), Moderne Dienstleistungen am Arbeitsmarkt. Vorschläge der Kommission zum Abbau der Arbeitslosigkeit und zur Umstrukturierung der Bundesanstalt für Arbeit. Berlin: Bundesministerium für Arbeit und Sozialordnung.

Harvey, D. (2011). The Enigma of Capital. And the Crises of Capitalism. London: Profile Books.

Hassel, A. & Schiller, C. (2010). Der Fall Hartz IV: Wie es zur Agenda 2010 kam und wie es weitergeht. Frankfurt: Campus Verlag.

Haugh, H. (2006). Social enterprise: Beyond economic outcomes and individual returns. In: Mair, J., Robinson, J. & Hockerts, K. (eds.) *Social entrepreneurship*. Basingstoke: Palgrave Macmillan, pp. 180–205.

Heidbrink, L & Seele, P. (2010). Einleitung: Vom Nutzen und Nachteil des Unternehmertums. In: Heidbrink, L & Seele, P. (eds.) *Unternehmertum: Vom Nutzen und Nachteil einer riskanten Lebensform*. Frankfurt: Campus Verlag, pp. 7–26.

Hein, R. (2021). Typisch Social Entrepreneurship: Arbeitsgestaltung und Wirkung von Arbeit bei Sozialunternehmer*innen in Deutschland. Wiesbaden: Springer Gabler.

Heinze, R, Schneiders, K. & Grohs, S. (2011). Social Entrepreneurship im deutschen Wohlfahrtsstaat – Hybride Organisationen zwischen Markt, Staat und Gemeinschaft. In: Hackenberg, H. & Empter, S. (eds.) *Social Entrepreneurship – Social Business: Für die Gesellschaft unternehmen*. Wiesbaden: Springer VS, pp. 86–104.

Heinze, R. (1998). Die blockierte Gesellschaft. Sozioökonomischer Wandel und die Krise des "Modell Deuschland", Wiesbaden: Westdeutscher Verlag.

Heinze, R., Schönauer, A., Schneiders, K., Grohs, S. & Ruddat, C. (2013). Social Entrepreneurship im etablierten Wohlfahrtsstaat. Aktuelle empirische Befunde zu neuen und alten Akteuren auf dem Wohlfahrtsmarkt. In: Jansen, S., Heinze, R. & Beckmann, M. (eds.) *Sozialunternehmen in Deutschland. Analysen, Trends und Handlungsempfehlungen*. Wiesbaden: Springer VS, pp. 315–346.

Hirseland, A. (2007). Rezension zu: Margarete Jäger & Siegfried Jäger (2007). Deutungskämpfe. Theorie und Praxis Kritischer Diskursanalyse. *Forum Qualitative Sozialforschung / Forum: Qualitative Social Research*, 8 (2), Art. 27, doi: 10.17169/fqs-8.2.259.

Hockerts, K. (2006). Entrepreneurial opportunity in social purpose business ventures. In: Mair, J., Robinson, J. & Hockerts, K. (eds.) *Social entrepreneurship*. Basingstoke, UK: Palgrave Macmillan, pp. 142–154.

Hulgard, L. (2010). Discourses of Social Entrepreneurship – variations of the same theme? *EMES European Research Network Working Papers*, 10 (1), pp. 1–20.

Hulgard, L. (2011). Social economy and social enterprise: an emerging alternative to mainstream market economy? *China Journal of Social Work*, 4 (3), pp. 201–215.

Hunter, S., Riggs, D. & Feo, R. (2019). Australian news media constructions and categorisations of primary caregiving fathers. *Discourse & Society*, 30 (6), 622–635.

Impact Hub Berlin (2022). Vision & Mission. [online] Available at: https://berlin.impacthub.net/de/ueber-uns/vision-und-mission/ (Accessed 21 September 2022).

Impact Hub Germany (2022). Locations. [online] Available at: https://impacthub.de/#cities (Accessed 6 September 2022).

Informationsgemeinschaft zur Feststellung der Verbreitung von Werbeträgern e.V. (IVW) (2020). Ranking der auflagenstärksten überregionalen Tageszeitungen in Deutschland im 3. Quartal 2020. [online] Available at: https://de.statista.com/statistik/daten/studie/73448/umfrage/auflage-der-ueberregionalen-tageszeitungen/ (Accessed 8 January 2021).

Informationsgemeinschaft zur Feststellung der Verbreitung von Werbeträgern e.V. (IVW). (2021a). Ranking der auflagenstärksten Regionalzeitungen in Deutschland im 2. Quartal 2021. Statista. Statista GmbH. [online] Available at: https://de.statista.com/statistik/daten/studie/1080894/umfrage/auflage-der-regionalzeitungen/ (Accessed 4 January 2021).

Informationsgemeinschaft zur Feststellung der Verbreitung von Werbeträgern e.V. (IVW) (2021b). Ranking der auflagenstärksten überregionalen Tageszeitungen in Deutschland im 3. Quartal 2021. Statista. Statista GmbH. [online] Available at: https://de.statista.com/statistik/daten/studie/73448/umfrage/auflage-der-ueberregionalen-tageszeitungen/ (Accessed 4 January 2021).

Informationsgemeinschaft zur Feststellung der Verbreitung von Werbeträgern e.V. (IVW) (2021c). Verkaufte Auflage der Tages- und Wochenzeitungen in Deutschland im 3. Quartal 2021. Statista. Statista GmbH. [online] Available at: https://de.statista.com/statistik/daten/studie/171774/umfrage/verkaufte-auflage-der-zeitungen-in-deutschland/ (Accessed 4 January 2021).

International Centre of Research and Information on the Public, Social and Cooperative Economy (CIRIEC) (2020). History. [online] https://www.ciriec.uliege.be/en/who-we-are/historique/ (Accessed 6 September 2022).

Jacques, M. (2016). The death of neoliberalism and the crisis in western politics. *The Guardian* [online] Available at: https://www.theguardian.com/commentisfree/2016/aug/21/death-of-neoliberalism-crisis-in-western-politics (Accessed 27 August 2020).

Jäger, M. & Jäger, S. (2007). Deutungskämpfe. Theorie und Praxis kritischer Diskursanalyse. Wiesbaden: Springer VS.

Jäger, S. (1999). Kritische Diskursanalyse. Eine Einführung, 2nd ed. Duisburg: Duisburger Institut für Sprach- und Sozialforschung.

Jäger, S. & Diaz-Bone, R. (2006). Siegfried Jäger im Gespräch mit Rainer Diaz-Bone: Kritische Diskursanalyse: Zur Ausarbeitung einer problembezogenen Diskursanalyse im Anschluss an Foucault. *Forum Qualitative Sozialforschung / Forum: Qualitative Social Research*, 7 (3), Art. 21, doi:10.17169/fqs-8.2.259.

Jähnke, P., Christmann, G. & Balgar, K. (eds.) (2011). *Social Entrepreneurship Perspektiven für die Raumentwicklung*. Wiesbaden: Springer VS.

Jansen, S. (2013). Begriffs- und Konzeptgeschichte von Sozialunternehmen: Differenztheoretische Typologisierungen. In: Jansen, S., Heinze, R. & Beckmann, M. (eds.) *Sozialunternehmen in Deutschland. Analysen, Trends und Handlungsempfehlungen*. Wiesbaden: Springer VS, pp. 35–78.

Jansen, S., Heinze, R. & Beckmann, M. (eds.) (2013). *Sozialunternehmen in Deutschland. Analysen, Trends und Handlungsempfehlungen*. Wiesbaden: Springer VS.

Karis, T. (2010). Foucault, Luhmann und die Macht der Massenmedien: Zur Bedeutung massenmedialer Eigenlogiken für den Wandel des Sagbaren. In: Landwehr, A. (ed.) *Diskursiver Wandel*. Wiesbaden: Springer VS, pp. 237–251.

Karre, P. (2021). Social Enterprise in Belgium, Germany and the Netherlands: Where the Old Meets the New. In: Defourny, J. & Nyssens, M. (eds.) *Social Enterprise in Western Europe*. London: Routledge, pp. 288–300.

Kay, A., Roy, M. & Donaldson, C. (2016). Re-imagining social enterprise. *Social Enterprise Journal*, 12 (2), pp. 217–234.

Keller, R. (2011). Diskursforschung, 4th ed. Wiesbaden: Springer VS.

Kendall, G. (2007). What Is Critical Discourse Analysis? Ruth Wodak in Conversation with Gavin Kendall. *Forum Qualitative Sozialforschung / Forum: Qualitative Social Research*, 8 (2), Art. 29, doi:10.17169/fqs-8.2.255.

Kerchner, B. & Schneider, S. (2006). "Endlich Ordnung in der Werkzeugkiste". Zum Potenzial der Foucaultschen Diskursanalyse für die Politikwissenschaft – Einleitung. In: Kerchner, B. & Schneider, S. (eds.). *Foucault: Diskursanalyse der Politik*. Wiesbaden: Springer VS, pp. 9–32.

Kerlin, J. (2010). A Comparative Analysis of the Global Emergence of Social Enterprise. *Voluntas*, 21, pp. 162–179.

Kerlin, J. (2013). Defining Social Enterprise Across Different Contexts: A Conceptual Framework Based on Institutional Factors. *Nonprofit and Voluntary Sector Quarterly*, 42 (1) pp. 84–108.

Kerlin, J. (2018). Social Enterprise: What the U.S. and European Experience Can Teach Us – And Where to Now? *Nonprofit Quarterly*, 25 (2).

Kewes, T. (2017). Ann-Kristin Achleitner im Porträt: Mit aller Macht. [online] Availabe at: https://www.handelsblatt.com/unternehmen/management/ann-kristin-achleitner-im-portraet-sie-war-die-perfekte-kandidatin/19663640-4.html (Accessed 30 August 2020).

Kollmann, T., Kleine-Stegemann, L., Then-Bergh, C., Harr, M., Hirschfeld, A., Gilde, J. & Walk, V. (2021). Deutscher Startup Monitor. [online] Availabe at: https://startupverband.de/fileadmin/startupverband/mediaarchiv/research/dsm/dsm_2021.pdf (Accessed 16 September 2022).

Korosec, R. & Berman, E. (2006). Municipal support for social entrepreneurship. *Public Administration Review*, 66 (3), pp. 448–462.

Krugman, P. (2009). How Did Economists Get It So Wrong? *The New York Times*, 2. September 2009 [online] Availabe at: https://www.nytimes.com/2009/09/06/magazine/06Economic-t.html (Accessed 17 September 2019).

Kurtenbach, S. (2018). Ausgrenzung Geflüchteter. Eine empirische Untersuchung am Beispiel Bautzen. Wiesbaden: Springer Fachmedien.

Lautermann, C. (2012). Verantwortung unternehmen! Die Realisierung kultureller Visionen durch gesellschaftsorientiertes Unternehmertum. Eine konstruktive Kritik der 'Social Entrepreneurship'-Debatte. Marburg: Metropolis.

Leppert, T. (2008). Social Entrepreneurs in Deutschland – Ansätze und Besonderheiten einer spezifischen Definition. Hamburg: social startup – Beratung für soziale Bewegungen/ Universität Hamburg.

Leppert, T. (2011). Zur Wahrnehmung eines Phänomens: Förderpolitische Bedingungen für Social Entrepreneurship in Deutschland. In: Jähnke, P, Christmann, G. & Balgar, K. (eds.) *Social Entrepreneurship: Perspektiven für die Raumentwicklung*. Wiesbaden: Springer VS, pp. 133–148.

Lohmeyer, N. & Jackson, G. (2018). The business case as new vocabulary of motive: Discourse coalitions around CSR in Germany, 1970–2014, Academy of Management Proceedings, 2018 (1), 14169.

Longhurst, N., Avelino, F., Wittmayer, J., Weaver, P., Dumitru, A., Hielscher, S., Cipolla, C., Afonso, R., Kunze, I. & Morten, E. (2016). Experimenting with alternative economies: four emergent counter-narratives of urban economic development. *Current Opinion in Environmental Sustainability*, 22, pp. 69–74.

Luhmann, N. (2004). Die Realität der Massenmedien, 3rd ed. Wiesbaden: Springer VS.

Maaß, F. & Schneck, S. (2017). Soziales Unternehmertum: Denkpapier. Bonn: Institut für Mittelstandsforschung Bonn.

Maier, F. (2013). Feministische Ökonomie ist immer auch Kritik der herrschenden Wirtschaftstheorien. *Feministische Studien*, 31 (1), pp. 131–135.

Mair, J., & Marti, I. (2006): Social entrepreneurship research: A source of explanation, prediction, and delight. *Journal of World Business*, 41 (1), pp. 36–44.

Mair, J., Robinson, J. & Hockerts, K. (2006). Introduction. In: Mair, J., Robinson, J. & Hockerts, K. (eds.) *Social Entrepreneurship*. Basingstoke: Palgrave Macmillan, pp. 1–13.

Mason, C. (2012). Up for grabs: A critical discourse analysis of social entrepreneurship discourse in the United Kingdom. *Social Enterprise Journal*, 8 (2), pp. 123–140.

Mason, C. & Moran, M. (2019). The tale of the veil: unweaving Big Society and the social enterprise myth. In: Dey, P. & Steyaert, C. (eds.) *Social Entrepreneurship: An Affirmative Critique*. Cheltenham: Edward Elgar, pp. 75–99.

McRobbie, A. (2020). Feminism and the Politics of Resilience. Essays on Gender, Media and the End of Welfare. Cambridge: Polity Press.

McRobbie, A., Strutt, D. & Bandinelli, C. (2019). Feminism and the Politics of Creative Labour: Fashion Micro-enterprises in London, Berlin and Milan. *Australian Feminist Studies*, 34 (100), pp. 131–148.

Metzger, G. (2019). Social Entrepreneurs in Deutschland: Raus aus der Nische – 154.000 "junge" Sozialunternehmer im Jahr 2017. Frankfurt: KfW Research.

Meyen, M. (2013). »Wir haben freier gelebt«. Die DDR im kollektiven Gedächtnis der Deutschen. Bielefeld: transcript.

Mills, S. (1997). Discourse. London: Routledge.

Mirowski, P. & Plehwe, D. (2009). The Road from Mont Pelerin. Cambridge, MA: Harvard University Press.

Nicholls, A. (2010). The Legitimacy of Social Entrepreneurship: Reflexive Isomorphism in a Pre-Paradigmatic Field. *Entrepreneurship Theory and Practice*, 34 (4), pp- 611-633.

Nicholls, A. & Teasdale, S. (2017). Neoliberalism by stealth? Exploring continuity and change within the UK social enterprise policy paradigm. *Policy & Politics*, 45 (3), pp. 323–341.

Nonhoff, M. (2006). Politischer Diskurs und Hegemonie. Das Projekt »Soziale Marktwirtschaft«. Bielefeld: transcript.

Ostermeyer, F. (2015). Deutschlands machtigste Clans: Familie Mohn. *Welt* [online] Available at: https://www.welt.de/iconist/unterwegs/article177192846/Deutschlands-maechtigste-Clans-Familie-Mohn.html (Accessed 17 September 2022).

Papi-Thornton, D. (2016). Tackling Heropreneurship. *Stanford Social Innovation Review*, doi:10.48558/997W-YB97.

Parkinson, C. & Howorth, C. (2008). The Language of Social Entrepreneurs. *Entrepreneurship & Regional Development*, 20, pp. 285–309.

Pearce, J. (2003). Social Enterprise in Anytown. London: Calouste Gulbenkian Foundation.

Peredo, A. & McLean, M. (2006). Social entrepreneurship: A critical review of the concept. *Journal of World Business*, 41, pp. 56–65.

Polanyi (2015 [1944]). The Great Transformation. Frankfurt: Suhrkamp.

Przyborski, A. & Wohlrab-Sahr, M. (2014). Qualitative Sozialforschung: Ein Arbeitsbuch, 4th ed. München: Oldenbourg.

Ranville, A. & Barros, M. (2021). Towards Normative Theories of Social Entrepreneurship. A Review of the Top Publications of the Field. *Journal of Business Ethics*, doi:10.1007/s10551-021-04867-4.

Redclift, M. (2005). Sustainable development (1987–2005): an oxymoron comes of age. *Sustainable Development*, 13 (4), pp. 212–227, doi:10.1002/sd.281.

Ridley-Duff, R. & Bull, M. (2011). Understanding Social Enterprise. London: SAGE.

Rose, N. (1999). Powers of Freedom: Reframing Political Thought. Cambridge: Cambridge University Press.

Rummel, M. (2011). Wer sind Social Entrepreneurs in Deutschland? Wiesbaden: Springer VS.

Saad-Filho, A. (2020). From COVID-19 to the End of Neoliberalism. *Critical Sociology*, 46 (4–5), pp. 477–485.

Sassmannshausen, S.-P. & Volkmann, C. (2018). The scientometrics of social entrepreneurship and its establishment as an academic field. *Journal of Small Business Management*, 56 (2), pp. 251–273.

Schelkle, W. (2007). 'Sick Man of Europe' or 'Midlife Crisis in Europe'? Germany's Woes since the Mid-1980s – a Comment. In: Hölscher, J. (ed.) *Germany's Economic Performance*. Basingstoke: Palgrave Macmillan, pp. 167–172.

Scheper, J. (2021). Was die Ampel für Social Entrepreneurs bedeutet. *Enorm* [online] Available at: https://enorm-magazin.de/gesellschaft/politik/demokratie/was-der-koalitionsvertrag-fuer-social-entrepreneurs-bedeutet (Accessed 6 September 2022).

Scheuerle, T., Glänzel, G., Knust, R. & Then, V. (2013). Social Entrepreneurship in Deutschland – Potentiale und Wachstumsproblematiken. Heidelberg: Centrum für soziale Investitionen und Innovationen.

Schneiders, K. (2020). Sozialwirtschaft und Soziale Arbeit. Stuttgart: Kohlhammer.

Schubert, K. & Klein, M. (2020). Das Politiklexikon. 7th ed. Bonn: Bundeszentrale für politische Bildung.

Schwarz, Sabine (2014): Social Entrepreneurship Projekte. Unternehmerische Konzepte als innovativer Beitrag zur Gestaltung einer sozialen Gesellschaft. Wiesbaden: Springer VS.

Schweiger, C. (2010). Towards convergence? New Labour's Third Way and the SPD's Agenda 2010 in comparative perspective. *Sozialer Fortschritt – German Review of Social Policy*, 59 (9), pp. 244–253.

Seibring, A. (2019). Editorial. *Aus Politik und Zeitgeschichte*, 69, (44–45), p. 3.

Senatsverwaltung für Wirtschaft, Energie und Betriebe (SenWEB) (2020). Neues Projekt "Social Economy Berlin" stärkt und vernetzt die Soziale Ökonomie Berlins. [online] Availabe at: https://www.berlin.de/sen/web/presse/pressemitteilungen/2020/pressemitteilung.990297.php (Accessed 19 September 2022).

Shaw, E. & de Bruin, A. (2013). Reconsidering capitalism: the promise of social innovation and social entrepreneurship? *International Small Business Journal*, 31 (7), pp. 737–746.

Sievers, S. (2016). Fragile heterotopias – a case study of a Danish social enterprise. *Community Development Journal*, 51 (1), pp. 77–94.

Silverman, D. (2015). Interpreting Qualitative Data, 5th ed. London: SAGE.

Social Economy Berlin (2020). Über uns. [online] Available at: https://socialeconomy.berlin/ueber-uns/ (Accessed 6 September 2022).

Social Entrepreneurship Netzwerk Deutschland e.V. (SEND) (2019). Social Entrepreneurship – Entstehung und Bedeutung. [online]. Available at: https://www.send-ev.de/wp-content/uploads/2021/03/definition_socialentrepreneurship.pdf (Accessed 22 September 2022).

Social Entrepreneurship Netzwerk Deutschland e.V. (SEND) (2021a). Social Entrepreneurship Netzwerk Deutschland [Facebook]. Available at: https://www.facebook.com/SocEntNetDe/videos/?ref=page_internal (Accessed 3 September 2022).

Social Entrepreneurship Netzwerk Deutschland e.V. (SEND) (2021b). Über uns. [online] Available at: https://www.send-ev.de/startseite/ueber-uns/ (Accessed 6 September 2022).

Social Entrepreneurship Netzwerk Deutschland e.V. (SEND) (2021c). Unsere Kernforderungen. [online] Available at: https://www.send-ev.de/social-entrepreneurship/unsere-kernforderungen/ (Accessed 6 September 2022).

Social Entrepreneurship Netzwerk Deutschland e.V. (SEND) (2021d). Sozialinnovator Hessen. [online] Available at: https://www.send-ev.de/projekte-items/sozialinnovator-hessen/ (Accessed 6 September 2022).

Social Entrepreneurship Netzwerk Deutschland e.V. (SEND) (2021e). emp:our now – Gemeinsam stark für ein vielfältiges Morgen. [online] Available at: https://www.send-ev.de/projekte-items/empour-now/ (Accessed 22 September 2022).

Social Entrepreneurship Netzwerk Deutschland e.V. (SEND) (2022a). 4. Deutscher Social Entrepreneurship Monitor 2021/22.

Social Entrepreneurship Netzwerk Deutschland e.V. (SEND) (2022b). NRW-Landtagswahl 2022: Antworten auf die Wahlprüfsteine von GWÖ und SEND. [online] Available at: https://www.send-ev.de/2022/05/10/nrw-landtagswahl-2022-antworten-auf-die-wahlpruefsteine-von-gwoe-und-send/ (Accessed 21 September 2022).

Social Impact gGmbH (2022a). Social Impact Labs. [online] Available at: https://socialimpact.eu/labs (Accessed 6 September 2022).

Social Impact gGmbH (2022b). Über uns. [online] Available at: https://kompetenzzentrum-soziale-innovationen.com/ueber-uns (Accessed 22 September 2022).

Social Impact gGmbH (2022c). About us. [online] Available at: https://si-allian ce.eu/about-us (Accessed 22 September 2022).

Somers, A. (2013). The Emergence of Social Enterprise Policy in New Labour's Second Term. Doctoral thesis, Goldsmiths, University of London.

Spohr, F. (2019). Germany's Labour Market Policies: How the Sick Man of Europe Performed a Second Economic Miracle. In: Compton, M. & Hart, T. (eds.) *Great Policy Successes*. Oxford: Oxford University Press, pp. 283–303.

Statistisches Bundesamt (2018). Bildung und Kultur: Private Hochschulen. [online] Availabe at: https://www.destatis.de/DE/Themen/Gesellschaft-U mwelt/Bildung-Forschung-Kultur/Hochschulen/Publikationen/Downloa ds-Hochschulen/private-hochschulen-5213105177004.pdf?__blob=publica tionFile (Accessed 11 September 2022).

Steyaert, C. & Dey, P. (2019). The books on social entrepreneurship we edit, critique and imagine. In: Dey, P. & Steyaert, C. (eds.) *Social Entrepreneurship: An Affirmative Critique*. Cheltenham: Edward Elgar, pp. 1–18.

Stiglitz, J. (2019). The end of neoliberalism and the rebirth of history. [online] Available at: https://www.socialeurope.eu/the-end-of-neoliberalism-and-the-rebirth-of-history (Accessed 27 August 2020).

Tagesschau. (2019). Tampons werden billiger. [online] Availabe at: https://www .tagesschau.de/inland/bundesrat-233.html (Accessed 18 September 2022).

Teasdale, S. (2012). What's in a Name? Making Sense of Social Enterprise Discourses. *Public Policy and Administration*, 27 (2), pp. 99–119.

Teasdale, S., Lyon, F. & Owen, R. (2019). A methodological critique of the social enterprise growth myth. In: Dey, P. & Steyaert, C. (eds.) *Social Entrepreneurship: An Affirmative Critique*. Cheltenham: Edward Elgar, pp. 19–39.

Teasdale, S., Bellazecca, E., de Bruin, A. & Roy, M. (2022). The (R)evolution of the Social Entrepreneurship Concept: A Critical Historical Review. Nonprofit and Voluntary Sector Quarterly, https://doi.org/10.1177/0899764022 113069.

Technologie-Netzwerk Berlin e.V. (TechNet). (2022). Team. [online] Available at: https://www.technet-berlin.de/team (Accessed 8 September 2022).

Tracey, P. & Jarvis, O. (2007). Toward a theory of social venture franchising. *Entrepreneurship Theory & Practice*, 31 (5), pp. 667–685.

Traue, B., Pfahl, L. & Schürmann, L. (2014). Diskursanalyse. In: Baur, N. & Blasius, J. (eds.) *Handbuch Methoden der empirischen Sozialforschung*. Wiesbaden: Springer VS, pp. 493–508.

Unterberg, M., Richter, D., Jahnke, T., Spiess-Knafl, W., Sänger, R. & Förster, N. (2015). Herausforderungen bei der Gründung und Skalierung von Sozi-

alunternehmen. Welche Rahmenbedingungen brauchen Social Entrepreneurs? Hamburg: Evers & Jung.
van Dijk, T. (1997). Discourse as Interaction in Society. In: van Dijk, T. (ed.) *Discourse as Social Interaction (Discourse Studies: A Multidisciplinary Introduction. Vol. 2)*. London: SAGE, pp. 1–37.
van Dijk, T. (2007). Editor's introduction: The study of discourse: an introduction. In: van Dijk, T. (ed.) Discourse Studies. London: SAGE, pp. 16–42.
van Treeck, T. & Urban, J. (2017). Einleitung. In: van Treeck, T. & Urban, J. (eds.) *Wirtschaft neu denken: Blinde Flecken der Lehrbuchökonomie*, 2nd ed. Berlin: iRights.Media, pp. 8–19.
Voß, E. (2015). Wegweiser Solidarische Ökonomie. Neu-Ulm: SPAK-Bücher.
Warnke, I. (2013). Urbaner Diskurs und maskierter Protest – Intersektionale Feldperspektiven auf Gentrifizierungsdynamiken in Berlin Kreuzberg. In: Roth, K. & Spiegel, C. (eds.) *Angewandte Diskurslinguistik. Felder, Probleme, Perspektiven*. Berlin: Akademie Verlag, pp. 189–221.
Welter, F. (2011). Contextualizing Entrepreneurship – Conceptual challenges and ways forward. *Entrepreneurship Theory and Practice*, 35 (1), pp. 165–184.
Welter, F. & Baker, T. (2021). Moving Contexts Onto New Roads: Clues From Other Disciplines. *Entrepreneurship Theory and Practice*, 45 (5), pp. 1154–1175.
WeQ Institute (2020). Vision Summit – Leitkonferenz & Agendasetting-Konferenz. [online] Available at: https://weq.institute/vision-summit/ (Accessed 6 September 2022).
Wihlenda, M., Brahm, T., & Greger, L. (2020). Social Innovation Education – Transformierende Lernprogramme für Hochschulen. Tübingen: Tübingen Library Publishing.
Wodak, R. & Meyer, M. (eds.) (2001). *Methods of Critical Discourse Analysis*. London: SAGE.
Zimmer, A. & Bräuer, S. (2014). The Development of Social Entrepreneurs in Germany. University of Münster: EFESEIIS National Country Report.
Zimmermann, K. (2013). Agenda 2010: Was Europa von Deutschland lernen kann. *Cicero* [online] Available at: https://www.cicero.de/aussenpolitik/agenda-2010-was-europa-von-deutschland-lernen-kann/53823 (Accessed 6 September 2022).

Philipp Kenel (Dr.), born in 1987, is a Researcher and Lecturer at the Alice Salomon Hochschule in Berlin. After studying politics, economics, education, English and social entrepreneurship in Mainz, Valencia, London and Berlin, he received a PhD from Goldsmiths, University of London.